Signs
of the
Spirit

Other Books by Howard A. Snyder

One Hundred Years at Spring Arbor

The Problem of Wineskins: Church Structure in a Technological Age

The Community of the King

The Radical Wesley and Patterns for Church Renewal

Liberating the Church: The Ecology of Church and Kingdom

Under Construction: Ephesians Study Guide

A Kingdom Manifesto

The Divided Flame: Wesleyans and the Charismatic Movement (with Daniel Runyon)

Foresight (with Daniel Runyon)

HOWARD A. SNYDER

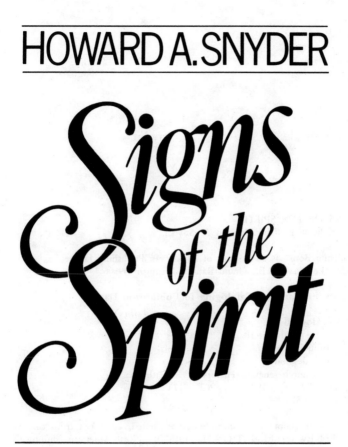

Signs of the Spirit

HOW GOD RESHAPES THE CHURCH

Academie
Books Grand Rapids,
Michigan
Zondervan Publishing House

SIGNS OF THE SPIRIT
Copyright © 1989 by Howard A. Snyder

Academie Books is an imprint of Zondervan Publishing House,
1415 Lake Drive, S.E., Grand Rapids, Michigan 49506.

Library of Congress Cataloging in Publication Data

Snyder, Howard A.
    Signs of the Spirit.
    Bibliography: p.
    Includes index.
    1. Church renewal–History.   I. Title.
BV600.2.S596   1988   262'.0017'09   88-8059
ISBN 0-310-51541-6

Edited by Tom Raabe

Printed in the United States of America

89   90   91   92   93   94   95 / PP / 10 9 8 7 6 5 4 3+1 M2 1

To my teachers

Contents

Introduction

Signs and wonders were a notable part of the experience of the early church. Typical is the statement in Acts 2:43, "Everyone was filled with awe, and many wonders and miraculous signs were done by the apostles." In the early days of the church God worked "signs, wonders and various miracles, and gifts of the Holy Spirit distributed according to his will" (Heb. 2:4).

We thank God when he works in such dramatic ways. Yet it is well to remember that Jesus said, "By this all people will know that you are my disciples, if you love one another" (John 13:35, my translation). The most wonderful sign of the Spirit's power in the first century was the new community of Christian disciples which so demonstrated Jesus' love that the Gospel spread powerfully across the Roman Empire.

God works by his Spirit to create Christian community and to renew his people when they fall into unfaithfulness. In varying degrees the story of the early church has been replayed down through the ages of church history. This book tells a part of this story of renewal and revival in the church. It shows how God is at work renewing and reshaping the church.

Books abound on revival in the church. The stories of the great revivals of the past have been told and retold. Yet there is a large, untold story about the inner dynamics of renewal movements throughout church history—a very significant story which still remains largely hidden.

In this book we will look closely at several renewal movements in church history. First we will tell the story of the movement, then we will note the way the movement's key leaders understood the church. We will also examine each movement's internal dynamics, seeking keys that may still fit the doors of

9

renewal today. We will see how these movements fit into the fascinating flow of history, forming the background for our own experience of the church.

We will first look briefly at Montanism, the church's "first charismatic movement." Later we will focus in detail on three post-Reformation movements, German Pietism, Moravianism, and Methodism, showing both their distinctiveness and their historical interrelatedness.

We might plug into church history at any number of points to study God's renewing work: the early monastic movement; periodic renewals in the various church orders; the Waldensians or early Franciscans; or modern revivalism and renewal movements. However, from the broad spectrum of church history I have chosen to examine four movements which both illuminate the issues in renewal and offer insights which I believe apply more or less directly to the church today.

Pietism, Moravianism, and Methodism shared a number of common characteristics as well as many actual historical links. These movements were also part of a larger context of currents and movements in seventeenth- and eighteenth-century Europe. English Puritanism was certainly a part of this broader picture as were, somewhat more remotely, Jansenism, Quietism, Jewish Hasidism, and some developments within the Jesuits.[1] Dale Brown suggests that "Jansenism was in some respects to Catholicism what Pietism was to Lutheranism" and notes that " 'Hasidism' is the Hebrew equivalent for 'pietism.' "[2] And John T. McNeill notes in *Modern Christian Movements:* "Not only do the same genes run through Puritanism, Pietism, and Evangelicalism, but the whole series of fresh awakenings in the modern history of Christianity, however divergent in purpose, bear a family resemblance. They share the cultural atmosphere common to the period from the Puritan to the atomic age."[3]

While our purpose is not to enquire into the meaning or extent of this cultural atmosphere, it should be borne in mind, especially as we attempt to construct a theology of renewal. The context reminds us that every renewal movement is, in some way, linked to others in history, and that somehow both socio-cultural dynamics and the Holy Spirit are at work down through history.

We begin with a brief look at Montanism, setting the stage for our discussion, showing how from very early days the church has faced questions of renewal. The next chapter shows how church history itself is the story of renewal and examines seven ways of viewing or interpreting renewal movements, ranging from revivalism theories to sect/church typologies.

We then turn our attention to the stories of Pietism, Moravianism, and early Methodism. In concluding chapters we draw lessons for understanding renewal generally and for working for vital Christian congregations today. One of the questions I am most frequently asked is, "How can an institutional church be renewed?" I attempt to answer that in the last chapter.

This book is based primarily on my doctoral dissertation at Notre Dame, published here for the first time. An earlier book, *The Radical Wesley and Patterns for Church Renewal* (Francis Asbury Press, Zondervan, 1987) drew somewhat from my doctoral research into Methodism. Some overlap between that book and the treatment of Methodism in this book has been unavoidable, though the material here has been considerably revised. Chapter 8 was previously published in a somewhat different form as "Renewal That Lasts," *Leadership* (Summer, 1984), 90–93.

The story and comparison of key renewal movements in church history as related here can open new doors and windows. This has been true for me, and I hope it will be for others also.

NOTES

[1] Dale W. Brown, *Understanding Pietism* (Grand Rapids: Eerdmans, 1978), 25–27.

[2] Ibid., 26.

[3] John T. McNeill, *Modern Christian Movements* (Philadelphia: Westminster, 1954), 13.

Chapter One

The First Charismatic Movement

Chapter One

The First Charismatic Movement

She was only twenty-two, too young to die in the arena. How would her nursing son survive? Her unbelieving father begged her to recant, but she said, "I cannot deny what I am, and I am a Christian."

It was early spring in the year 203. The North African city of Carthage, a prominent metropolis of the Roman Empire, was in turmoil over the crackdown on the growing sect of Christians. For one and one-half centuries the church had spread like a flame across the empire, but now persecution was rising. Recently Emperor Septimius Severus had forbidden conversions to Christianity. And so Vibia Perpetua, at twenty-two, became a martyr, a confessor of the faith. Cultured and refined, from a well-known family, she died for her faith in Jesus Christ—leaving behind a tiny infant and a brief diary account which became one of the classics of Christian literature, "the most beautiful of all the records of Christian martyrdom."[1] Otherwise we might never have known of her.

Not only was Perpetua a Christian; she may well have been part of the first charismatic movement to sweep the church. Some thirty years earlier this movement, called the New Prophecy, was born in the backwoods Roman province of Phrygia. It stressed the ministry of the Holy Spirit, the Paraclete, especially in the giving of prophetic gifts. *The Passion of St. Perpetua* begins by quoting Acts 2:17 and adds, "We who recognize and honour equally the prophecies and the new visions which were alike promised, deem the other powers of the Holy Spirit to be for the equipment of the Church, to whom He has been sent administering all gifts to all, according as the Lord hath allotted to each. . . ."[2]

Perpetua was a new believer when she and several others were arrested and thrown into prison. With her were Felicitas and Revocatus, probably a slave couple from her father's household, and two other young believers, Saturninus and Secundulus. The slave Felicitas was pregnant and delivered her child in prison before her martyrdom. Perpetua, until her sentence was pronounced, was allowed to nurse her infant son in the prison. Meanwhile the little group had been joined voluntarily by Saturus, the man who apparently had led Perpetua and the others to Christ and was discipling them. He chose to share their fate.

One day at breakfast time Perpetua and the others were taken suddenly to the forum for public trial. Crowds gathered to watch the spectacle. Perpetua's father appeared with her infant and appealed to her, "Pity your child!" Hilarion, a Roman official, told her, "Spare your father's gray hairs, spare your infant boy. Sacrifice for the safety of the Emperor." But Perpetua said she was a Christian and would not renounce her faith. She and her friends were sentenced to face the wild animals in the arena.

Some days later Perpetua, Felicitas, and the others were led to the amphitheater to die for their faith. "Perpetua followed with bright step as a bride of Christ, as the darling of God, with the flash of her eyes quelling the gaze of the populace."[3] The martyrs protested being costumed—the men as priests of Saturn and the women as devotees of Ceres—and were thus allowed to enter the arena in their own clothes.

Bears, leopards, and wild boars were alternately set loose upon Saturninus and Saturus. Saturus, as he had foreseen, died of one bite from a leopard. Perpetua and Felicitas were tossed about by a maddened cow. Perpetua said to the others, "Stand fast in the faith and let all love each other; and let not our sufferings be a stumbling block to you." At the end of the spectacle, the martyrs who were still alive were dispatched by gladiators. *The Passion of St. Perpetua* concludes, "They had already before this mutually exchanged the kiss, in order to complete the martyrdom by the solemn rite of the peace. The rest were unable to move and received the sword in silence. Saturus . . . was the first to yield his spirit; for he was waiting for Perpetua [as foreseen in a vision she had had]. And she, in order to taste somehow of sorrow, was moaning amongst the pierced bones, and guided the uncertain hand of the clumsy gladiator to her own throat. Perchance so noble a woman, who was feared by the unclean spirit, could not have otherwise been put to death except she herself wished it."[4]

Were Perpetua and her friends part of the New Prophecy movement? We cannot say for sure. Frederick Klawiter writes: "Without a doubt the document was authorized by a member of the New Prophecy, and Perpetua and Saturus stand forth as noble martyrs in that movement."[5] Some scholars concur; others dispute this.[6]

THE RISE OF THE NEW PROPHECY MOVEMENT

In any case, we know the New Prophecy movement had spread rapidly through much of the Roman Empire in the decades just preceding Perpetua's martyrdom. Within sixty or seventy years of the apostle John's apocalyptic visions on the Isle of Patmos, this first renewal movement to stir the Christian church broke out in Phrygia, Asia Minor. Called "the New Prophecy" (and later "Montanism"), the movement was the first widespread outbreak of renewal currents and the first serious challenge to the institutionalizing tendencies in the church.

Historian W. H. C. Frend sets the context for the rise of Montanism. In the wake of Paul's missionary journeys, two types of ministry developed in the church: residential and itinerant (or traveling) ministries. Each Christian community was familiar both with traveling preachers and prophets who visited periodically and with its local leaders or elders. Each Christian community had its "residential ministry, consisting probably of presbyter-bishops [that is, overseeing elders], each with an allotted function, that administered its affairs, taught, and celebrated the liturgy."[7] The flexible, more or less fluid New Testament pattern of team eldership evolved in many places over the first two centuries into a three-part hierarchy of bishop, presbyter/priest, and deacon. At one level, the New Prophecy was a reaction to this hardening of leadership categories and to the development of the concept of "office" in the church.

At other levels, the New Prophecy was both a response to persecution and evidence of the heightening of the apocalyptic and prophetic strain within early Christianity. Frend notes that "prophecy, asceticism, and martyrdom, the hallmarks of Montanism, all belong to the second-century Christian tradition."[8] This was especially true in Asia Minor, where the Gospel of John and the Revelation were much revered and where there was widespread Jewish presence. Frend points out that "the place occupied by the Paraclete in Montanist theology, their hopes of martyrdom, and the coming of the millennium are purely Johannine."[9]

About A.D. 170 three Christian prophets in Phrygia—Montanus and two women, Maximilla and Priscilla—claimed to receive new revelations from the Holy Spirit and knowledge of an imminent appearance of the Holy City. Montanus, a relatively new convert and reportedly a former priest of Cybele, said the heavenly Jerusalem seen by John would soon descend near the Phrygian town of Pepuza, ending the present age.[10] The prophetess Priscilla declared, "Christ came to me in the form of a woman clothed with a long, gleaming, flowing robe, and placed wisdom in me and revealed to me that this place is sacred and that in this place the heavenly Jerusalem shall descend."[11] Sparked by a fresh emphasis on the ministry and gifts of the Holy Spirit, the movement called itself the New Prophecy. (Only two centuries later did the movement become known as Montanism.)

Like the book of Revelation, to which it felt especially attracted, the New Prophecy movement arose in an atmosphere of persecution and trials. New decrees about A.D. 175 permitted provincial officials to plunder and kill Christians throughout Asia. This "oppressive condition of persecution created the atmosphere in which the flame of the New Prophecy burned brightly."[12] Frend notes that the new prophetic message "was heard gladly. The prophets spoke of the millennium; people abandoned homes, families, and work, and streamed out into the countryside. Wars and rumors of wars were freely foretold, death as a martyr was accepted, and this was to be prepared for by fasting and abstinence at the command of the Holy Spirit."[13] In the face of persecution, the New Prophecy taught believers to confess Christ openly and accept martyrdom gladly. "Do not hope to die in bed," the prophets urged, "but as martyrs."[14] So virile was the new movement that it made some Christians question whether John's *Apocalypse* was really divinely inspired and acceptable among the received authoritative writings of the church.

Frend adds, "All told, with the large and long-established Jewish communities scattered around the province, the influence of an apocalyptic-minded church at Philadelphia, and a native religious tradition which tended towards violent and orgiastic religious manifestations, the emergence of Montanus' movement in Phrygia is not surprising. The orthodox clergy ran scared."[15]

Women were particularly prominent in the New Prophecy movement, especially as prophetesses. "It is highly probable that from the beginnings of Montanism, women were permitted to rise to ministerial status through their role as confessor-martyrs in the

19

early Christian church."[16] Frend notes that while women "had traditionally played a role in prophecy," there was "always opposition from representatives of institutional religion."[17] The free exercise of women's prophetic gifts in the New Prophecy probably heightened opposition to the movement. Maximilla, before her death about 179, lamented, "I am driven as a wolf from the sheep. I am not a wolf. I am word, spirit and power."[18]

The new movement soon organized itself as a church with alternate forms of leadership. It formed close-knit communities of believers modeled, they thought, on the first Christian community in Jerusalem.[19] "Many of the accusations leveled [against the Montanists] merely suggest that the Montanists were behaving like the Church, *were* in fact the Church in large areas."[20] Bishop Epiphanius of Salamis, writing some two hundred years after the beginning of Montanism, gives us one of the more graphic accounts of the movement. Writing in his "Medicine Box" (*Panarion*) against heresies, Epiphanius says,

> The members of this sect held Quintilla and Priscilla in great honor and called them "prophetesses." To justify the admission of women into the clergy, they . . . referred to the daughters of Philip who prophesied. Frequently a procession of seven virgins, carrying torches and dressed in white, is seen entering their assemblies. Under the power of prophetic delirium, they lamented the miseries of the human condition and surrendered themselves to noisy penitential demonstrations, so that the assistants also cried with them. But that is not all—they had women bishops and presbyters, since, as they said, they did not discriminate with regard to sex, to be in accord with the statement of Paul: "In Christ Jesus, there is neither male nor female."[21]

THE SPREAD AND INFLUENCE OF THE NEW PROPHECY

The new movement grew rapidly, spreading through Phrygia, into Thrace and as far as Gaul. By 200 it was stirring the church in such major centers as Rome and Carthage, though initially its major impact seems to have been in less sophisticated rural areas. Frend comments that "Montanus's movement demonstrated that Christianity among the rural populations of the empire might retain a radical apocalyptic and prophetic outlook, long after the established communities in the cities were coming to terms with their environment. It also established a precedent as a regional movement 'of the Phrygians.' "[22]

In North Africa the New Prophecy movement became linked with the name of the famous Christian apologist Tertullian (c. A.D. 165–220), who espoused the new movement about A.D. 206. Tertullian presumably was attracted to the movement because of its stress on the Holy Spirit and on purity and discipline. "Tertullian believed that the new and greater things which the Spirit promised by Jesus would reveal were stricter standards for the church and the Christian in pagan society."[23] Frend notes, "From 207 he began to quote the New Prophecy as having the same authority as Scripture."[24] He adds, "Thanks to Tertullian the North African church was and remained a gathered church concerned with the maintenance of its integrity."[25]

Writing in *Against Praxeas,* Tertullian pointed out that the bishop of Rome had first "acknowledged the prophetic gifts of Montanus, Prisca, and Maximilla" and given the new movement his blessing, but had changed his mind due to false accusations brought by the heretic Praxeas. By his heretical views concerning the relationship of God the Father and the Son and his opposition to Montanism, Tertullian complained, Praxeas "did a twofold service for the devil at Rome: he drove away prophecy, and he brought in heresy; he put to flight the Paraclete, and he crucified the Father."[26]

The New Prophecy was opposed in part because of its stress on the prophetic and ecstatic gifts. One opponent, Asterius Urbanus (probably a bishop), said he found "the church in Pontus greatly agitated by this new prophecy, as they call it, but which should rather be called this false prophecy." And he speaks of "the impropriety of a prophet's speaking in ecstasy."[27] Ecstatic gifts and visions certainly occurred in Montanism; Tertullian wrote near the end of his life, "We have now among us a sister who has been granted gifts of revelations, which she experiences in church during the Sunday services through ecstatic vision in the Spirit."[28] Following the worship service the woman would report her visions to the leaders, who would examine "all her communications . . . with the utmost scrupulous care, in order that their truth may be probed."[29]

This did not mean, however, that Tertullian favored widespread leadership of women in the church. He felt ecclesiastical functions, including teaching, should be limited to men. As a Montanist, however, he did recognize the legitimacy of women as prophets in the church.[30]

Official opposition to the New Prophecy grew. In 230 the Synod of Iconium refused to recognize Montanist baptism, virtually excommunicating the movement. Yet "Montanism continued as an underground movement, chiefly as a protest against growing formalism and worldliness in the official church."[31] The church in Thyatira was entirely Montanist for nearly a century[32] and in some areas Montanism survived for 300 years or more.[33]

THE NEW PROPHECY AS A RENEWAL MOVEMENT

What was the net influence of the New Prophecy? Frend notes that while "Montanism had shaken the authority of the episcopate momentarily, . . . at the end of the century established hierarchies were in firmer control of Christian communities than ever before."[34] And Henry Chadwick comments, "The chief effect of Montanism on the Catholic Church was greatly to reinforce the conviction that revelation had come to an end with the apostolic age, and so to foster the creation of a closed canon of the New Testament."[35]

22

David Wright concludes that the Montanists were "fanatics but not heretics." He adds, "The church lost much by excluding them. Despite their excesses, the Montanists stood for the conviction that the Spirit was active in the church as at the beginning; greater manifestations, not lesser, were promised for 'the last days.' "[36] And historian Paul Johnson comments, "The Montanists were evidently sincere, holy and probably humble and abstemious people."[37]

According to Klawiter, the New Prophecy was rejected not because it was theologically unorthodox but "because in the new situation in which the Christians were openly pursued, it took a position on martyrdom which the church deemed to be suicidal, irrational and destructive to the life of the church. Thus, the extreme position of voluntary martyrdom distinguishes the New Prophecy from its ecclesiastical opponents."[38] Writing from the perspective of the Methodist renewal in eighteenth-century England, John Wesley declared that Montanus was "one of the best men then upon earth" who, "under the character of a Prophet, as an order established in the Church, appeared (without bringing any new doctrine) for reviving what was decayed, and reforming what might be amiss."[39]

The New Prophecy movement testifies to both the decline of spiritual vitality in the church and the faith's inherent tendency and push toward new life and fresh energies. In the New Prophecy we see the first (or one of the first) of many recurring waves of renewal that were to stir the church. Some movements were local and limited; others touched the church more broadly or deeply. Each had its unique features; yet each demonstrated certain recognizable patterns or tendencies, as we shall see.

Many would argue that the New Prophecy did more harm than good. The reaction it provoked pushed the church further toward institutionalism, the bureaucratization of charismatic power, and a clergy-dominated church. At present, all we wish to say is that no renewal movement is unambiguous. Neither its initial reception nor its longer-range impact is predetermined. In any case

IMPORTANT

it is significant and thought-provoking to see a renewal movement shaking the church within one and one-half centuries of Pentecost. And the movement raises issues that we need to examine as we look more broadly at church history.

LESSONS FOR CHURCH RENEWAL

The story of the New Prophecy provides both insights and questions concerning the nature of the church and the dynamics of church renewal. Themes emerge which we will see recurring often in history, and today as well. We may note the following marks of Montanism which recur in other movements:

1. The movement was grounded in a thirst for renewal, for recovery of an earlier dynamic, or for "better times" in the life of the church. This is how renewal movements arise. A perception grows that the church has declined from its early purity or power, and that somehow the vitality and perhaps the patterns of the early church must be recovered. This is often called "primitivism": the wish to recover the vitality of the early (or primitive) church.

2. A stress on the immediate operation or "new work" of the Holy Spirit in the present day. The Holy Spirit is seen to be active in the present, in new ways. The work of the Spirit recorded in Scripture is seen not only as important for the past but also as a model and expectation in the present.

3. Relatedly, an institutional/charismatic tension appears in the church. Whenever the Holy Spirit is perceived to be doing a new work in the present, tension with existing patterns is almost inevitable. Suddenly the status quo is questioned. Is the "new thing" of the Spirit or not? And if it is, what kind of judgment is this on existing patterns?[40]

4. A concern with being a countercultural community over against the world; a strong sense of *being* the community of the church. Renewal movements call the church to a more radical commitment and a more active tension with the world.

5. Nontraditional or nonordained leadership in the church,

including openness to the gifts and leadership of women. Renewal movements often are led by people with no recognized leadership status in the church who usually emerge through a new burst of charismatic gifts. In this freer, less institutionally regulated environment, women are often more noticeably active than in the church generally.

6. Ministry to the poor, or those at the lower end of the socioeconomic scale. Often (though not always) renewal movements are movements of the masses, or the unlettered or uncultured. The New Prophecy was not exclusively a movement of the poor, but it was "of the Phrygians," and was known as such. To associate the movement with Phrygia was to discredit it; "Phrygians were considered stupid, boorish, and cowardly, and their name was almost a synonym for these negative qualities."[41] The movement was popular, "of the people," rather than of the church's more cultured sectors.

7. The energy and dynamic of a new movement. One of the most fascinating features of any renewal movement is the energy it demonstrates and its ability to excite and enlist others as leaders and participants. This is significant sociologically and raises questions theologically: Do this energy and dynamic derive from God, from Satan, or merely from human will and emotion and social dynamics? And how does one tell?

For now, these are questions—issues to be faced. They are questions of history and interpretation, to which we will later return.

Down through history people have been hopefully curious about renewal, reform, and revival in the church. What brings about genuine renewal? Are there any handles to help us understand it? Before proceeding to a deeper analysis of specific movements, we will examine the different ways renewal itself may be understood and interpreted.

NOTES

[1] J. Armitage Robinson, *The Passion of St. Perpetua* (Cambridge: University Press, 1891), vii.

[2] *The Passion of St. Perpetua,* in T. Herbert Bindley, *The Epistle of the Gallican Churches Lugdunum and Vienna* (London: SPCK, 1900), 62. Note the reference to 1 Corinthians 12 and Ephesians 4:11.

[3] *Passion of St. Perpetua,* Bindley, 72.

[4] Ibid., 76.

[5] Frederick C. Klawiter, "The Role of Martyrdom and Persecution in Developing the Priestly Authority of Women in Early Christianity: A Case Study of Montanism," *Church History* 49 (September 1980): 257.

[6] The New Prophecy movement came to be known as Montanism. J. Armitage Robinson felt that *The Passion of St. Perpetua* had a "distinctly Montanistic tone," particularly in its emphasis "on the present work of the Holy Spirit in the Church and especially in Martyrdoms" (Robinson, 51; Robinson believed Tertullian edited the account). A number of other scholars concur. However, in a recent examination of the evidence, William Weinrich concludes that Perpetua probably was not a Montanist and that "the evidence argues against Tertullian as the redactor of the *Passio*." His evaluation is as follows: "There is, therefore, no reason to assume that the redactor of the *Passio* was a Montanist or that he tended toward Montanism. What the *Passio* shows is that within the Church at Carthage there was a dispute concerning the continuance of certain phenomena of the Spirit within the Church. One party denied that the Spirit still worked in the selfsame manner as in earlier periods. . . . The other party—to which the redactor of the *Passio* would have belonged—affirmed that the Spirit continued to act in the Church as it [*sic*] had always acted. The relationship of Montanism with this conflict cannot be determined with any precision. Possibly the introduction of Montanism into Carthage elicited the conflict" (William C. Weinrich, *Spirit and Martyrdom: A Study of the Work of the Holy Spirit in Contexts of Persecution and Martyrdom in the New Testament and Early Christian Literature* [Washington, D.C.: University Press of America, 1981], 224, 225, 235–36).

[7] W. H. C. Frend, *The Rise of Christianity* (Philadelphia: Fortress, 1984), 139. *Presbyter (presbyteros)* is the Greek term for *elder,* and *bishop* means *overseer.*

[8] Ibid., 254.

[9] Ibid.

[10]F. L. Cross and E. A. Livingstone, eds., *The Oxford Dictionary of the Christian Church,* 2d ed. (London: Oxford University Press, 1974), 934; Elsa Gibson, *The "Christians for Christians" Inscriptions of Phrygia* (Missoula, Montana: Scholars Press, 1978), 125; Klawiter, "Martyrdom and Persecution," 253.

[11]Klawiter, "Martyrdom and Persecution," 253.

[12]Ibid.

[13]Frend, *Christianity,* 254.

[14]David F. Wright, "The Montanists," in Tim Dowley, ed., *Eerdmans Handbook to the History of Christianity* (Grand Rapids: Eerdmans, 1977), 74.

[15]Frend, *Christianity,* 255.

[16]Klawiter, "Martyrdom and Persecution," 251.

[17]Frend, *Christianity,* 255.

[18]Ibid., 256.

[19]David F. Wright, "The Montanists," *The Lion Handbook of Christian Belief* (Hertfordshire, England: Lion, 1982), 427.

[20] Paul Johnson, *A History of Christianity* (New York: Atheneum, 1976), 49–50.

[21]Roger Gryson, *The Ministry of Women in the Early Church,* trans. Jean LaPorte and Mary Louise Hall (Collegeville, Minn.: The Liturgical Press, 1976), 77–78. It is hard to know how much weight to give Epiphanius' description, though (as Gryson notes) "Despite what some scholars say, there is not sufficient reason to reject this testimony" (p. 78).

[22]Frend, *Christianity,* 256.

[23]Wright, "The Montanists," *Lion Handbook of Christian Belief,* 428.

[24]Frend, *Christianity,* 349–50.

[25]Ibid., 350.

[26]Tertullian, "Against Praxeas," Alexander Roberts and James Donaldson, eds., *The Ante-Nicene Fathers* (Grand Rapids: Eerdmans, 1976), 3:597.

[27]*The Ante-Nicene Father,* 7:335, 337.

[28]Paul Johnson, *A History of Christianity,* 50.

[29]Tertullian, *De Anima,* quoted in Gryson, *Ministry of Women,* 20.

[30]Gryson, *Ministry of Women,* 17–19.

[31]H. D. C. McDonald, "Montanism," in J. D. Douglas, ed., *The New International Dictionary of the Christian Church* (Grand Rapids: Zondervan, 1974), 674.

[32]Henry Chadwick, *The Early Church* (Middlesex, England: Penguin Books, 1967, 1976), 52.

[33] Wright, "The Montanists," *Eerdmans Handbook to the History of Christianity*, 74.

[34] Frend, *Christianity*, 285.

[35] Chadwick, *The Early Church*, 53.

[36] Wright, "The Montanists," *Eerdmans Handbook to the History of Christianity*, 74.

[37] Johnson, *A History of Christianity*, 50.

[38] Klawiter, "Martyrdom and Persecution," 254.

[39] John Wesley, "The Real Character of Montanus," in Thomas Jackson, ed., *The Works of John Wesley*, (London: John Mason, 1829–31), 11:479.

[40] Montanism, in fact, became the battleground and rallying point for the church's struggle between institution and charisma, between hierarchical authority and prophetic inspiration, and between strict discipleship and open inclusiveness—in sum, between sect and church (in the Troeltschian sense).

[41] Gibson, *Inscriptions of Phrygia*, 125.

Chapter Two

The Study of Renewal
Movements

Chapter Two

The Study of Renewal Movements

Over and over again renewal has stirred the church. Montanism was only the first of a long and continuing series of renewal movements.

Today one hears of charismatic renewal, lay renewal, theological renewal, or liturgical renewal. And renewal, or revitalization in the broader sense of social or cultural movements, is also a topic of scholarly interest. These various uses of the term *renewal* are all linked, for whatever else the church may be, it is at least a body of people with some common characteristics who are undergoing change. Whatever else it is, the church is a social and cultural phenomenon.

Yet because renewal happens, or is perceived to happen in the church, it is a theological consideration. And because the church is a movement in history, church renewal is a historical consideration. The phenomenon of renewal in the church thus deserves historical and theological study. W. A. Visser 't Hooft, former general secretary of the World Council of Churches, once wrote:

. . . we have practically no studies of Church history written from the point of view of the renewal of the Church. This is most regrettable. For the most important contribution which the study of its own history can and should make to the life of the Church is to teach it how its Lord operates through judgment and renewal. If a Church historian . . . would give us a story of the renewals of the Church, we would come to see far more clearly . . . how the Holy Spirit intervenes in the life of the Church. . . . Such a presentation of Church history would show the extraordinary capacity for renewal which characterizes the Christian Church. . . . Though it could of course not prove that the Holy Spirit is at work in that history. . . , it would inevitably raise the challenging questions: What is it that makes for the rebirth of the Church when everything . . . would seem to point to its approaching death? Why is it that the great attempts to suppress it have so often led to its renewal?[1]

Beginning in the next chapter, we will look in detail at three renewal movements which arose in Europe in the seventeenth and eighteenth centuries: German Pietism, Moravianism, and British Methodism.

THE PROBLEM

Pietism, Moravianism, and Methodism were movements within large established church communions. These movements and their principal leaders (Philipp Jakob Spener and August Hermann Francke, Count Nikolaus von Zinzendorf, and John Wesley) did not intend to start new sects, but to revitalize the established church. Yet they touched off dynamics which either resulted in or threatened to produce separate denominations.

There are direct historical links between Spener, Francke, Zinzendorf, and Wesley, and at the levels of theology and practice a number of parallels and interrelationships are traceable. Most of these concern, in one way or another, matters of ecclesiology. Among common features of the three movements were an emphasis on the new birth; intensity of personal religious experience; a focus on personal piety, holiness, and discipline; an emphasis on Scripture; primitivism and an "oppositive element" regarding the established church; and religious idealism.[2] From an ecclesiological perspective, two characteristics of these movements are especially interesting and seem to be fundamental to the function of these groups as agencies of renewal: The emphasis on and practice of some form of "more intimate fellowship" for prayer, Bible study, and personal sharing, and the practical expression (not always articulated) of the priesthood of believers through ecclesiastically unordained or "lay" leadership. We will focus particularly on these two issues.

The formation of intimate renewal communities within the larger church (whether locally or trans-locally) raises fundamental questions of ecclesiology. It is usually seen as implying a negative judgment on the spirituality and sometimes the legitimacy of the larger church community and structure. Therefore tension and controversy often arise precisely over this issue. And since such renewal communities or subcommittees often become the context for the emergence of new, unauthorized leadership, the question of unordained or "lay" leaders is a closely related issue.

These dynamics are found in very interesting ways in Pietism, Moravianism, and Methodism. All three movements were, in effect, *ecclesiolae in ecclesia*—both in the broader sense, as movements within established ecclesiastical communions, and in the narrower sense, as subgroups within local parishes. Pietism had its *collegia pietatis*; the Moravians organized distinct communities; and the Methodists were organized into "societies." Further, Moravians and Methodists subdivided into smaller, more tightly knit groups, called "bands." As such community structures developed, so did new patterns of leadership. Spener advocated greater emphasis on "the spiritual priesthood" as a means of reform, and Zinzendorf and Wesley had rather elaborate theories of ministry or the church, as we shall see, which allowed for the use of various kinds of "lay" ministers.

The issues raised by such renewal movements are both

historical and theological. The historical questions focus on the development of "lay" leadership and renewal communities in Pietism, Moravianism, and Methodism and the interrelationships among the three movements. The theological questions concern the place of renewal communities and unordained leadership in the theology of the church and church renewal and raise the issue of the legitimacy or validity of such phenomena—whether evaluated biblically, sociologically, or by other criteria.[3]

SOME DEFINITIONS

Pietism, Moravianism, and early Methodism are here treated as "renewal" or "revitalization" movements. Although the term *renewal* is not precise, it comes closest, in the popular sense of "church renewal," to the meaning intended here. More specifically, by "renewal movement" I mean a sociologically and theologically definable religious resurgence which arises and remains within, or in continuity with, historic Christianity, and which has a significant (potentially measurable) impact on the larger church in terms of number of adherents, intensity of belief and commitment, and/or the creation or revitalization of institutional expressions of the church. Gerlach and Hine define *movement* as "a group of people who are organized for, ideologically motivated by, and committed to a purpose which implements some form of personal or social change; who are actively engaged in the recruitment of others; and whose influence is spreading in opposition to the established order within which it originated." They see its five key factors as being (1) "a segmented, usually polycephalous, cellular organization" with various personal, structural, and ideological ties; (2) "face to face recruitment by committed individuals" from their already existing social relationships; (3) personal commitment which marks off the convert from the prevailing order and commits him or her to the movement and its patterns of behavior; (4) an integrating and motivating ideology; and (5) "real or perceived opposition."[4] This definition fits the movements we are discussing here.

INTERPRETIVE FRAMEWORKS

How does one go about studying renewal movements? The task can be approached from several angles. In fact, the various ways of looking at church renewal movements may be classified into seven interpretive frameworks. These frameworks employ or imply somewhat different models of renewal. Neither the frameworks themselves nor the models of renewal implied therein are necessarily mutually exclusive.

These seven perspectives may be sketched as follows. (I have largely omitted the various dispensational and millennial theories [both ancient and modern] which might be included here as being only marginally relevant since they tend to be based on ahistorical frameworks.)

Ecclesiola in Ecclesia

The church, (*ecclesia*), composed of large numbers of people all of whom profess faith in Christ but who in fact demonstrate varying degrees of commitment, needs as a normative structure a form of "a church within the church" or a "little church" (*ecclesiola*) as a place the occasion for more intimate fellowship and spiritual growth. From this perspective, both the *ecclesia* and the *ecclesiola* are viewed as normative, complementary structures which together provide for a greater measure of spiritual health and vitality in the church.

As a specific theory or concept, the *ecclesiola* idea is often traced back to Martin Luther. In his Preface to the German Mass of 1526 Luther proposed "a truly evangelical order" which would meet in private, not "in a public place for all sorts of people." Thus, those who want to be Christians in earnest and who profess the gospel with hand and mouth should sign their names and meet alone in a house somewhere to pray, to read, to baptize, to receive the sacrament, and to do other Christian works. According to this order, those who do not lead Christian lives could be known, reproved, corrected, cast out, or excommunicated, according to the rule of Christ, Matthew 18. Here one could also solicit benevolent gifts to be willingly given and distributed to the poor, according to St. Paul's example, II Corinthians 9. Here would be no need of much and elaborate singing. Here one could set up a brief and neat order for baptism and the sacrament and center everything on the Word, prayer, and love. Here one would need a good short catechism on the Creed, the Ten Commandments, and the Our Father.

In short, if one had the kind of people and persons who wanted to be Christians in earnest, the rules and regulations would soon be ready. But as yet I neither can nor desire to begin such a congregation or assembly or to make rules for it. For I have not yet the people or persons for it, nor do I see many who want it. But if I should be requested to do it and could not refuse with a good conscience, I should gladly do my part and help as best I can. . . . And to train the young and to call and attract others to faith, I shall—besides preaching—help to further some public services for the people, until Christians who earnestly love the Word find each other and join together. For if I should try to make it up out of my own need, it might turn into a sect.[5]

Here is a rather complete description of the purpose and function of an *ecclesiola in ecclesia* (although Luther does not use the term here), as well as the reasons why Luther never put this idea into practice.

As we will see, both Spener and Zinzendorf made use of the *ecclesiola in ecclesia* idea. Spener's *collegia pietatis* were commonly identified as *ecclesiolae* and Zinzendorf drew on Spener and the *ecclesiola* concept in developing his own distinctive ecclesiology.

In Continental Lutheran circles especially the *ecclesiola in ecclesia* idea has received some attention, primarily with reference to Luther himself. The question, as Gerhard Hilbert puts it, is "to what extent Luther himself had thought about the structure or form of the Church and [Christian] community."[6] Hilbert concludes that Luther in fact desired both the established church and the voluntary smaller covenantal community—rather than, as some have argued, exclusively one or the other. Luther accepted the state church, but "he also earnestly had wished for the *ecclesiola in ecclesia*."[7] Luther saw the *ecclesiola* concept as a realistic option; "he never understood this 'ideal' as false, even though he had not embodied it practically."[8]

In general, Lutheran and Reformed writers seem uncertain what to make of Luther's idea of an evangelical covenant order. Dietrich Bonhoeffer saw "great danger" in the *ecclesiola* idea; it would almost inevitably lead to an equation of the "church within the church" with the true church. "The church within the church is not separable from the empirical church community, and is itself such a community. If the separatist attitude is nevertheless adopted, the result is the establishment of factions. It is thus advisable to proceed cautiously. . . ."[9] Yet Bonhoeffer's later experience with expressions of Christian community in Nazi Germany took forms very similar to what Luther was advocating in 1526.[10]

Karl Barth criticized the *ecclesiola* idea even more strongly:

> We are obviously thrown back entirely on faith even if in a supposed awareness of the mixed character of the Church union we try to seek an "inner circle" of true believers or to make common cause with certain others as *sancta ecclesiola in ecclesia*. It is evident that Luther did occasionally toy with this idea. But fortunately he neither developed it systematically nor attempted to apply it in practice. For who is to decide and who is able to decide who belongs or does not belong to this *ecclesiola*?[11]

The concern of Barth and others was that the "church within the church" might be understood as, or come to mean, the true church within the nominal church in a way that proves divisive or is presumptuous. This apparently was Luther's concern as well. As a strategy for church life or renewal, however, the *ecclesiola* may be seen not as an attempt to separate the wheat from the tares but as a normative means for providing the intimacy and discipline of community which contribute to the health of the whole church. The *ecclesiola* is a voluntary subcommunity providing the option of a more deeply earnest experience of the Christian faith for those believers who sense such a need. Whether such *ecclesiolae* can in fact function without creating factions or schism, and whether it is ever legitimate to allow for what may amount to two levels of discipleship in the church, are the two major questions raised by the *ecclesiola* approach.

The idea of *ecclesiola* can, however, be applied to the Roman Catholic context as a way of looking at Catholic orders. Dean Kelley has suggested that religious orders such as the Dominicans, Franciscans, and Jesuits may be seen as *ecclesiolae:*

> These movements typify the *ecclesiola in ecclesia* . . . which have infused new vigor and resilience into the churches throughout the centuries. The Roman Catholic Church has shown exceptional ingenuity in harnessing and internalizing these reform movements for the good of the Church as a whole through the device of the religious order existing alongside the secular (parish and diocesan) structure but largely independent of it. Thus the *ecclesiola,* responsible directly to the pope rather than to the local bishop, served as a legitimated but not subservient source of example, criticism, goading, and competition to the rest of the Church. It raised the general level of demand and commitment by its own greater strictness (an injection of new stringency rather than an imposition of stricture), but it also felt the equal and opposite reaction of the resistant environing masses.[12]

It is clear that the idea of *ecclesiola in ecclesia* functioned significantly as part of the renewal strategy of Continental Pietism and early Moravianism. And in Great Britain both the Anglican religious societies from about 1675 on and the Methodist societies functioned in fact as *ecclesiolae.* Furthermore, the concept is still operative today. Many of the Latin American Roman Catholic *comunidades de base,* or base ecclesial subcommunities, apparently see themselves as *ecclesiolae*,[13] and J. M. Ford uses the *ecclesiola* motif as a point of criticism against some tendencies in the Catholic charismatic renewal today.[14]

Sect/Church Typologies

The well-known sect/church typology derives initially from Max Weber and Ernst Troeltsch. This is essentially a historical and sociological approach to the phenomenon of the different social forms of Christianity. It is based on the premise that all church groups tend either toward the highly committed, exclusivistic, antiestablishmentarian sect or toward the inclusive, more institutional, established church which is more or less identical with society. The relevance of the typology for the present study is its identification and analysis of two distinctly different kinds of groups, with adult voluntary commitment being a primary differentiating factor between the two. Sociologically, at least, the *ecclesiola* and the sect have much in common and may in some cases signify the same thing, while the *ecclesia,* when defined as the larger church within which the *ecclesiola* functions, tends toward the church side of the sect/church distinction.

When the *ecclesiola* is viewed positively as a normative pattern, the major difference between the *ecclesiola in ecclesia* and sect/church concepts appears at once. *Sect* and *church* describe forms of the Christian community which are mutually exclusive, whether viewed as discrete types or as opposite poles on a continuum. In contrast, the *ecclesiola* concept holds by definition that both "sect" and "church" are normative patterns; that the more intense, committed group does or should function within the larger "church" context—for the health of both. The sect/church distinction raises a very serious question, however, whether such a symbiosis is in fact possible on any kind of sustained basis. Are *ecclesiola* and *ecclesia* like opposite poles of a magnet, which inevitably repel each other? This question underscores the criticism of those who reject the *ecclesiola* concept as inherently undesirable or unworkable.

While the sect/church typology has some value as a tool for analysis, it does not seem appropriate as the primary framework for our study here. Also, the considerable disagreement over the precise meaning of these terms and the inability of scholars to reach any consensus on specific categories indicate serious problems with the typology.

Believers' Church Theories

Another interpretive framework emerges from those who advocate a Believers' Church understanding of the Christian community. This is essentially a biblical-theological-historical approach: biblical in that it sees the New Testament teachings and believing community as providing the normative model of what the church is always to be; theological and historical in that it interprets church history in the light of this model, usually viewing Constantinianism as the fall of the church and calling for its restitution to the New Testament pattern.

The Believers' Church position has been articulated with considerable force in recent decades as Anabaptism and the Radical Reformation have been "rediscovered" and given more sympathetic scholarly treatment. The position is advocated especially by Franklin Littell, Donald Durnbaugh, and John Howard Yoder.[15]

In defining the Believers' Church both Durnbaugh and Yoder cite Luther's suggestion in 1526 of a "truly evangelical order" as indicating the essential elements of what the church ought to be. The Believers' Church is "the covenanted and disciplined community of those walking in the way of Jesus Christ. Where two or three such are gathered, willing also to be scattered in the work of their Lord, there is the believing people."[16]

A Believers' Church model of seven elements may be synthesized from the writings of several advocates of this position.[17] As a type or model somewhat distinct from its various historical manifestations, the Believers' Church demonstrates most basically the following characteristics:

1. Voluntary adult membership based on a covenant-commitment to Jesus Christ, emphasizing obedience to Jesus as necessary evidence of faith in him. Believers' baptism has usually been the sign of this commitment, but not essentially.

2. A community or brotherhood of discipline, edification, correction, and mutual aid, in conscious separation from the world, as the primary visible expression of the church.

3. A life of good works, service, and witness, as an expression of Christian love and obedience, incumbent on all believers—thus an emphasis on the ministry of the laity, rather than a special ministerial class; the church as a "missionary minority."

4. The Spirit and the Word as comprising the sole basis of authority, implying a de-emphasis on or rejection of church traditions and creeds.

5. Primitivism and restitutionism: belief in the normative nature of the early church, with an attempt to restore the essential elements of early church life and practice; also implying some view of the fall of the church.

6. A pragmatic, functional approach to church order and structure.

7. A belief in the universal church as the body of Christ, of which the particular visible believing community is but a part.

The Believers' Church model is immediately attractive in studying renewal movements because of the similarity of concerns between the Believers' Churches and reform movements within established church communions. The Believers' Church perspective, for instance, stresses the priority of an authentic visible expression of the believing community; mounts a radical critique of the institutional church; and values highly the daily life and practice of believers in terms of community, obedience, discipline, mutual support, and service. This tends to be true as well of reform groups within the larger church. It could be argued, of course, that reform groups, if consistent, would break with the institutional church and go the full route of the Believers' Churches—or, conversely, that Believers' Church groups err in carrying their views to too radical an extreme, thus breaking with the larger church, causing schism. One way of mediating these two views might be to raise the question of the particular historical and cultural circumstances which tend either to push a group toward separation or to hold it within the larger church. This raises an important question with regard to the three groups we are studying—a question that will require attention as we analyze and compare these movements in detail.

The Believers' Church position has been criticized as failing to appreciate the positive side of the historic or institutional church, as being divisive or sectarian, and as potentially leading to withdrawal or isolation from the world. As an interpretive framework, its main difference from the two discussed above is that it focuses primarily, if not exclusively, on one side of the duality that characterizes the *ecclesiola/ecclesia* and sect/church viewpoints. On the other hand, Believers' Church proponents do not necessarily claim that theirs is the only authentic expression of the church (although they tend to see it as normative).

Revivalism Theories

The history of the church and of God's work in the world can be understood in terms of a series of divinely inspired religious revivals. This is a somewhat more popular and less academically sophisticated interpretive framework, and one which has operated in the church for many years.

In general, revivalism theories hold that by more or less direct divine intervention, but with more or less human agency or cooperation, the church is periodically renewed by outbreaks of revival. Such revivals may fit into a pattern of common characteristics; these may vary somewhat according to the interpreter. An ebb and flow, or oscillation, of revival currents is often posited.

Revivalism is often associated particularly with the modern

era since the eighteenth century and especially with the North American scene.[18] As a way of looking at the renewal of the church, however, the revivalism viewpoint clearly has broader application. J. Edwin Orr, for instance, has applied an essentially revivalistic viewpoint in describing a series of "evangelical awakenings" throughout the world.[19] Orr uses the terms *revival* and *awakening* virtually synonymously, defining an evangelical awakening as "a movement of the Holy Spirit bringing about a revival of New Testament Christianity in the Church of Christ and in its related community."[20] Its "major works" are invariably "some repetition of the phenomena of the Acts of the Apostles" (especially "the 'upper room' type of praying and the pentecostal sort of preaching"), "followed by the revitalizing of nominal Christians and by bringing outsiders into vital touch with the Divine Dynamic causing all such Awakenings—the Spirit of God." The divine origin of such revivals is evidenced by the "presentation of the evangelical message declared in the New Testament and its reenactment of the phenomena therein in the empowering of the saints and conversion of sinners."[21] According to Orr, an accelerating progression of awakenings beginning just prior to the Protestant Reformation has "moved the Church by degrees back to the apostolic pattern." "What may be called the General Awakenings began in the second quarter of the eighteenth century, among settlers in New Jersey and refugees from Moravia about the same time. The First Awakening ran its course in fifty years, and was followed by the Second Awakening in 1792, the Third in 1830, the Fourth in 1858–59, the Fifth in 1905."[22] Thus for Orr, evangelical awakenings are essentially a Protestant phenomenon.

It is understandable that persons who are key figures in religious renewals should attempt to explain them by a theory or theology of revival. We may think especially of Jonathan Edwards (1703–58), the New England scholar and revivalist who played a key role in the Great Awakening in America. Edwards increasingly came to see the New England awakenings from 1734 on as a key to understanding the work of God in history. In his *Faithful Narrative of the Surprising Work of God* (1736), *The Distinguishing Marks of a Work of the Spirit of God (1741)*, *Thoughts on the Revival in New England* (1742), and other works, Edwards attempted not only to understand these awakenings but to view them within the broad sweep of God's redemptive active.

Edwards intended eventually to write "a great work, which I call a History of the Work of Redemption, a body of divinity in an entire new method, being thrown into the form of a history,"[23] but this design was cut short by his death in 1758. However, a 1739 series of his sermons was posthumously published as *A History of the Work of Redemption* (Edinburgh, 1774). In these writings the outlines of Edwards' views on renewal are clear. Perry Miller summarizes:

> In the History of the Work of Redemption Edwards saw the over-all design of history as a steady progress from the fall of Adam to Christ, then a reversal of direction with the coming of the Saviour, and thereafter "a finishing state," where all is spent "in finishing things off which before had been preparing, . . . in summing things up, and bringing them to their issues." But in each of the two phases, though work is steadily carried on, there is a constant rising and falling, not deviations or repetitions, but the zigzag course of a ship making head against the wind, every tack putting it farther on its voyage. The systole and diastole of time is like that within the person: it "has its ups and downs," but all the while, "in general, grace is growing." A declension, thus, should be interpreted as a preparation for the next and greater exertion: "the event is accomplished in a further degree than in the foregoing." As there are ebbs, so there are floods, each mounting higher toward the goal of history.
>
> Though the larger design is constant progress, from Adam to Christ, from Christ to the Judgment, within these segments of time the morphology is retreat and advance, and the work "has mainly been carried on by remarkable pourings out of the Spirit of God." History moves through a pulsation of "special seasons," interspersed with exhaustion and backsliding. The prophets were revivalists, early Christianity was a revival, and

so was the Reformation. The intervals are necessary in the design as times for the gathering of forces; in each resurgence more men are changed (or men are more changed) than in the preceding.[24]

Edwards paints this drama, in part, in terms of the kingdom of God, "that evangelical state of things in his church, and in the world, wherein consists the success of Christ's redemption" in the final period of history.[25] "The setting up of the Kingdom of Christ is chiefly accomplished by four successive great events" or dispensations: Christ's appearing in the apostolic age; the "destruction of the heathen Roman empire" under Constantine; the destruction of Antichrist; and "the last judgment, which is the event principally signified in Scripture by Christ's coming in his kingdom."[26] According to Edwards, "Christ's coming in Constantine's time, was accompanied with a glorious spiritual resurrection of the greater part of the known world, in a restoration of it to a visible church state from a state of heathenism."[27]

Edwards developed these ideas on a postmillennial framework and intimated that the millennial age of the church was beginning to dawn in his own day. By positing alternating periods of advance and decline, however, he was able to admit some of the dangers, weaknesses, or superficialities of awakenings or renewals while still seeing these movements as legitimate and strategic components in the divine strategy.

A century after Edwards, Charles G. Finney (1792–1875), converted lawyer, rose to prominence in North America as a widely effective evangelist. His success and the "new measures" he introduced (the "mourner's bench," the "protracted meeting") have given him the reputation as the "Father of Modern Revivalism." Conceiving of revivals more narrowly than Edwards did, Finney analyzed the phenomenon of revivalism in a series of lectures in 1835 which were later published and widely distributed as *Lectures on Revivals of Religion*. A decade later Finney wrote a less well-known series of letters on revivals published in the

Oberlin Evangelist in 1845 and 1846; these have recently been republished as *Reflections on Revival*.[28]

Finney did not build his theory of revivals into an overall theology of redemption but did set about to analyze the factors which promote revivals and saw revivals as necessary for the progress of the church. The church has "so little firmness and stability of purpose," he wrote,

> that unless it is greatly excited, it will go back from the path of duty, and do nothing to promote the glory of God. The state of the world is still such, and probably will be till the millennium is fully come, that religion must be mainly promoted by means of revivals. . . . The Church is so little enlightened, and there are so many counteracting causes, that the Church will not go steadily to work without a special excitement. As the millennium advances, it is probable that these periodical excitements will be unknown. Then the Church will be enlightened, and the counteracting causes removed, and the entire Church will be in a state of habitual and steady obedience to God.[29]

More open to Arminian influence than was Edwards, Finney insisted that a revival is "not a miracle" but is "as naturally a result of the use of the appropriate means as a crop is of the use of its appropriate means."[30] However, he strongly stressed prayer and being filled with the Spirit. In his more mature reflection ten years later, he placed relatively more emphasis on God's sovereignty and the normal life of the local congregation and said opposition to social reform was a hindrance to revival.[31]

Building on Edwards' views but looking very broadly at the whole phenomenon of personal and corporate renewal in the church, Richard Lovelace published in 1979 a volume entitled *Dynamics of Spiritual Life: An Evangelical Theology of Renewal*. Lovelace argues that "different groups within the church are at odds with one another because their models of the Christian life . . . are so diverse."[32] "The Christian life is being offered in diverse packages, but what is inside is the same—newness of life in Christ."[33] He therefore calls for a "unified field theory" of spirituality that can make sense of the various ways of viewing spiritual life and renewal and expresses the hope that his book may serve as "an updating of Philipp Spener's *Pia Desideria*."[34]

Lovelace attempts to develop and refine Edwards' view of alternating periods of renewal and decline leading to final triumph of the kingdom of God. He outlines biblical models of both cyclical and continuous renewal and the preconditions of continuous renewal. He suggests that the "primary elements" of continuous renewal are justification, sanctification, the indwelling Holy Spirit, and authority in spiritual conflict. He sees "secondary elements" as being orientation toward mission, dependent prayer, the community of believers, theological integration, and disenculturation.

While the views of Edwards, Finney, Orr, and Lovelace vary considerably both at specific points and in their levels of sophistication, they are all revival theories in that they posit some pattern of periodic revivals as normal, or at least to be expected, in the life of the church. All argue that authentic revival movements are a primary source of social reform, although they vary in the relative stress they place on this dimension. Edwards, Finney, and Lovelace call for the active participation of Christians in social reform as an aspect of God's renewing work.

Compared with the interpretive frameworks already discussed, revivalism theories tend to stress the dramatic and unusual aspects of spiritual renewal over the normal, day-by-day life of the church. They tend to say little about the normative life of the local congregation, largely bypass the question of structure, and tend to see the revival of the church in more or less global terms rather than in terms of the particular situation of each congregation of believers. This is in contrast to the *ecclesiola in ecclesia* perspective (with its focus on the question of structure) and to the Believers' Church perspective which stresses that the church must be a covenanted, disciplined, visibly functioning community of believers. In general, revivalism theories tend also to presuppose a kind of individualism in understanding church life and renewal which contrasts with other views. At all these points, however, Lovelace's treatment is more carefully balanced and nuanced than are the views of earlier revivalist writers.

Revitalization Movements

A considerably different interpretive framework is supplied by discussions in anthropological circles of "revitalization movements." These discussions grow primarily out of a 1956 essay by Anthony F. C. Wallace entitled "Revitalization Movements: Some Theoretical Considerations for Their Comparative Study."

Wallace defined a revitalization movement as "a deliberate, organized, conscious effort by members of a society to construct a satisfying culture." It is "a special kind of culture change phenomenon" leading deliberately to a new cultural system. Wallace has investigated several hundred such movements, ranging from Ikhnaton's new religion in ancient Egypt to modern religious and cultural renewal movements in Africa and among North and South American Indians. He specifically includes among these movements the origin of Christianity and early Methodism under John Wesley.[35]

Wallace sees a human society as "a definite kind of organism" of interrelated subsystems ranging from the literal cells and organs of persons to the social relationships of the group. He uses the term *mazeway* to describe the mechanism by which each individual fits into this social organism. A mazeway "includes perceptions of both the maze of physical objects of the environment . . . and also the ways in which this maze can be manipulated by the self and others in order to minimize stress."[36]

When persons experience stress within their society (for whatever reasons), they choose either to tolerate the stress or to run the risk of challenging the mazeway and its related social system. "The effort to work a change in a mazeway and 'real' system together so as to permit more effective stress reduction is the effort at revitalization; and the collaboration of a number of persons in such an effort is called a revitalization movement."[37] Wallace classifies revivalistic, nativistic, and other movements as subclasses within this comprehensive category. He suggests that all organized religions may be seen as "relics of old revitalization movements."[38]

Wallace posits five somewhat overlapping stages in the revitalization process: (1) steady state, (2) period of individual stress, (3) period of cultural distortion, (4) period of revitalization, and (5) new steady state. During the period of revitalization, religious revitalization movements must perform at least six functions: (1) mazeway reformulation (led by a prophetic figure who proposes "a new mazeway Gestalt"); (2) communication of this vision by the leader to others; (3) organization involving "three orders of personnel": the prophet, his disciples, and the followers; (4) adaptation in the face of resistance, giving the movement "a better 'fit' to the population's cultural and personality patterns"; (5) cultural transformation; and (6) routinization in which the movement becomes established and institutionalized.[39] There are certain similarities here to the sect/church typology, and in fact part of Wallace's analysis is a development of ideas first put forth by Max Weber.

William G. McLoughlin employs Wallace's scheme in discussing "Awakenings as Revitalizations of Culture" in his book, *Revivals, Awakenings, and Reform.*[40] He traces four great awakenings in America, the first (1730–60) followed by successive occurrences in 1800–30, 1890–1920, and 1960–90(?).

McLoughlin sees "the conversion of great numbers of people from an old to a new world view" as "a natural and necessary aspect of social change" involving "the awakening of a people caught in an outmoded, dysfunctional world view to the necessity of converting their mindset, their behavior, and their institutions to a more relevant or more functionally useful ways of understanding and coping with the changes in the world they live in."[41]

McLoughlin suggests that the study of such revitalizing awakenings is important for historians and social scientists, not just religionists, for such movements change the face of society. "It was through following the new guidelines of our revitalization movements that Americans abandoned allegiance to the king, abolished human slavery, regulated business enterprise, empowered labor unions, and is [sic] now trying to equalize the rights of women, blacks, Indians, and other minorities."[42]

McLoughlin's main point, however, is the deeper social significance of such awakenings. Rather than setting society on a fundamentally new course, revitalization movements (in Wallace's sense) provide the necessary energy to renew the society's sense of direction and purpose. "They restore our cultural verve and our self-confidence, helping us to maintain faith in ourselves, our ideals, our 'covenant with God' even while they compel us to interpret that covenant in the light of new experience."[43] In short, such revitalizations are a culture's way of renewing itself (again, the organismic metaphor is basic) in the face of the challenges and stresses of social change. Thus "to understand the functions of American revivalism and revitalization is to understand the power and meaning of America as a civilization."[44]

From one perspective, Wallace's and McLoughlin's interpretation could be called a secularization or "desacralization" of the Christian renewal phenomenon in that it suggests that such upheavals are really quite natural social phenomena. One need not bring God into the picture at all. Similar movements occur in Christian and non-Christian contexts. On the other hand, any valid or fruitful description of how renewal occurs or how renewal in the church parallels similar phenomena in non-Christian settings is obviously important data for the Christian historian and theologian.

This is recognized by Charles H. Kraft in his study *Christianity in Culture: A Study in Dynamic Biblical Theologizing in Cross-Cultural Perspective*.[45] Kraft's book is essentially an attempt to understand the dynamics of crosscultural Christian communication, or what he calls "Christian ethnotheology." He notes the importance of revitalization movements in such Christian communication, treating them in essentially the same way as does Wallace, and noting Wallace's analysis.[46] Kraft also notes the apparent analogy between individual conversion and the process a society undergoes when experiencing revitalization.[47]

Similarities between religious revitalization movements and broader socio-cultural patterns are suggested also by comparing religious renewals and "scientific revolutions." Kraft notes that the phenomena of revitalization movements "are often of the same nature as the 'scientific revolutions' described by Kuhn."[48] Thomas S. Kuhn describes "the structure of scientific revolutions" in terms of a "paradigm shift" within a scientific community. The fundamental models or paradigms by which that community understands itself and its work undergo a change which in turn produces new insights. "Led by a new paradigm, scientists adopt new instruments and look in new places. Even more important, during revolutions scientists see new and different things when looking with familiar instruments in places they have looked before."[49] Such altered perceptions due to changed models or paradigms seem analogous to the changes persons experience in religious renewals, or to the new perceptions of biblical content that often accompany the rise and progress of a renewal movement (or new theological current) in the church.

The value of the revitalization movement framework is precisely that it raises questions and suggests perceptions which might otherwise be overlooked. It both provides a useful tool for analysis and itself constitutes a "paradigm shift" in the way renewal movements are studied. It may enable the investigator to "see new and different things" when looking in familiar places. As an interpretive framework, this perspective suggests that Christian renewal movements at least partake of a broader set of dynamics that are a part of all significant movements of social change.

Modality/Sodality Typology

Protestant missiologist Ralph D. Winter has elaborated a theory of two normative structures in the church, using the terms *modality* and *sodality*.[50] The sodality in Winter's definition is a distinct subcommunity within the larger church (the modality), and is highly mission-oriented. Medieval preaching orders and modern Protestant missionary societies are seen as examples of such sodalities. This is thus an interpretive framework which, like the *ecclesiola in ecclesia* and the sect church typology, underscores the duality of groupings or structures that often emerges in the church, based in part on intensity of commitment.

Winter believes that these two structures can be found throughout church history and even in the New Testament. What we normally think of as the New Testament church was essentially a Christian synagogue and was supplemented in its missionary outreach by small missionary bands, probably also patterned after Jewish models. Later in Roman culture these two patterns emerged as the parish church and the monastic order, respectively.[51]

In Winter's view, the missionary sodality and the modality (congregation) are quite different. Whereas the congregation is comprised of all the believers, including families, and must therefore concern itself with a broad range of worship and nurture functions, the sodality is an elite, more explicitly committed group focused on a particular mission. "A sodality is a structured fellowship in which membership involves an adult second decision beyond modality membership, and is limited by either age or sex or marital status. In this use of these terms, both the denomination and the local congregation are modalities, while a mission agency or a local men's club are sodalities."[52]

Winter sees "the harmony between the modality and the sodality achieved by the Roman Church" in the Middle Ages as the most significant characteristic of the church's life and growth during that period and "Rome's greatest organizational advantage to this day." It was the variety and vitality of Catholic sodalities which accounted for much of the renewal and missionary outreach of the church during its first 1,500 years. Winter believes "the greatest error of the Reformation" and its greatest structural weakness was that in reacting against monasticism it made no room for sodality structures. Winter notes however the position of the Anabaptists and considers the Believers' Church as "a most significant experiment in Christian structure" which "stands in a certain sense, midway between a modality and a sodality, since it has the constituency of the modality (involving full families) and yet, in its earlier years, may have the vitality and selectivity of a sodality."[53]

Charles J. Mellis has elaborated Winter's typology in somewhat more depth in his book *Committed Communities*.[54] He briefly examines Pietism and Moravianism as sodality structures (seeing the Moravians as the fruit of the merging of Protestant Pietism and the earlier radical Christianity of the *Unitas Fratrum*) but does not discuss Methodism. He notes the emergence in recent decades of such youth-oriented Protestant missionary sodalities as Youth With a Mission and Operation Mobilization.

Several authors have discussed essentially this same model in recent years, although sometimes with different terminology. Gordon Cosby speaks of "mission groups," based on the experience of the Church of the Savior in Washington, D.C.[55] Donald Bloesch sees intentional Christian communities as forming, together with the larger church, "two patterns of discipleship," both of which are needed.[56] In this connection he quotes Dietrich Bonhoeffer's call for "a new kind of monasticism, which will have only one thing in common with the old, a life lived without compromise according to the Sermon on the Mount in the following of Jesus."[57]

The modality/sodality approach to church structure may be seen as a systematization or elaboration of the *ecclesiola in ecclesia* pattern, provided the *ecclesiola* is viewed as more than merely a pietistic growth cell. While Winter and Mellis apply the modality-sodality pattern primarily to missions, at the structural level this pattern applies equally to renewal movements. Thus Stephen B. Clark in his book *Unordained Elders and Renewal Communities* is really dealing with the same issue. Writing from within the contemporary Catholic Charismatic Renewal, Clark sees historical precedents for today's renewal communities and their leaders in the Catholic monastic tradition. Like Winter, Mellis, and Bloesch, Clark holds that subcommunities are and should be a normative pattern in the church, although his concern is with "movements in which the central thrust is towards a more fervent and effective living of the Christian life" rather than specifically with missionary outreach.[58] This seems, however, to be a difference of focus, not of structure.

The modality/sodality construct employs a primarily historical and theoretical perspective rather than a theological one. It grows mainly out of a pragmatic concern with the renewal or mission of the church. Like the *ecclesiola in ecclesia* pattern, it sees both the modality and the sodality as normative and complementary. It thus seeks to hold together the "sect" and "church" tendencies in dynamic, constructive tension. The sodality may be seen, in effect, as an attempt to maintain the character and dynamism of the Believers' Church (and of the sect) within the confines of the larger church. Many sodalities which originated in or assumed the character of a movement could be considered "revitalization movements" in the sense discussed above. Several such movements (especially within the Protestant context) would be considered "revival movements" in the sense discussed earlier in this chapter, but that designation fails to deal adequately with the dynamic of the relationship of such movements to the larger church context.

Catholic Anabaptist Typology

In his study of renewal groups in the Christian tradition, Stephen Clark suggests that "Renewal communities always tend to pattern themselves on the New Testament Church."[59] He adds, "When renewal communities that have grown out of the charismatic renewal have done something similar, they have, at times, been accused of modeling themselves on (or being influenced by) the Protestant 'Believers Church' (the Anabaptist tradition)."[60] Clark claims the charismatic communities are really more similar, however, to the early ascetic communities than to the Believers' Churches.

The comparison between renewal communities and Believers' Church groups does, however, raise some interesting questions which have been explored by several writers. Of significance here are both the suggested parallels between Catholic renewal or monastic communities and the Believers' Churches, and the role or function of such groups in relation to the larger Roman Catholic or Protestant traditions, respectively.

Four Roman Catholic writers (Josephine Ford, Rosemary Ruether, Jane Russell, and Michael Novak) have raised the question of such parallels in somewhat different ways and almost totally independently of each other. Josephine Ford employs the comparison negatively as a way of criticizing the Catholic charismatic renewal. She distinguishes "two forms or types" within the charismatic movement: Type I, which is characterized by "a para-ecclesial structure; a teaching, advisory, and executive magisterium; and a disciplinary system," and has important affinities with Anabaptism; and Type II, which by contrast is "unstructured and free," places less stress on separate community experience, and "is fully integrated with the theology and sacramentality" of Roman Catholicism.[61] Ford believes Type II is more authentic and legitimate, while Type I represents a dangerous schismatic tendency, as demonstrated in part by its affinities with Anabaptism, or Radical Protestantism.

Ford sees a basic difference between Anabaptist communities and legitimate renewal subcommunities, based on their relationship and attitude toward the institutional church. Thus Type I groups resemble Anabaptism while the more authentic Type II communities are similar to "early Franciscan and Dominican spirituality." Similarities between Anabaptism and Catholic renewal communities are thus viewed negatively. (Ford does not discuss the fact that Catholic orders generally with time became quite structured.)

Michael Novak takes a considerably different approach in an essay entitled, "The Meaning of 'Church' in Anabaptism and Roman Catholicism: Past and Present." Noting "similarities between the inspiration of the Anabaptist conception of the church and the inspiration of the Roman Catholic conception of the special religious community," Novak calls attention especially to the early Franciscans. "If, for a moment, we conceive of 'the Roman Catholic Church' only as a generic name like 'the Protestant Church,' and look upon the different modes of Catholic life as sects or denominations within the larger whole, the relationship between evangelical Anabaptist piety and Franciscan piety seems . . . striking."[62]

As Ford suggests that the charismatic "baptism in the Spirit" is the functional equivalent of believers' baptism, so Novak sees the religious vow and believers' baptism as being functionally equivalent. "The dynamism of living faithful to a freely taken religious vow . . . appears to be very like the dynamism of living faithful to believers' baptism."[63] Novak goes on to suggest several parallels between the Anabaptist view of the church and the Catholic view of religious vocation: "Such a life is a free, voluntary commitment; it forms a band of the 'more perfect'; it has discipline; it encourages the piety of abandonment to God's will; it is undertaken as a living martyrdom, founded on renunciation of the world and on the doctrine of the cross."[64] Thus Novak suggests:

> Anabaptism represents a laicizing of the Catholic monastic spirituality; it is a transferal of the focus of the "state of perfection" from a monastic brotherhood, bound by vow and cloistered by walls, to a lay, married brotherhood bound by believers' baptism and separated from the world by the ban. Its

root is not a sense of sin, trust in personal justification, and aggressive social reform (classical reformers); its root is the desire to follow God completely, to withdraw from the world, and to respond to a call to a new and higher form of Christian life (Catholic religious vocation).[65]

Novak points out two crucial differences, however, between the Catholic religious and the Anabaptist. First, the Catholic religious sees himself or herself as living a special form of the Christian life within the larger community of the church, while the Anabaptist tends to see the church as restricted to the covenant community of adult believers. Second, Anabaptism inevitably faces the problem of the second generation and therefore the dangers of relaxation and accommodation, while the religious order more easily maintains its dynamism and focus since "new candidates . . . must come from without, by free choice."[66] (We may add however that the history of monastic orders shows that this fact alone is not sufficient to prevent eventual decline in vigor or accommodation to the world.)

Novak does not discuss this comparison in terms of church renewal, nor, in fact, does he develop it as a typology for the life of the church or of renewal communities. His concern is primarily to point out the similarities noted above, to explore some of the dynamics, and to suggest that in some respects Anabaptists are becoming more catholic, and Catholics are moving somewhat in an Anabaptist direction (principally in the rejection of Constantinianism). The juxtaposition of these two conceptions of the Christian life does, however, suggest a Catholic Anabaptist typology that could be applied more specifically to the question of church renewal. Novak suggests that "Anabaptist emphasis upon the free act of faith, the covenant, and the consensus, introduce [sic] into Christian polity an admirable way of living out the freedom of the Gospels under communal discipline."[67] These themes are all important for questions of renewal and renewal movements.

Rosemary Ruether makes a conceptually similar comparison,

SIGNS OF THE SPIRIT

though without explicitly referring to historical Anabaptism, in her essay, "The Free Church Movement in Contemporary Catholicism." Speaking of various renewal currents in Catholicism (not primarily of the charismatic renewal), Ruether describes the "free church" and the institutional church as "interdependent polarities." She writes:

> The free church, in the sense that I am using it, is the free community within historical Christianity. It is founded on a view of the church which denies that hierarchical institutionalization belongs to the essence of the church. The church is seen essentially as the gathered community of explicit believers in which sacramental distinctions between clergy and laity are abolished, priestly roles become purely contextual and functional; the whole community arising by joint covenant entered into by the existential analogue of believer's baptism; that is to say, by voluntary adult decision. This concept of the believer's church is, I believe, the authentic church, and it is the understanding of the church which ever reappears in the avant garde at the moments of real church renewal. It is the avant garde and full expression of the church of renewal.[68]

Ruether says the "free church" cannot however "simply replace the institutional church." The institutional church is essential but secondary. "It is necessary precisely for that dimension of historical perpetuation of the church's message as tradition which continually makes the gospel available to a new generation." The free church, in contrast, "cannot perpetuate itself" and simply becomes another institution if it tries to do so. Thus:

> The two are really interdependent polarities within the total dialectic of the church's existence. The charismatic community can be free to be itself when it can resign the work of transmission to the institution and allow itself to form its life and let go of its life only so long as the vital spirit lasts within it. The historical church, in turn, remains vital and is constantly renewed through its ability to take in and absorb the insights of the believer's church. But in order to receive the fruits of the believer's church, it must be willing to accept whatever freedom the believer's church feels is necessary for the flowering of its

own experimental spirit. It must be willing to let communities
arise autonomously and without any specific kind of institutional ties to work out their own gifts, and yet still to remain in
the kind of open communication with these free communities
which will allow their fruits to be given to the church as a
whole. Only in this way does the whole dialectic of historical
Christianity work as it should.[69]

Ruether admits that in fact, however, this dialectic never
completely works out as it should because of the fallenness of
humankind and the church. "Hence we constantly block the free
movement of the dialectic of renewal in the church and fall into
alienation and schism." Implicit in Ruether's argument is the
caution that unless room is given for this "free church" expression,
the Spirit's renewing work "flees outside the bonds of historical
Christianity and takes up its work elsewhere."[70]

While Ruether does not explicitly develop the "free church"
or "believer's church" side of her typology in terms of historic
Anabaptism, her terminology and the way she develops her
analysis in terms of "interdependent polarities" is conceptually
similar enough to be classified under the Catholic Anabaptist
typology. In general, her approach is more conceptual and
theoretical than historical in that the "free church" in her analysis
appears to be rather ahistorical, whereas it is the institutional
church which "represents the historical dimension of the church's
existence."[71] Structurally, Ruether's model also displays close
affinities with that of Winter and Mellis, which posits the need for
normative sodality structures for mission and renewal analogous
to Catholic religious orders.

Jane Russell explicitly employed an Anabaptist model as an
aid in evaluating contemporary Catholic renewal movements in
her 1979 dissertation, "Renewing the Gospel Community: Four
Catholic Movements with an Anabaptist Parallel." Although
admitting the difficulties with such an approach, she concludes
that "the problems of classification and evaluation entailed in a
Catholic Anabaptist comparison do not outweigh the advan-

tages. . . . If the Anabaptist comparison serves to illuminate some features in our contemporary movements which we otherwise would not have noticed, that will be service enough."[72] She uses this approach in describing and evaluating the Catholic Charismatic Renewal, the base ecclesial communities (*comunidades de base*) in Latin America, and two Roman Catholic sisterhoods.

Russell concludes (similarly to Ford and Novak) that there are many "functional equivalents" between these Catholic renewal movements and Anabaptism. She notes:

> The key elements . . . common to all the Catholic movements were also present in the Anabaptist vision of Christian renewal: i.e., that renewal must turn around the core of Christianity, the Lordship of (or discipleship to) Jesus Christ; that only adult decision commits one fully into the Christian Church; that the Church should be above all a community of brothers and sisters who love one another and who serve one another in various ministries; and that each Christian, and each Christian community, is on mission to spread the good news. The chief difference between Anabaptists and our Catholic renewals with regard to these convictions is the degree of urgency and polemic with which the former pursued their course.[73]

Her final evaluation is that, in general, "between Catholicism as herein portrayed (renewed and reforming) and Anabaptism there is much more kinship than difference."[74]

While none of these authors fully elaborates a Catholic Anabaptist typology *per se,* they provide the perspective from which such a typology might be developed and applied to Pietism, Moravianism, and Methodism. On the one hand, Roman Catholicism and Radical Protestantism represent two polar positions and two seemingly antithetical views of the church and church renewal. On the other hand, the similarities between Radical Protestant sects and Roman Catholic religious orders suggest that similar dynamics are at work in movements of renewal, whether within the Catholic fold or within the more nebulous and fragmented world of Protestantism. The movements we are studying here may be seen as attempts at *mediating positions* between the Catholic and Anabaptist polarities. And this polarization itself provides a helpful framework for study and evaluation. Key questions about the dynamics which lead a renewal movement either to remain within or separate from the larger church context arise out of this kind of discussion.

Developed into a theory of renewal, the Catholic Anabaptist typology would hold that renewal movements within the "Catholic" Church (whether Roman Catholic or Protestant) tend to display the marks and dynamics of an Anabaptist or Believers' Church model. In this sense this typology may be seen as a variant of Believers' Church theories. On the other hand, in its affirmation of the principle of complementarity between the renewal body and larger "Catholic Church," this model has affinities with the *ecclesiola in ecclesia* and modality-sodality models. Like them, it would tend to see the dynamics suggested by the sect church typology as complementary, not mutually exclusive.

Using the motif of renewal, the Catholic Anabaptist typology could be seen as compatible with a relatively sophisticated revivalist theory (such as that of Lovelace) and would suggest that modern "revivals" are not unique but may be viewed simply as more recent examples of renewal patterns that recur in the history of the church, varying somewhat according to the socio-historical circumstances. More broadly, such "anabaptist" movements within the "catholic" church can be seen as revitalization movements in the anthropological sense discussed earlier in this chapter, and indeed as being examples within the Christian context of similar socio-religious phenomena which occur in all cultures.

SUMMARY

The discussion of these seven interpretive frameworks suggests at least three things of importance in studying renewal movements such as Pietism, Moravianism, Methodism, and Montanism. First, it suggests that the life of the church through history, viewed from almost any angle, presents an oscillating pattern of rise and fall, renewal and decline—however this pattern may be evaluated. Second, the discussion raises the question, at least, of similar or basically identical patterns in the life of renewal movements. Finally, the discussion underscores the importance of seeing church history not in static, linear terms, but as dynamic, living, and fluctuating. From this perspective, renewal movements in the church are neither isolated nor peripheral phenomena but lie at the heart of what the church is and how it functions in culture and history. If it is true, as Wallace suggests, that "all organized religions are relics of old revitalization movements, surviving in routinized form in stabilized cultures,"[75] then in the case of Christianity such movements are fundamentally and seminally important in understanding both the rise and the growth and continuance of the church. The authentic role of the Spirit and the Word in this process in the church, and in the light of apparent similarities between church renewal movements and revitalization movements in culture generally, of course becomes a question for later theological reflection and analysis.

This analysis may also explain why more has not been written historically from the perspective of the renewal of the church or from a perspective which would give major attention to renewal movements. Wallace refers to the "steady state" stage in the life of cultures and religions. In the case of Christianity, this presumably is a period of relative stability, of consolidation and institutionalization, and of scholastic orthodoxy. This is the time of doctrinal consolidation and of writing "standard" doctrinal treatises. It is therefore the period also in which the normative or orthodox understanding of the church and its history emerges.

Since such writings naturally reflect the period in which they were written, histories and doctrines of the church written during the "steady state" period are likely to reflect a relatively static understanding of the church, emphasizing its divine or eternal character and placing relatively little stress on periods of renewal or revival. Renewal periods or movements are likely to be treated in a stylized or programmatic way rather than as real movements in history. They become part of the "mythology" of the church, used to justify the status quo. It is assumed that the present situation of the church is the legitimate and logical product of the period of renewal, and real, significant differences between the status quo and the original impulse of the renewal movement are either unperceived or glossed over.

If this interpretation is valid, it explains why the history of the church has usually not been written from the angle of church renewal, and why historical (or pseudohistorical) interpretations such as those of Joachim of Fiore or Gottfried Arnold have emerged either at the periphery of the institutional church or in the context of periods of renewal or at least ferment.

This understanding further underscores the importance of giving adequate attention today to renewal movements, both for their inherent importance and as a corrective to the dominant interpretation of the life of the Christian community in history.

These observations and interpretive perspectives should be borne in mind as we turn now to the stories of Pietism, Moravianism, and Methodism.

NOTES

[1] W. A. Visser 't Hooft, *The Renewal of the Church* (London: SCM Press, 1956), 67–68.

[2] F. Ernest Stoeffler discusses several of these as distinctive marks of Continental Pietism in *The Rise of Evangelical Pietism* (Leiden: E. J. Brill, 1965), 13–23.

[3] A strict distinction between historical and theological research and analysis has intentionally not been observed in this study. It is my conviction, and therefore a methodological consideration here, that all theology must be seen as historically grounded; that the Christian faith is essentially historical (God choosing to reveal himself in human history); and that theological analysis should be understood in large measure as the church's reflection on its own history.

[4] L. P. Gerlach and V. H. Hine, *People, Power, Change: Movements of Social Transformation* (New York: Bobbs-Merrill, 1970), 370–77.

[5] Martin Luther, *Luther's Works,* ed. *Ulrich Leupold (Philadelphia: Fortress, 1965),* 53–54.

[6] Gerhard Hilbert, *Ecclesiola in Ecclesia: Luthers Anschauungen von Volkskirche und Freiwilligkeitskirche in ihrer Bedeutung für die Gegenwart* (Leipzig: A. Deichert, 1920), 1.

[7] Ibid., 3.

[8] Ibid., 3–4. Compare Ludwig Thimme, *Kirche, Sekte und Gemeinschaftsbewegung,* 2d ed. (Schonberg: Friedrich Bahn, 1925), 254–58.

[9] Dietrich Bonhoeffer, *The Communion of Saints,* trans. R. Gregor Smith (New York: Harper and Row, 1960), 169–70.

[10] See, for example, Donald F. Durnbaugh, *The Believers' Church: The History and Character of Radical Protestantism* (New York: Macmillan, 1968), 185 and following.

[11] Karl Barth, *Church Dogmatics,* 41, trans. Geoffrey W. Bromiley (Edinburgh: T. and T. Clark, 1956), 698.

[12] Dean M. Kelley, *Why Conservative Churches are Growing* (New York: Harper and Row, 1972), 114.

[13] Jane Elyse Russell, "Renewing the Gospel Community: Four Catholic Movements with an Anabaptist Parallel" (Ph.D. diss., University of Notre Dame, 1979), 306–09, 337.

[14] J. Massyngberde Ford, *Which Way for Catholic Pentecostals?* (New York: Harper and Row, 1976), 40.

[15] See especially Durnbaugh, *The Believers' Church;* Franklin H. Littell, *The Origins of Sectarian Protestantism* (New York: Macmillan, 1964); James Leo Garrett, Jr., ed., *The Concept of the Believers' Church* (Scottdale, Pa.: Herald Press, 1969); and Jane Russell's summary (Russell, "Renewing the Gospel Community," 65–73).

[16] Durnbaugh, *The Believers' Church,* 33.

[17] The typology presented here is drawn primarily from Durnbaugh, Littell, Yoder, William Estep, and Ross T. Bender.

[18] See, for example, Donald W. Dayton, "Revivalism," *New International Dictionary of the Christian Church,* (Grand Rapids: Zondervan, 1974), 844; Timothy L. Smith, *Revivalism and Social Reform* (New York: Abingdon, 1957).

[19] See J. Edwin Orr, *The Second Evangelical Awakening in Britain* (London: Marshall, Morgan, and Scott, 1949); *The Second Evangelical Awakening in America* (London: Marshall, Morgan, and Scott, 1953); *The Light of the Nations: Evangelical Renewal and Advance in the Nineteenth Century* (Grand Rapids: Eerdmans, 1965); and similar works.

[20] J. Edwin Orr, *Evangelical Awakenings in Africa* (Minneapolis: Bethany Fellowship, 1975), vii. Earle E. Cairns reflects a similar

perspective in his *Endless Line of Splendor: Revivals and Their Leaders From the Great Awakening to the Present* (Wheaton: Tyndale, 1986).

[21]Orr, *Evangelical Awakenings in Africa,* vii, viii.

[22]Ibid., x.

[23]Perry Miller, *Jonathan Edwards* (n.p.: William Sloane Associates, 1949), 307.

[24]Ibid., 315–16.

[25]Jonathan Edwards, *A History of the Work of Redemption Containing the Outlines of a Body of Divinity in a Method Entirely New* (Edinburgh, 1774; Philadelphia: Presbyterian Board of Education, n.d.), 219.

[26]Ibid., 219.

[27]Ibid., 220.

[28]Charles G. Finney, *Reflections on Revival,* comp. Donald W. Dayton (Minneapolis: Bethany Fellowship, 1979).

[29]Charles G. Finney, *Revivals of Religion* (Westwood, N.J.: Fleming H. Revell, n.d.), 2–3.

[30]Ibid., 5.

[31]Finney, *Reflections on Revival,* 17, 107, 113–19, 140–44, 151–60.

[32]Richard F. Lovelace, *Dynamics of Spiritual Life: An Evangelical Theology of Renewal* (Downers Grove, Ill.: InterVarsity Press, 1979), 16.

[33]Ibid., 17.

[34]Ibid., 12, 17.

[35]Anthony F. C. Wallace, "Revitalization Movements: Some Theoretical Considerations for Their Comparative Study," *American Anthropologist* 58 (April 1956): 264–65.

[36]Ibid., 265, 266.

[37]Ibid., 267.

[38]Ibid., 268.

[39]Ibid., 268–75.

[40]William G. McLoughlin, *Revivals, Awakenings, and Reform* (Chicago: University of Chicago Press, 1978).

[41]Ibid., 8.

[42]Ibid., 22–23.

[43]Ibid., 2.

[44]Ibid. Jeremy Rifkin makes somewhat similar claims for the significance of America's evangelical awakenings in his *The Emerging Order: God in the Age of Scarcity* (with Ted Howard) (New York: G. P. Putnam's Sons, 1979), 127–48.

[45]Charles H. Kraft, *Christianity in Culture: A Study in Dynamic Biblical Theologizing in Cross-Cultural Perspective* (Maryknoll, N.Y.: Orbis, 1979).

[46] Ibid., 57, 368, 371–77.

[47] Ibid., 370.

[48] Ibid., 371.

[49] Thomas S. Kuhn, *The Structure of Scientific Revolutions,* 2d ed. International Encyclopedia of Unified Science, 2:2 (Chicago: University of Chicago Press, 1970), 111.

[50] Ralph D. Winter and R. Pierce Beaver, *The Warp and the Woof: Organizing for Mission* (South Pasadena, Calif.: William Carey Library, 1970) (especially chapter 5, "The Warp and the Woof of the Christian Movement," 52–62, by Winter); Winter, "The Two Structures of God's Redemptive Mission," *Missiology* 2:1 (January 1974): 121–39.

[51] Winter, "Two Structures," 121–30.

[52] Ibid., 127.

[53] Ibid., 127–30.

[54] Charles J. Mellis, *Committed Communities: Fresh Streams for World Missions* (South Pasadena, Calif.: William Carey Library, 1976).

[55] Gordon Cosby, *Handbook for Mission Groups* (Waco, Tex.: Word, 1975).

[56] Donald G. Bloesch, *Wellsprings of Renewal: Promise in Christian Communal Life* (Grand Rapids: Eerdmans, 1974), 19.

[57] Ibid., 99–100.

[58] Stephen B. Clark, *Unordained Elders and Renewal Communities* (New York: Paulist, 1976), 2.

[59] Ibid., 47.

[60] Ibid., 91.

[61] Ford, *Which Way for Catholic Pentecostals?,* 1, 67.

[62] Michael Novak, "The Meaning of 'Church' in Anabaptism and Roman Catholicism: Past and Present," C. B. Robertson, ed., *Voluntary Associations: A Study of Groups in Free Societies* (Richmond, Va.: John Knox, 1966), 91, 96. A different version was published as "The Free Churches and the Roman Church," *Journal of Ecumenical Studies* 2 (1965): 426–27.

[63] Ibid., 101.

[64] Ibid.

[65] Ibid., 99.

[66] Ibid., 101.

[67] Ibid., 105.

[68] Rosemary Ruether, "The Free Church Movement in Contemporary Catholicism," in Martin E. Marty and Dean G. Peerman, eds., *New Theology No. 6* (New York: Macmillan, 1969), 286.

[69] Ibid., 286–87.

[70] Ibid., 287.

[71] Ibid., 286.

[72] Russell, "Renewing the Gospel Community," 14–15. Russell makes reference to the discussions by Ford, Clark, and Novak referred to above.

[73] Ibid., 412. See also 391–93.

[74] Ibid., 418.

[75] Wallace, "Revitalization Movements, 268.

Chapter Three

The Rise of Pietism

Chapter Three

The Rise of Pietism

Our story begins in the early 1600s with a German Lutheran pastor, Johann Arndt, and continues for nearly two centuries, till the death of John Wesley in 1791. First we need to trace the story of Pietism.

JOHANN ARNDT AND PIETIST BEGINNINGS

A decade after the death of the great reformer Martin Luther (1483–1546), Johann Arndt was born. Toward the end of Luther's life, Lutheran doctrine was codified in *The Augsburg Confession* and *The Apology for the Augsburg Confession* (both 1530), and *The Smalcald Articles* (1538). The Peace of Augsburg, giving Lutheranism legal status within the Holy Roman Empire, was signed in 1555, the year of Arndt's birth.

This was an unsettled time, both theologically and politically, in Europe. Doctrinal controversies raged for decades, most having to do with the relation of faith and works, Gospel and Law, and

71

the nature of justification. They were part of Lutheranism's struggle to define itself vis-à-vis Roman Catholicism and Calvinism. Most of the theological controversies were largely laid to rest by the *Formula* and *Book of Concord* (1577, 1580).

The price paid for these theological battles was the period of Protestant Scholasticism—roughly the century from 1580 to 1680. While Protestant Scholasticism was marked by considerable erudition and did not totally neglect the concerns of personal piety, it developed a precise methodology and vocabulary rooted partly in Melanchthon's *Loci Communes* and partly in the earlier scholasticism influenced by Aristotelianism. Scriptural authority was emphasized, but increasingly in a mechanically logical and speculative way. The period was marked by a "pervasive traditionalism" in which Luther was revered but little known or understood: "The orthodoxists remade Luther in their own image."[1] Concerns with doctrinal fidelity and precision overshadowed concerns of personal and corporate religious experience. The dominant ecclesiastical concern was with theological orthodoxy, even though interest in personal piety, especially at the popular level, had by no means died out.

Theodore Tappert characterizes the dominant Lutheran view of ministry, at this time, in a way that is illuminating for the themes of this study. He notes:

> People of the upper strata of society insisted on reception of Holy Communion separate from that of the common people, or at least with the use of a separate cup. It was then that the term "Herr Pastor" became prevalent. The divine rights of rulers was paralleled by a notion of the divine character of the ministry which, contrary to Luther, placed the ministry on a plane above that of "secular callings." Duties were carefully differentiated, and it was deemed a great offense for one person to invade the office of another.[2]

Johann Arndt grew up during the earlier period of Lutheran orthodoxy. He was born on December 17, 1555, the son of the village pastor of Edderitz. Intending to study medicine, he went at twenty-two to the University of Helmstadt. When he became ill, however, he abandoned medicine and began to study Scripture and mystical theology. He studied theology at Wittenberg, Strassburg, and Basel, and was married in 1583.

Arndt served Lutheran pastorates from 1583 to the end of his life. He was appointed general superintendent in the city of Celle in 1611 and served there until his death in 1621.[3]

Arndt's pastoral work was colored by controversy, due in part to his refusal to abandon the rite of exorcism before baptism, in opposition to the more Calvinistic duke. It was his writings however which brought him wider attention. Everything he published had to do with spirituality and practical Christian living, but with a mystical bent. In 1597 he wrote a long introduction to and edited a new edition of the *Theologia Germanica* which Luther had published in 1518. His introduction critiqued the polemical nature of many of the publications of the day. This edition of the *Theologia Germanica* apparently met with success, for it was reprinted (together with the *Imitatio Christi* and a shorter introduction) in 1605, 1617, and 1621.

The work for which Arndt is best known, and which was very popular, was his *True Christianity (Wahres Christenthum)*. This was first published in 1605, with a corrected version in 1606. It grew in part out of the debilitating political-theological controversies in Braunschweig during his pastorate there. In a letter to Professor Johann Piscator he wrote, "Through this disintegration of true Christianity I was moved to write of love, under which circumstance the thoughts occurred to me, out of which my books came."[4]

Arndt soon added three additional "books" to his original manuscript and published the larger version by 1610 as *Four Books on True Christianity*. By the time of Arndt's death in 1621 the work had gone through some twenty editions, and over 125 printings were issued by the end of the eighteenth century.[5] Arndt also published a popular prayer book, *A Paradise Garden of Christian Virtues* (1612), and other works.

In his writings Arndt made extensive use of medieval and mystical sources. Like Luther, he was strongly attracted to the German Dominican mystic Johann Tauler (ca. 1300–1361), widely thought to be the author of the *Theologia Germanica*. Arndt quotes frequently from Tauler in the first three books of *True Christianity*. Tauler's spirituality was practical and pastoral, and in this he was closely followed by Arndt.

Though Arndt used mystical sources, his theme was more the new life in Christ than the mystical union with God. Stoeffler comments, "The central theme of Arndt was not that of union. For that reason he ought not to be referred to as a mystic. It was that of the new life, an emphasis which is of the very essence of Pietism."

> Love, for Arndt, is the ultimate manifestation of a unitive life of faith in imitation of Christ. It is directed toward neighbor and God; its end is perfect patience and praise. The only object worthy of man's love or praise is the chief good, God, to whom man is directed throughout life. In all this there is little one cannot find in Luther, but in Arndt the emphasis on the life of love allows a much larger scope for a mystical interpretation of progressive perfection toward the completion of the renewal of the image of God, and of contemplative prayer, than exists in the thought of Luther.
>
> Arndt agrees fully with Luther's accentuation of faith, but in his work the possibility for a perfected experience of the faith union is continually expressed in words that might well have sounded to Luther like those of the speculative mystics he so vehemently attacked. Arndt is no longer describing a union of the exact type discussed by Luther. Rather, the believer is directed to explore the nature of his union with Christ, he is admonished to cast aside all love for the creaturely and to learn progressively to have, in fullness, the God who has united himself with the believer.[6]

Arndt begins his *True Christianity* with a discussion of the image of God. Whereas Luther's main accent was faith and the Word of God, Arndt's was love and the image of God. According to Arndt, the Holy Trinity implanted its Image in Man in the Beginning; and . . . this was after such a Manner, as the Divine Holiness, Righteousness, and Goodness might shine forth in his Soul, and send forth Light abundantly in his Intellect, Will, and Affections, yea, even in his very outward Life also: And that all his Actions, both interior and exterior, might consequently breathe nothing but Divine Love, Divine Power, and Divine Purity; and Man might live upon Earth, no otherwise than the Blessed Angels do in Heaven, always doing the Will of his Heavenly Father.[7]

In concluding the first book Arndt says, "The whole Life of a Christian upon Earth, is properly nothing else but a *Renewing of the Image of God.*"[8]

Arndt states clearly that the purpose of his books is

the Propagation and Defence of our holy Reformed Religion, as it is chiefly taught in the Churches of the *Augsburg Confession,* . . . but more particularly to promote therewith *Purity and Holiness of Life.* For the Orthodoxy of our Faith will avail but little, without the Holiness of our Lives. Not that I would discourage anyone from defending the Purity of Faith and Doctrine; yet, methinks the greatest Zeal ought to be employed in the Reformation of our Lives and Manners. For what signifies great Knowledge, without Piety? He certainly does God more acceptable Service, who makes Men *Good,* than he that makes them *Learned.* Many contend earnestly for the *Doctrines of Jesus Christ;* but very few follow his Example, or tread in his Steps. . . .[9]

Bengt Hoffman notes that Arndt "stressed in his teaching and preaching the 'Christ for us' theology of orthodox Lutheranism. He represented 'a genuine Lutheran mysticism' . . . , orthodox with respect to pure doctrine, yet a proponent of inner 'heart theology.'"[10] In attempting to maintain and nourish a life of mystical spirituality within orthodox Lutheranism, Arndt "marks the beginning of a tradition in Lutheranism in which the medieval mystics are used as *Zeugen* [witnesses] in support of a specific wing within Lutheranism."[11]

Arndt thus combined a concern for personal holiness with a

call for reform—not in doctrine, but in the church's life. Calls for reform in church life were, in Arndt, joined with the revival of mysticism then occurring within Lutheranism to produce both critique and practical advice.

Arndt's recommendations, however, focused fairly exclusively on individual personal responsibility rather than on corporate church life. Arndt gives virtually no suggestions for the reform or improvement of the church's life together as a community. His role was to foster personal piety and the quest for holiness among the church's more devout members in an age when, outside of Anabaptist groups, little attention was given to the church's corporate life.

Arndt has often been called the father of Lutheran Pietism. Stoeffler says flatly, "Arndt's relation to Lutheran Pietism is to be found in the fact that he initiated it."[12] Wilhelm Koepp says that from 1700 to 1770 Arndt was "a constant and powerful, perhaps the most powerful, factor of Lutheranism, both from within and without, and for many he was its true essence and heart."[13] Here we find the primary source of the Pietist Movement which flourished nearly a century after Arndt through the influence of Philipp Spener and August Francke.

SPENER AND THE *PIA DESIDERIA*

Philipp Jakob Spener (1635–1705) was concerned with matters which, translated into today's terminology, have a remarkably contemporary ring: discipleship, "lay" ministry, the use of elders, cell groups, and equipping believers for ministry. In Spener's day, however, these views were considered radical and potentially subversive.

Spener was born on January 13, 1635, at Rappoltsweiler, Upper Alsace. He grew up during the final decade of the Thirty Years' War (1618–1648), but "in surroundings in which a mixture of Arndtian and Puritan piety set the tone for daily living."[14] From childhood on he seems to have had a fairly even, settled spiritual pilgrimage. "He is justly regarded as belonging to that class, who have preserved, unimpaired from childhood, their baptismal grace; and, by uninterrupted internal development, continually made deeper progress in the life of faith."[15] His spiritual awakening came at the age of thirteen when his godmother, Countess von Rappoltstein, to whom he was very close, passed away.

Spener matriculated at the University of Strassburg in 1651. He studied and lectured there until 1659, completing his master of arts degree. For his two-year *peregrinatio academica* he first studied Hebrew at Basel and then went to Geneva, where he remained for a year. After visiting other cities and universities he returned to Strassburg. There he was ordained and in 1663 completed a doctoral dissertation and was married.

After a brief period of preaching in Strassburg, Spener received a call in 1666 to become, at thirty-one, pastor and *senior ministerii* (senior or superintendent of the clergy) at Frankfurt am Main. He served there with considerable success for twenty years. It was during this period that his *Pia Desideria* was published and the German Pietist Movement really began.

Spener later served as court chaplain at Dresden (1686–91) and then as pastor of St. Nicholas Church at Berlin, where he remained until his death in 1705 (100 years after the first publication of Arndt's *True Christianity*).

Spener's Christianity was clearly in the mold of Arndtian Lutheranism, but with some additional Puritan and Reformed leavening. Spener was nurtured on Arndt's writings, and his *Pia Desideria* was originally published as a preface to a new edition of Arndt's *Postill,* or sermons on the appointed Gospels of the church year (and not, as is sometimes reported, as a preface to *True Christianity.*) As a youth, under the guidance of the Countess von Rappoltstein and especially Joachim Stoll (his tutor and future brother-in-law), Spener also read a number of books by English Puritan authors. These included especially Lewis Bayly's *Practice of Piety* (ca. 1610) and Immanuel Southom's *Golden Gem* or *Golden Treasure of the Children of God,* as well as some books by Jeremiah

Dyke, Richard Baxter, and others.[16] Spener observed later, "Especially was I moved by the setting forth of the state of the believers and the state of the godless in death as it is found in the *Practice of Piety*."[17] Tappert notes that in addition to advocating self-examination and holiness, "all these devotional books by English Puritans were critical of conventional Christianity."[18]

Spener's education at Strassburg was strictly Lutheran. Yet, due in part to cross-fertilization with the Reformed tradition and the lingering influence of Martin Bucer who had been active there a century earlier, practical pastoral care was given more attention in Strassburg than in many Lutheran areas. Stoeffler notes that "the religious instruction of children was taken more seriously . . . and pastoral visitation was accepted as normal."[19] Given this background, it is not surprising that Spener's year in Geneva would have a strong impact on him. There Spener studied Waldensian and early Reformed history with the Waldensian preacher Antonius Legerus and noted with admiration the structure of the Genevan church and the piety of her pastors.[20] Most important, he often went to hear the charismatic ex-Jesuit Reformed preacher Jean de Labadie (1610–74), then at the height of his popularity. Labadie's piety was "a mixture of the Christianity of Port Royal [Jansenism] and Reformed Pietism,"[21] notes Stoeffler. Spener would undoubtedly have become aware of Labadie's primitivism, his concern for intensive pastoral work, and possibly his use of cell groups or conventicles.

Spener's earnestness, stability, and rather cosmopolitan background prepared him well for his twenty-year tenure as senior of the clergy at Frankfurt am Main. He immediately gave himself to the catechization of children and the pastoral care of adults, within the limits allowed by the traditions and ecclesiastical regulations of the time.

Spener's duties as senior of the clergy included conducting the early service at the city's main church, presiding over meetings of the city's dozen or so clergy, ordaining and installing new pastors, and keeping pastoral records. His freedom to institute reforms, however, was severely limited because of the legal authority of the civil government over the church. This was a source of constant frustration for him. He complained, " . . . we are here in the greatest confusion, and have no power to introduce any improvements."[22]

In this setting, Spener preached a sermon in 1669 which contained the essence of his later reform tract, *Pia Desideria*. He declared:

> How much good it would do if good friends would come together on a Sunday and instead of getting out glasses, cards, or dice would take up a book and read from it for the edification of all or would review something from sermons that were heard! If they would speak with one another about the divine mysteries, and the one who received most from God would try to instruct his weaker brethren! If, should they be not quite able to find their way through, they would ask a preacher to clarify the matter! If this should happen, how much evil would he held in abeyance, and how the blessed Sunday would be sanctified for the great edification and marked benefit of all! It is certain, in any case, that we preachers cannot instruct the people from our pulpits as much as is needful unless other persons in the congregation, who by God's grace have a superior knowledge of Christianity, take the pains, by virtue of their universal Christian priesthood, to work with and under us to correct and reform, as much in their neighbors as they are able according to the measure of their gifts and their simplicity.[23]

This is Spener's earliest known reference to conventicles or *collegia pietatis*. The following year (1670) he began private meetings two days a week for the spiritually awakened. At these meetings the Sunday sermon was discussed, or selections from Scripture or devotional books were read and considered. Spener himself never made extensive use of such groups. His initial enthusiasm cooled somewhat when similar groups sprang up more or less spontaneously, some of which became divisive or turned separatist.

While the strength of Spener's impact was grounded in his

conscientious preaching and pastoral work, it was his extensive writings which brought him to broader public attention and soon embroiled him in controversy. He developed a wide-ranging correspondence which made him, in effect, "pastor to all Germany." His *Pia Desideria* caused such a stir when first published in 1675 that it was quickly reissued as a separate book (with supplemental material added) later the same year. It was reprinted again the next year and issued in a Latin translation in 1678.[24] The Latin edition, it has been suggested, was prepared for the use of people involved in the religious societies in England which began about this time.[25]

The *Pia Desideria* was a spark which touched off considerable correspondence and a larger pamphlet war over church reform. Initially the response was almost totally positive, but reactions became divided as the implications of Spener's proposals began to sink in.

Spener's *Pia Desideria* was but one of many books written about the same time calling for reform and greater piety in church life. Yet none had nearly the impact of Spener's tract. This suggests two things: a widespread perception of the need for change and renewal, and Spener's unique success in presenting a practical program with succinct clarity.

The proposals Spener put forth were rather simple and straightforward:

1. More extensive use of the Word of God, particularly in homes and in contexts beyond the traditional sermon.

2. The establishment and diligent exercise of the spiritual priesthood, as taught by Luther.

3. Stress on Christianity as the practice of love and good works.

4. Religious controversies should be conducted only with prayer and a gentle spirit (citing Arndt).

5. Pastors should be trained in true piety, using the Word, devotional books, and group meetings for the cultivation of spiritual life.

6. Sermons should be directed toward producing piety and holy living.[26]

To understand the force and controversial nature of Spener's pious proposals, we need to see them in the light of the times. Spener's program was radical and threatening, one may argue, for at least three reasons.

First, Spener was proposing in effect to upgrade the role of the laity—the dormant, powerless mass of church members—vis-à-vis the two centers of power in the church: the clergy and the civil authority. He saw where the political dominance of church affairs by the prince or civil authority had led. "Apparently he had lost all confidence in the first estate. It was his belief that if the desired reformation was to come it would have to result from the exertions of the clergy and laity."[27] Thus Spener's call for a renewed emphasis on the priesthood of believers, while stated positively, was an implicit attack not only on the clergy but even more on the civil authority.

Second, Spener's proposals in effect called for changes in local church structure. He felt every church should have a *collegium presbyterorum,* a council of elders, to assist the pastor in the spiritual oversight of the congregation. This tampered with the pastoral role as traditionally understood and seemed to introduce Calvinist elements into Lutheranism.

Third, Spener's proposals amounted to replacing the confessional with the conventicle. Spener felt that Roman Catholic *ex opere operatum* ideas had infiltrated the church's sacraments and practices so that the confessional had become more a hindrance than a help. Many who confessed were in fact unrepentant. What was needed were group meetings where believers could edify one another. Here again, Spener's positive proposal implied a negative critique.

These were some of the dynamics behind an extensive theological battle which raged especially from 1677 to the end of the century, eventually involving a wide range of specific issues.

Thus the German Pietist Movement was born. Technically,

neither Pietism nor the use of conventicles began with Spener. But with Spener we can begin to speak properly of a Pietist *movement* —certainly partaking of broader currents and streams, but distinct enough, theologically and especially sociologically, to be classed with other great renewal movements in history. Pietism as a renewal movement (in the sense of the focus of this book) began about 1675 with Spener, though its major force and form came later.

FRANCKE AND THE INSTITUTIONALIZATION OF PIETISM

The Pietist Movement entered a rather distinct second phase with August Hermann Francke and the development of a Pietist center in the city of Halle. We should note both the distinctiveness of Francke's views and work and the continuity between Spener and Francke.

Not least among the ties between Francke and Spener was the pervasive influence of Johann Arndt. Like Spener, Francke was raised in an atmosphere of Arndtian spirituality. Later it was Francke's influence, in part, which increased Arndt's popularity in the early 1700s and contributed to the translation of *True Christianity* into several languages.[28]

August Hermann Francke (1663–1727) was about twenty-eight years younger than Spener. He may be viewed as Spener's disciple and, after 1690, his successor as the dominant figure in Pietism. He was born at Lubeck, a very traditional free imperial city of 35,000, forty miles northeast of Hamburg, on March 22, 1663. His father was a lawyer in rather comfortable circumstances; the home was one of progressive Lutheran orthodoxy. Francke's father died when the boy was seven.

At sixteen Francke went to the nearby University of Erfurt and began studying logic and metaphysics. After one semester there, however, he transferred to the University of Kiel when his uncle obtained a stipend for him. At Kiel he resided in the home of

Christian K. Korthold, influential historical theologian at the university, a friend of Spener, and a man of piety concerned with the reform of the church.[29] Francke later wrote that Korthold endeavored "diligently and earnestly to warn the students against the offensive character of the world, and to make them fully aware of the difficult calling of a preacher."[30] It was under his influence that Francke experienced some degree of religious awakening and began to search for a personal religious faith.

Francke studied at Kiel for three years, concentrating on theology, history, philosophy, and physics. He spent some months studying Hebrew, Greek, and English. He was a brilliant student and excelled especially at linguistics. In the spring of 1684 he went to the prestigious University of Leipzig, a recognized center of Lutheran Orthodoxy, and studied there until 1687 under Johann B. Carpzov, Johann Dornfeld, and others. He received his master of arts degree in 1685 and lectured at Leipzig as a *privatdozent,* a teacher paid according to the number of students he had but not officially employed by the university. In 1691, at the instigation of Spener, Francke was appointed professor of Greek and Oriental languages at the newly founded University of Halle, where he was to remain until his death thirty-six years later.

By 1691 Francke had become a man of some notoriety and controversy due to a series of events beginning with his conversion experience in 1687.

During his days at the universities of Kiel and Leipzig, Francke applied himself to his studies, but his theological interest was more academic than spiritual. "My theology I set in my head and not in the heart," he said; "it was much more a dead science than a living belief."[31] While lecturing at Leipzig, Francke became involved in a small group for studying the Scriptures, a *collegium philobiblicum,* which first met on July 18, 1686, in the home of Professor Otto Mencken. This group of eight or so young scholars began meeting in part under the inspiration of Professor Carpzov, and Francke quickly became the leader.[32] The students met on Sunday afternoons to read and study the Bible in the original languages. Spener heard about the *collegium philobiblicum* and advised the scholars to study the Scriptures exegetically and to avoid giving excessive attention to difficult passages. This was of course in keeping with his suggestions in the *Pia Desideria*. Spener's advice was followed, with great significance for Francke, who was seeking answers to his own spiritual questions. One result was that Francke began to concentrate on exegesis rather than systematic theology in his studies. He wrote, "I can assure anyone, that, if I consider the benefit which has come to me as a result of it, I must regard this *collegium* as the most useful and best which I have ever held at any university."[33]

The gatherings of the *collegium philobiblicum* grew in popularity and soon became controversial in the Leipzig university community. Francke, however, decided to transfer to Luneberg the following year to further pursue his exegetical studies.

Francke arrived in Luneberg in October 1687, and shortly thereafter had a decisive conversion experience. The occasion was a request to preach in St. John's Church. Studying the text, John 20:31, Francke realized that he himself lacked the faith he would be preaching about. In great anxiety ("*solcher grosser Angst*"), he says,

> I went down upon my knees again and implored the God, whom I did not yet know and whom I did not believe, that, if there really is a God, he should save me from this wretched condition. Then the Lord, the living God, as I was still upon my knees, heard me upon his holy throne. So great was his fatherly love, that he did not relieve me gradually of such doubt and inquietude of heart, which would have been enough for me. But in order that I might be the more fully convinced, . . . he heard me suddenly. Even as one turns his hand, so all my doubts were gone. In my heart I was assured of the grace of God in Jesus Christ. . . . All sadness and restlessness of heart was taken way at once. On the other hand, I was suddenly overwhelmed by a flood of joy, . . . Upon standing up I was minded entirely differently from the way I had been when I knelt down. — That, then, is the time which I may really regard as my true conversion, for from that time on my Christianity has had substance.[34]

Francke stayed in Luneberg for only six months, but started a *collegium philobiblicum* there. He continued his studies at Hamburg (1687–88) before returning to Leipzig. During this time he was increasingly influenced by Spenerian Pietism. At Luneberg he studied under the guidance of Superintendent Caspar Sandhagen (1639–97), a personal friend and colleague of Spener. At Hamburg Francke stayed at the home of Pastor Johann W. Winckler (1642–1705), who had come to St. Michael's Church in 1684 on Spener's recommendation. Here he worked with poor and orphaned children and associated closely with leading Pietist pastors who were involved in the current controversy over Pietism. These contacts culminated in Francke's visit to Spener's home in Dresden over the Christmas holidays and until February 1689. According to Stoeffler,

> From here on a common bond united the two men and they were animated by the common purpose of furthering the pietistic understanding of Protestant Christianity. In his letters Francke now referred to Spener usually as "my dear father" and he signed himself as "your dutiful son." He made sure that he absorbed thoroughly the Spenerian understanding of Christianity and that he devoted his energies to its propagation by word and deed.[35]

Francke began lecturing at Leipzig in February 1689. His exegetical lectures became immensely popular, and several *collegia philobiblicum* were formed. Soon a spiritual awakening was underway among the students, provoking controversy and opposition from Carpzov and others. Carpzov said in a funeral oration that "Our mission as professors is to make students more learned and not more pious." He and Professor Loscher, a colleague at the university, complained that the study groups brought public worship into contempt, fostered spiritual pride and exclusiveness, degraded theological science, and threw souls into despondency through their subjective approach.[36] Francke's detractors succeeded in getting an edict from the civil authorities on March 10, 1690, designating "all conventicles and private meetings in which the Holy Scripture is explained, as dangerous, interdicting them on pain of imprisonment and recommending immediate enforcement of the law."[37]

From this point on Francke was embroiled in controversy. Leaving Leipzig, he went briefly back to Lubeck, but was forbidden to preach there. He accepted a position as pastoral assistant in Erfurt, but lost it a year later due to anti-Pietist opposition. He then spent some time with Spener before beginning his responsibilities as professor and pastor at Halle in January 1692.

At Halle Francke supported himself through his pastorate at Glaucha, a small suburb of Halle, while lecturing (at first without remuneration) at the infant university. He entered earnestly into his pastoral work, and under his influence the rather worldly town of Glaucha, "the cheap night spot of Halle,"[38] began to change. Francke preached on Fridays and twice on Sundays, revived catechetical instruction, visited regularly in homes, and opened his home for meetings of prayer, singing, and spiritual conversation. His reforms aroused opposition from the Halle ministerium, culminating in an investigation in November 1692. Significantly, the one change which came out of this inquiry was the agreement to move the evening meetings from the parsonage to the church building—indicating the depth of opposition to all conventicles.

In 1698 Francke again encountered opposition and another investigation following his publication of a sermon on true and false prophets. He continued his pastoral work without interruption, however, and with considerable success and growing influence. He pastored at Glaucha until 1715, and then at St. Ulrich's Church in Halle.

Meanwhile, Francke was at the center of the growth and rising influence of the University of Halle. He served as professor of Greek and Oriental languages until 1699, then as professor of theology until his death in 1727. Because of Spener's influence in recommending faculty for the university, Francke was joined by other men of Pietist leanings such as Joachim Lange (1670–1744),

Johann Michaelis (1668–1738), and others, so that Halle soon became the leading Pietist center. Eventually, from 800 to 1200 divinity students were enrolled at Halle annually, more than in any other German university at the time.[39] (While one may say that the main current of Pietism flowed through Halle, the movement also spread in other directions more or less independently. One important branch was Wurttemberg Pietism, in which Johann Albrecht Bengel [1687–1752] played a key role.)

Francke's influence spread especially through a series of institutions (*Stiftungen*) which he founded and guided. He tells the story of these in his *Pietas Hallensis,* written in 1702 and subsequently widely circulated. Most of these institutions were started partly in response to needs in Glaucha and the surrounding area after the plague of 1682–83, which reportedly reduced the population of the town by two-thirds.[40] Francke was so moved by the ignorance and poverty of the children of Glaucha that in 1695 he began a school for the poor which soon grew to over fifty students. This led to the founding of an orphanage in 1696, and eventually to a whole series of interrelated and mutually support-ive institutions. These included a *paedagogium* for the sons of the nobility (which the young Count Zinzendorf attended for six years), a Latin school to prepare students for the university, and German schools designed to provide a practical secondary educa-tion for boys and girls of ordinary citizens. In addition to the orphanage and schools, Francke founded a home for poor widows (1698), a bookstore, a chemical laboratory, a library, a museum of natural science, a laundry, a farm, a bakery, a brewery, a hospital, and other enterprises. He was instrumental also in founding the Canstein Bible House which was lodged in the new orphanage building, completed in 1698. By 1800 the Bible house had distributed nearly three million Bible and Scripture portions in several languages.

Although some of Francke's institutions were self-supporting, many depended on voluntary contributions and the faith of Francke and his associates. Francke staffed his schools largely with university students, using divinity students as teachers both to assist with their financial support and to give them practical experience. "By the time of his death in 1727 Francke was maintaining and employing almost four thousand persons in his institutions."[41]

Two things, especially, are worth noting about these institutions. First, they were part of a very intentional reform vision. Francke hoped to transform German society and influence the world through a thorough reform of the educational system as well as of the church. Francke was an educational innovator with a practical bent and a Spenerian concern that all education further the life of piety. He saw his schools as means for infiltrating all levels of society with Pietist influence. His educational methods and ideas were in fact applied very widely due to the success of the Halle schools.

Second, the developments at Halle became well known throughout Germany and in many other countries. This was due in part to Francke's wide-ranging correspondence with several hundred people, his close personal relations with the nobility, and the network of contacts he formed in London and elsewhere. A key contact was his former student, Anton Wilhelm Bohme (1673–1722), who had become chaplain-in-ordinary to Prince George of Denmark, the husband of Queen Anne of England from 1705.

Bohme came to London in 1701 and was settled in the influential position of chaplain-in-ordinary at the German Chapel in St. James, London, from 1705 till his death in 1722. During this time he acted as Francke's representative in England. Bohme arranged for the translation and publication of Francke's writings in English, published English translations of Arndt's *True Christianity* (as already noted) and other devotional literature, and was the intermediary for much of Francke's correspondence outside Germany. It was through him that a significant correspondence began in 1709 between Francke and the New England Puritan leader, Cotton Mather.[42]

Of related significance were Francke's contacts with the Society for Promoting Christian Knowledge (SPCK) in England. Francke was in regular contact with the SPCK virtually from its inception in 1698, and the society's founders were aware of Francke's work. Francke's representatives consulted with SPCK leaders in 1698, and by 1711 the SPCK was helping to support the two missionaries Bartholomaus Ziegenbalg and Heinrich Plutschau, former students of Francke sent to the Danish colonies in the East Indies in 1706 at the instigation of the king of Denmark.[43] Through these and related endeavors, Francke became "one of the outstanding personalities connected with the rise of Protestant missions."[44]

In his roles as pastor, educator, institutional innovator, administrator, publicist, and reformer, Francke channeled the energies of Pietist fervor in many practical directions, strongly affecting German society. He was, as Stoeffler says, the "originator, founder, and lifelong head of a charitable enterprise which has caught the imagination . . . of people the world over. Nothing like it could be found in the long history of the Christian church."[45]

Francke's tenure at Halle marks the institutionalization of Pietism in two senses. First, the founding and growth of the University of Halle under Pietist influence constituted the focal point and source of the institutional and theological strength of Pietism. Second, the network of institutions founded and guided directly by Francke strengthened the movement sociologically and provided the base for a sustained impact both in Germany and in many parts of the world.

Foundational to Pietism, however, was an important theological perspective. Spener and Francke's renewal efforts clearly presupposed a theology of the church, not just of individual Christian experience. Comparing the two reformers reveals both basic similarities and marked differences in ecclesiological perspective. These in turn give us a fuller understanding of Pietism.

SPENER'S DOCTRINE OF THE CHURCH

A significant note in Spener's thinking was his sense of the corporate nature of Christian faith and experience. This theme sets him off to some degree not only from Lutheran orthodoxy but also from the mystical tradition to which he was indebted. Spener's view of the church may be summarized by noting his definition of the church and three key themes in his theology with particular ecclesiological significance.

Spener's *Pia Desideria* assumes a view of the church which is elaborated more fully elsewhere in his writings. As a Lutheran, Spener took it as a maxim that the church exists where the Word of God is preached and the sacraments are rightly administered.[46] He noted in the *Pia Desideria,* "Although our Evangelical Lutheran Church is a true church and is pure in its teaching, it is in such a condition, unfortunately, that we behold its outward form with sorrowful eyes."[47] Yet Spener was convinced that "God promised his church here on earth a better state than this."[48] Here is a key spring for renewal.

In a sermon on Matthew 22:1–14, "Of the Christian Church," preached in 1687 and published the next year, Spener notes that by "church"

> one doesn't mean the building that is dedicated to the worship of God and is used for that purpose. Such churches of which we speak are "meeting houses." One understands by the word "church," however, the gatherings of Christians, in general as well as in certain special groups. The former is the universal; the latter are the singular churches.[49]

Again, the church is "a society or assembly of people who in a certain manner are bound together with one another"; she is a people (1 Peter 2:9) and a flock.[50] The church is the bride and kingdom of Christ.[51]

Two things are especially remarkable about this sermon: repeated references to the Epistle to the Ephesians and the prominence of organic language and figures. Although the text of the sermon is from Matthew, seventeen times Spener refers to Ephesians. Further, ten of the seventeen references speak of the church organically as a community, body, and wife (for example, Eph. 2:19–21, 4:11–16, 5:25–30; the wedding banquet referred to in Matthew 22 apparently provides the connection with Ephesians 5:25–30).

In effect, Spener here takes the orthodox understanding of the church and infuses it with new life by de-emphasizing the church's institutional side and stressing her essential character as a people, community, and body. The church comes from Christ; she is "born out of Christ, for she is the seed which he is supposed to have and which was promised to him (Isaiah 53:10)."[52] As the human race derives from Adam, "so all believers, who are therefore the church, come from the second Adam . . . through the new birth in spiritual fashion." Believers become "one church or community (*gemeine*) of God."[53] "Through the New Birth we enter the fellowship of the true church."[54]

Spener's discussion abounds with organic images and also with the awareness of the difference between the "inner" and "outer" church. The "inner" church consists of

> the righteous believers who have the true, divine, living faith, and therefore find themselves not only in the outer assembly, and confess themselves to Christ, but who through such faith in him, cleave to the true head, and out of him, as the branches out of the vine (John 15:4, 5), receive living sap and spirit, and bring forth fruit out of the same. Thus we can imagine "the entire outer Christian church as a tree which has dry and green branches."[55]

Spener concentrates on the imagery of Ephesians 4:

> Christ will be named the head in a likewise natural way as the head is related to the physical body. The head not only rules the physical body with wisdom, but power for all living movements must come from it to the members of the body. In this fashion is Christ the head of the congregation—that all spiritual life and power to do good, yes, even the Holy

> Spirit, . . . must flow in and out of one member into another
> when he from one to another builds up the bodily members.[56]

Such an ideal, though biblical, clearly was far from the common experience of the church in Spener's day. Recognizing this, Spener resorted to using the visible/invisible distinction, or more characteristically to distinguishing between the "inner" and "outer" church.[57] Now by God's design true believers are "the salt which preserves the rest from universal rottenness." Wheat and tares grow together but will be separated at the Judgment.[58]

Spener's stress on New Testament images of the church reveals the primitivist motif that pervades his ecclesiology. Spener saw himself as attempting to institute New Testament church patterns and was accused of a "ridiculous aping" of the early church.[59] He saw the period of church history before Constantine as "the brilliant age of Christendom, when the church had not yet fallen into secularization," as Deeter notes.[60] Spener viewed himself as a reformer striving to complete the Reformation begun by Luther in the areas of life, morality, and the corporate experience of the church. The church had so far failed to carry the Reformation through to its logical conclusion.[61]

While this was Spener's general understanding of the church, three key themes gave his ecclesiology a distinctive flavor: his emphasis on the new birth (*Wiedergeburt*), the universal priesthood, and the importance of small groups (*ecclesiolae* or *collegia pietatis*).

The New Birth

The theme of *Wiedergeburt* (rebirth or new birth) was a key element in Spener's ecclesiology, as has been increasingly recognized in recent years.[62] While Spener clearly held to the orthodox doctrine of justification by faith, the organic concept of new birth was the dynamic element in his understanding of Christian experience.

Spener often preached on the new birth. As his writings, and especially the sixty-six sermons published as *Der Hockwichtige Articul von der Wiedergeburt* in 1696 show, rebirth was an important theme for Spener—"the center around which everything else has to be ordered."[63] According to Martin Schmidt, *Wiedergeburt* is the "inner meaning" of Spener's thought and "the ground-theme of Pietist theology."[64]

Spener gave an orthodox interpretation to baptism and justification but saw much of the church in a backslidden condition needing regeneration. As John Weborg notes,

> For Spener, the "backslider" is one who had by his life rejected the new covenantal life, received in baptism. The *Wiedergeburt* is a return to the household of God and to the Covenant. . . . The *Wiedergeburt* was secondary to baptism and was not a demand for all provided they remained within the grace of baptism.[65]

Spener's new birth/rebirth concept was not merely one element in his theology. Rather, it became a central motif through which Spener came to see not only personal spiritual experience but the whole course of the church. In his use of organic rather than primarily legal language and metaphors one finds a distinct difference from Luther—in fact a "paradigm shift," in Thomas Kuhn's sense, which lies at the heart of the Pietist Movement.

Rebirth according to Spener involves three stages: the kindling of faith, justification and adoption as children of God, and the completion of the new man.[66] "Spener's regeneration-concept is not a simple but a complex concept";[67] not a moment or single act but in effect a process marked by stages and crises.

This new birth emphasis profoundly shaped Spener's ecclesiology in at least two ways. First the stress on organic figures and models meant a concern with the present life and fellowship of the church, not just with one's theological/juridical standing before God or one's eternal destiny. This was of course in keeping with Arndt and the mystical tradition. Second, and perhaps more importantly, Spener's rebirth theology was closely linked with his overall hope for a general church renewal.

Spener held out the hope for "better times" (*besserer Zeiten*) for the church—based on God's promises and a renewed faithfulness of God's people.[68] He hoped to see *the church herself* reborn and renewed. His stress on perfection meant the relative perfection of the church, not just of individual experience:

> We do not understand the perfection which we demand of the church in such a way that not a single hypocrite is any longer to be found in it, for we know that there is no field of grain in which there are no weeds. What we mean is that the church should be free of manifest offenses, that nobody who is afflicted with such failings should be allowed to remain in the church without fitting reproof and ultimately exclusion, and that the true members of the church should be richly filled with many fruits of their faith. Thus the weeds will no longer cover the grain and make it unsightly, as is unfortunately often the case now, but the weeds will be covered by the grain and made inconspicuous.[69]

Wallmann and others have pointed to Spener's "hope of better times" as the core of his eschatology. Scripture promises better times—a renewal of the church—and so we can and must work for such a renewal in hope and faith. "For Spener, the ideas of the 'better church' and the 'better man' closely paralleled each other, and the former presupposed the latter."[70] In other words, Christians may expect not only spiritual rebirth in individual experience but also a rebirth or renewal of the church.[71] What can be true in personal experience can be true as well for the whole church. Here is, in embryo at least, a theology of church renewal, not just of individual experience.

The Spiritual Priesthood

This vision for church renewal was reinforced by Spener's renewed stress on the priesthood of believers. Spener had made "the establishment and diligent exercise of the spiritual priest-hood" a cardinal point in his reform program: "All spiritual functions are open to all Christians without exception. Although the regular and public performance of them is entrusted to ministers appointed for this purpose, the functions may be performed by others in case of emergency. Especially should those things which are unrelated to public acts be done continually by all at home and in everyday life."[72]

As with the doctrine of regeneration, Spener here takes an element of Luther's theology and gives it new prominence and meaning. The universal priesthood became for Spener a funda-mental category for understanding the church herself. The church, including all members, *is* a priesthood under the High Priesthood of Jesus Christ. Spener combines the teachings of Ephesians 4:11–12 and 1 Peter 2:9 to bring out the practical meaning of this priesthood: Teachers and preachers are "the ordained workers and master-builders on whom the church is built," given so "that the saints will be prepared for the work of ministry" (Eph. 4:11–12). But other Christians, he continued,

> based on their spiritual priesthood, . . . may and should strive to build the church, . . . not only with prayer and good example, but according to each person's measure of grace, with instruction, admonition, warning, punishment and consolation. (1 Peter 2:9) All you Christians, not only the preachers, "are a chosen race, a royal priesthood, a holy people, . . . " through which . . . they are supposed always to encourage their brethren and all others to enlist themselves so much more diligently (in the fellowship and blessings of the church).[73]

Spener's publication in 1677 of a tract on "The Spiritual Priesthood" shows both the importance of this theme in his ecclesiology and its practical link to his reform program. The tract was published in part to give a theological-biblical justification to the use of conventicles, or cell groups (*collegia pietatis*), in which both lay man and lay women took a prominent part.[74] Spener defines the spiritual priesthood as "the right which our Saviour

Jesus Christ has purchased for all men, and for which He anoints all believers with His Holy Spirit, in virtue of which they may and shall bring sacrifices acceptable to God, pray for themselves and others, and severally edify themselves and their neighbors."[75]

Spener argued that the spiritual priesthood was based on "the new birth in baptism" and the anointing of Christ. The conception here is highly Christological: the universal priesthood derives from the High Priesthood of Jesus. Spener argues that "All Christians without distinction, 1 Peter 2:9, old and young, male and female, bond and free, Gal. 3:28," are spiritual priests. In fact, "the name priest is a general name for all Christians," not specifically for ministers who, "according to their office, are not properly priests."[76]

Spener details the "offices" of the spiritual priesthood as (1) sacrifice, (2) praying and blessing, and (3) the divine Word.[77] While public ministry is reserved to "the office of the ministry" and requires "a special call," all believers have the right and duty to exercise these priestly functions privately and personally among themselves. Believers should use the Word of God "for themselves and among or with others." They are to "search the Scriptures, so that they may test the teaching of their preacher."[78]

From this basis Spener leads into the need for "mutual edification" and the application of the Word by believers within the church in fulfillment of believers' "duty to care for the salvation and edification of others."[79] The communion of saints is an earthly fellowship, not just a heavenly reality. In the "one spiritual body" of the church, believers have the duty to build up one another: " . . . believing Christians are to use the Scriptures to all these intents and to teach, convert from error, admonish, reprove and comfort, as the Scriptures themselves everywhere indicate."[80] This is to be done "according to the gifts bestowed by God upon each one"—not publicly, but "privately as occasion offers and without hindrance to the public office of the regular ministry."[81] Clearly, this is a prescription for house groups as well as for the teaching of the Word within the family. Spener gives concrete practical advice:

> When godly hearts come together and read in the Scriptures, each one should modestly and in love tell for the edification of the others what God has enabled him to understand in the Scriptures, and what he thinks will be serviceable for the edification of the others.[82]

All these duties concern all Christians, "not only in the sense that fathers and mothers should faithfully do these things among their children and domestics, but that every Christian has the power and right to do these things among his brethren on other occasions. . . ."[83]

Spener is explicit here about the role of women:

> 60. But do women also share in these priestly offices:
> Assuredly; for there is neither Jew nor Greek, bond nor free, male nor female, but all are one in Christ Jesus, Gal. 3:28. In Christ, therefore, the difference between man and woman, in regard to what is spiritual, is abolished. Since God dignifies believing women also with the spiritual gifts, Joel 2:28, 29; Acts 21:9; 1 Cor. 11:5, the exercise of them in proper order cannot be forbidden. The apostles themselves make mention of those godly women, who worked together with them and edified their fellow men; . . .
> 61. But are women not forbidden to teach?
> Yes; namely in the public congregation. But that it is permitted to them outside of the public congregation, is clear from the passages and apostolic examples cited, I Cor. 14:34 sq.; 1 Tim. 2:11, 12.[84]

Spener goes on to explicitly endorse the *collegia pietatis* idea and to instruct pastors how they may encourage such groups while maintaining proper order.

An interesting and ecclesiologically rich aspect of Spener's stress on the spiritual priesthood is the link he makes to the sacraments. Baptism is entrance into the spiritual priesthood,[85] and the Holy Communion, "as it is a feast of love, and as we all partake of one bread, . . . signifies that we are one body."[86] Based on the sacrifice and priesthood of Christ, the spiritual priesthood is a sacramental fellowship. Thus Spener's sacramental theology is set within the context and ecclesiological meaning of the priesthood of believers. As Weborg comments,

> The importance of the Lord's Supper is not determined by merely arriving at a theology of the sacrament. Its importance is seen most clearly when it is placed in the context of the larger doctrine of the priesthood of believers. The Lord's Supper is a feast celebrated within this priesthood. Christ, by instituting this meal, defined the character of the priesthood.[87]

Thus "Holy Communion is an act performed by Christ the High Priest whereby he . . . purifies and sustains the identification with Christ and simultaneously with one another. Holy Communion is Christ feeding the believer, solidifying the unity of the priesthood."[88]

In this stress on the spiritual priesthood Spener was not only putting new emphasis on a Reformation doctrine, but was in fact recasting ecclesiology in more vital, less institutional terms. This was consistent with his essential definition of the church and his stress on *Wiedergeburt*. A distinctive ecclesiology emerges out of Spener's concern for (and practical pastoral involvement in) the renewed life of the church. The doctrine of the priesthood of believers, and with it the sacraments, are reshaped and given new life by this paradigm shift in Spener's ecclesiological thinking. A more charismatic, less institutional ecclesiology emerges stressing *koinonia,* mutual edification and discipline, and to a limited extent the gifts of the Spirit.

Collegia pietatis

Spener's proposal for *ecclesiola* structures, the *collegia pietatis,* should be seen in the context of these distinctive accents. For Spener such conventicles were not merely a matter of pastoral strategy (though they clearly were that); rather they were firmly embedded in the reformer's fundamental ecclesiology.

In the *Pia Desideria* Spener introduced his proposal for such house gatherings with an appeal to the early church, proposing "to reintroduce the ancient and apostolic kind of church meetings."[89] 1 Corinthians 14:26–40 was to serve as the model. In Spener's view, the best hope for renewal of the church was the recovery of the Word of God in the context of a gathered expression of the spiritual priesthood. Not only preaching but also "reading, meditating, and discussion (Ps. 1:2)" of the Word "must be the chief means for reforming something. . . . The Word of God remains the seed from which all that is good in us must grow." Through eager and diligent searching of the Scriptures together, believers "will become altogether different people."[90]

As noted above, Spener grounded the *collegia pietatis* theologically in the universal spiritual priesthood and pragmatically in the need for believers to build up one another in the Spirit through the Word. In *The Spiritual Priesthood* Spener advises,

> it cannot be wrong if several good friends sometimes meet by appointment to go over a sermon together and recall what they heard, to read in the Scriptures, and to confer in the fear of the Lord how they may put into practice what they read. Only the gatherings should not be large, so as not to have the appearance of a separation from a public assembly. Nor should they, by reason of them, neglect the public worship or condemn it, or disdain the ordained ministers.[91]

Spener did not hold that those who gathered in such conventicles were more truly the church than those who did not; rather his concern was the reformation from within of the whole church based on the spiritual priesthood. Weborg comments: "The conventicle is the fellowship of the converted only relatively for there may be many Christians of fervent faith outside the conventicle. The conventicle was not the locale of the 'hidden church' but it was the opportunity for the 'hidden church' to renew the 'visible church.' . . . The Church, like God, is both hidden and revealed."[92] Stoeffler similarly comments that the *collegia pietatis*

> were to be instrumentalities through which the Church was to be brought again to reflect the image of the early Christian community. . . . [They] were not meant to be means to separate "true" Christians from others and of imbuing the former with a pharisaical self-image. They were meant to constitute one of the major facets of the new reformation. Through them, pastors and dedicated laymen were intended to work in concert to add to the reformation of doctrine the reformation of life. . . . The institution was opposed so fiercely by Spener's enemies precisely because of this reformatory implication.[93]

As noted above, Spener advocated forming a local eldership (*collegium presbyterorum*) in the church to assist pastors in their discipling work and to turn the priesthood of believers into a functioning reality. In Spener's view the *collegium pietatis* was a step in the direction of such a council of elders.[94] It is essentially this kind of internal congregational structure—in essence, a network of cell groups pastored and coordinated by a council of elders—which has grown up in many of the new Christian churches and intentional communities in North America over the past fifteen to twenty years.

In summary, Spener's writings show that he was concerned not only with the inner spiritual experience of believers but with the renewal of the whole church, and that he developed both a theology and an embryonic strategy for achieving such a general renewal. Inner spiritual experience was the primary focus for Spener, but his ecclesiology and reform program were intended to foster the growth and extension of such spirituality throughout the church.

FRANCKE'S DOCTRINE OF THE CHURCH

As the spiritual son of Spener and eventually his heir as the leading figure of German Pietism, Francke espoused a theology which was essentially that of his mentor. Nourished, like Spener, on the Lutheran-Arndtian tradition, Francke clearly was a Pietist in the Spenerian mold. Yet certain accents and shifts in emphasis may be noted in Francke, some of which touched upon his view of the church.

Francke's Pietism was marked especially by three emphases: (1) Particular stress on the conversion experience, and more generally what would be called today the psychology of Christian experience; (2) Christian nurture, especially in terms of discipline, training, and rules for living; and (3) the duty to do good to one's neighbor and to the poor and needy. These accents were to be found in Pietism generally, but were given special prominence by Francke.

Francke's views may be summarized as follows:

1. *Francke gave less prominence to ecclesiology than did Spener, assuming the base Spener had laid.*

The Pietists believed they were creating no new doctrines. Concerned above all to revive the life of the church, they gave little attention initially to fundamental theology beyond affirming their adherence to orthodox Lutheran creeds. Francke, like Spener, considered himself an orthodox Lutheran. He accepted Spener's emphasis and program of reform, and we may therefore assume he accepted Spener's conception of the church presupposed in the *Pia Desideria* and elaborated elsewhere. He could assume, further, that among Pietists, Spener's program was to some degree being put into practice. Thus he was building on the foundation Spener had laid.

Precisely because Francke assumed Spener's foundation, his thinking was less ecclesiologically oriented than was Spener's. Francke seems to have had a less profound concept of the priesthood of believers and less intense subjective or existential apprehension of the corporate significance of the new accents (the paradigm shift) in Spener's program and thinking. Francke put almost no stress on the priesthood of believers in comparison with Spener.[95] "His main concern was the Christian life of the individual believer."[96] His passion was to carry through and extend the Pietist reformation, especially through his significant power base in the university and Pietist institutions in Halle.

Spener was concerned with initiating reform in the church, and for this a theology of church renewal and therefore of church was needed. Francke's concern was to extend and broaden the reform impulse released by Pietism; this called for a theology of Christian experience more than a theology of church.

2. *Francke transmuted Spener's rebirth theme, putting it at the center of his theology of Christian experience and giving it a more psychological, less ecclesiological meaning.*

It has often been said that the key theme in Francke's theology was *Bekehrung* (conversion) and particularly the penitential struggle (*Busskampf*) that frequently accompanies it.[97] The contrast between Spener and Francke at this point may be seen by comparing Spener's *Pia Desideria* with Francke's widely circulated *Nicodemus* (1701). Like the *Pia Desideria, Nicodemus* was intended for ministers of religion and uses the image of the body of Christ.[98] Yet rather than proposing reforms, Francke holds up "the fear of man" as the great problem in the church. "Thus the fear of man is made the opposite of real Christianity," notes Schmidt, and must be overcome by a deeper experience of God healing the divided heart. "This psychological formulation of the problem determines the whole direction of the thought."[99]

Manfred Kohl notes that

> it is the active term *Bekehrung* which expresses Francke's concept, whereas Spener uses the more passive term, *Wiedergeburt*. Again and again [Francke] refers to the *Busskampf,* the wrestling of the old man with the new within the soul; he believed that only through very strong birth pangs, *Busskampf* and *Reue* [a form of penance], can the new man come to the foreground.[100]

Several writers have drawn attention to the "psychologizing tendencies"[101] in Francke; his focus on the process and inner experience accompanying and following conversion. Francke balanced Luther's stress on salvation as a gracious gift with a focus on the believer and his or her ethical responsibility. Sattler observes that "self-examination plays a large role in the psychological life of the Halle Pietist. The heart, mind, and conscience are constantly plowed up and pored over, dissected under the light of Scripture and the Pietist understanding of the Christian life."[102]

Holding that "no doctrine in Christianity is more necessary than the doctrine of rebirth," Francke argued that the new life in Christ "must be a true 'becoming new'—and a true renewal of the image of God in the person, even though what concerns the renewal does not occur in this life all at once, but rather in stages, and the person presses ever further and further into it."[103]

In the prominence and spiritual-psychological interpretation given to conversion, reflecting perhaps his own experience, Francke was somewhat different from Spener. As Brown comments, Francke's "dramatic conversion experience and his introspective analyses of feelings of guilt, anxiety, sorrow, and joy resulted in a greater emotionalization and subjectivism in his theology of experience than in the theology of Spener."[104] Ecclesiologically this marks a shift away from the stress on *koinonia* and corporate life and discipleship in Spener and toward individualism and greater subjectivism.

3. *Francke put particular stress on discipline, education, and rules for living.*[105]

As Pietism gained ground and Halle increasingly became a Pietist bastion, Francke became more a propagandist and educational reformer and less a church reformer and builder.

One notes an inner consistency between Francke's theology and ministry at this point. For Francke everything turned on education and discipline (enabled, of course, by the new birth), and Francke's reform efforts were primarily in terms of training and education. As Kohl notes, "The wrong upbringing of youth, which he considered to be the source of all corruption, was his reason for founding his famous institutions, and not merely the needs of orphans."[106] Francke intended nothing less than raising up a new generation of youth based on Pietist principles, and for this he developed a theology, educational theories, actual model institutions, and a very effective propaganda network (based, in time, on the far-scattered alumni of the Halle institutions). Francke, notes Kohl,

> hoped that through the provisions of prolonged, in-depth Christian influence . . . a better generation would be forthcoming. Francke and his staff worked toward this ultimate goal, demanding strict discipline in all spheres of life. . . . The tightly knit system of education as demonstrated at Halle was Francke's way of forming, ordering, and protecting the life of man, and it is within this system that one must see the concept of *Busskampf.*[107]

While conversion and especially real, inner spiritual experience of God were central in Francke's theology, the conversion experience was set within a larger process—a process which could be guided so as to increase the likelihood of the desired result. "At the risk of oversimplification," Kohl notes, "one might say that man has to erect by himself (although to some extent with God's help) two columns called *Busse* and *Bekehrung;* over these God places an arch, *Wiedergeburt.*"[108] Francke saw God's commandments as addressed primarily to the unconverted in order to lead to conversion. Kohl notes,

> For Francke, it was necessary for man to enter an educational program which began with the commandments, continued with the recognition of one's invalidity on the one hand and God's mercy on the other, which led naturally to repentance, self-denial, and the acceptance of divine forgiveness, and concluded with faith. Only then was the process of leading man to sanctification completed; one step followed the other in a kind of organic development.[109]

Here again one notes a shift from the church to the school; from ecclesiology to pedagogy. We remember also that Francke was a lifelong educator (though also a pastor), and that his initial and formative experience of *ecclesiola* was in the form of a university *collegium philobiblicum,* rather than a *collegium pietatis* in a parish setting. In general, Spener saw renewal as coming through church reform while Francke saw it coming through educational reform. While these two approaches may have been in fact complementary, they also reflect significantly different ecclesiologies.

In sum, Spener and Francke were alike in stressing spiritual experience, the new birth, and the importance of Scripture as the source of life and not just of doctrine; a generally more organic and less institutional understanding of the church and the Christian life; and an optimism as to the possibilities of reform. They were different in that Francke placed more emphasis, in theory and practice, on *individual* Christian experience, on education and training, and on the reform of society through educational programming.

THE INTERNAL DYNAMICS OF PIETISM

Kohl notes that "the object of revival, in Pietist theology, was always the individual; the ultimate goal of revival, however, was the transformation of the world through the conversion of the individual and the renewal of the church."[110]

The two-pronged thrust of church renewal and educational reform did with time have considerable impact. McNeill notes that Pietism "gave . . . an impulse to popular education in Germany comparable to that given by Puritanism and Nonconformity in England, and of greater relative importance. The Pietists first used the vernacular in university lectures, and they promoted the technical, vocational aspects of education in a most significant way."[111]

There can be no doubt that the Pietism of Spener and Francke, especially, owed much to the rise of Prussian political power and to other external factors.[112] The focus here however is on the internal dynamics of Pietism as a movement. What structure, activities, and perceptions undergirded the rise and extension of the movement? It will be useful to examine the various forms of *ecclesiolae* or *collegia* under Spener and Francke and the internal structure of Halle Pietism.

The Pietist *collegia pietatis* never became the dominant, central structural feature of Pietism that the class meeting became in Methodist organization. Yet it seems clear that much of the spiritual energy of Pietism as a movement was released through the network of *collegia* originally formed by Spener and others. Both Spener and his critics quickly saw the potency inherent in the "radical" practice of bringing simple believers together to delve more deeply into their faith. Deeter notes: "Most of Spener's program for Pietism was so successful that it won its way into the everyday life of many Christian communions. Thus the revolutionary upheaval caused by [Spener's] writing in its own time is scarcely understandable to those who take many of his points for granted as essential characteristics of Christianity."[113]

We saw that the Pietist use of *collegia* began with Spener in his parish at Frankfurt am Main in 1670, five years before the publication of the *Pia Desideria*. Already at this time Spener's adult catechism classes and preaching were receiving a strong positive response. After a sermon by Spener on the righteousness of the Pharisees, a number of his parishioners came to him for further guidance on how they could make the Bible their central guide as Spener had advocated. Spener initially proposed small Bible-study groups independent of pastoral control, but after discussion with fellow pastors he decided to lead the groups himself to check the dangers of separatism. "To this plan both his fellow pastors and the religious overseers from the city council gave their full approval and cooperation."[114]

Spener soon began twice-weekly informal meetings for discussion and prayer in his home. Deeter notes,

> A general practice gradually became fixed in these meetings in which in the Monday *collegia* Spener would repeat briefly the main points of his Sunday sermon and its Biblical teaching and the group would discuss the concrete applications of the

message to their lives and their community and daily work. Then in the Wednesday meeting a certain portion of Scripture would be explained briefly and then discussed with a large amount of time being set aside also for prayer.[115]

Spener himself explained:

I either repeated in summary fashion the sermon held the previous Sunday or repeated from the New Testament a few verses . . . and then the men present discussed these things without contention or disquiet. . . . All of the people had free access to these exercises, often as many as the place would hold, nevertheless the women were separated from the men so that the latter could not see them. The subject was at all times the text at hand. Since their goal was to become more godly and not more learned, difficult passages were not treated so much with scientific efforts at understanding as approached with the humility and desire to be obedient in acknowledging the truth and receiving new motivation. Extremely difficult passages that seemed not to have value for edification were simply set aside.[116]

This general pattern apparently continued for some twelve years (1670–82), during which time the *Pia Desideria* was published. At first people of the humbler classes predominated, but as the meetings grew in number and popularity, the more learned and cultured began to dominate the discussions. In the face of criticism that even under his leadership these meetings were separatist, and as the group became too large for his home, Spener moved the meetings to the church buildings—although, said Spener, "not without detriment, in that some of the middle class who had often spoken something for their own and others' upbuilding in the home, ceased to speak in such a public place and thus a certain part of the previous fruitfulness was lost."[117] It is clear that the change in size and place produced a change in the internal dynamics of the *collegia* with the loss of the intimacy and spontaneity which are part of the peculiar dynamic of a cell group or house fellowship—certainly a lesson for today.

Eventually these gatherings came to be accepted and were

widely copied across Germany and in Scandinavia. In Spener's day however they were revolutionary. Deeter notes,

> The major problem of the colleges of piety was that they stimulated certain participants to a radical Christianity which could not be generally spread throughout the larger body of the church. Then after repeated frustrations at the slowness of many fellow church goers to accept a more radical Christian living, the unsatisfied converts often became separatistic. They would thus tend to equate the more intimate fellowship of the "collegium" or "cell" with the church. . . . [and] would form the nuclei of separatist pietistic groups meeting and working quite independently of the larger body of the Church. . . . Some of Spener's close friends and early disciples were among these separatists who left the church.[118]

Spener's enthusiasm for such groups cooled somewhat as a result of these developments, and he later made little use of the *collegia*. Württemberg Pietism employed the *collegium* pattern extensively, however, following Spener's example. There the groups were called *Stunden* or devotional hours, were often led by laymen, and were tied closely to the worship life of the church.[119]

Such home meetings spread quickly across Germany and became the inner dynamic of the movement. Kohl notes,

> These group sessions might be considered a combination of Bible study and a form of spiritual group therapy. Revival was expected not so much as a result of a church service as in these simple meetings, most often held in individual homes. Here everyone was challenged to perform spiritual priestly acts. Here all could admonish, chastise, and comfort each other. Pietism was always concerned with reaching the common people with a simple message, given, if possible, by those on their own spiritual level and in their own language.[120]

It has been argued that the openness and egalitarianism of such groups tended to break down distinctions and hastened the process of defeudalization. "In Pietism the stress was on equality."[121] Tappert argues,

Not only did the inherited differences between clergy and laity lose some of their significance as a result of the emphasis on the spiritual priesthood of believers, but other class distinctions became less sharp in the intimate fellowship of masters and slaves, rulers and subjects, and the rich and poor, which was sometimes cultivated in Pietistic conventicles.[122]

Although the *collegia* took somewhat different forms in different areas, the following generally were common features: (1) a relatively small number of people, such as could conveniently meet in a private home; (2) a combination of the three ingredients of Bible study, prayer, and discussion of spiritual matters with a view toward mutual edification; (3) a more informal atmosphere than the normal worship services; (4) some degree of mixing of the social classes; (5) an apprehension of the theoretical and practical meaning of the priesthood of believers; and, often but not exclusively, (6) lay leadership. Kohl makes the significant point that in exercising the function of the confessional the *collegia* brought many ordinary believers to a place of spiritual leadership in the church:

> In the context of the groups, sometimes the pastor, but more often a fellow parishioner, might act as a father confessor, since everyone was advised to seek a spiritual advisor (*Geistlicher Vater*). These fathers and mothers in Christ, as they have often been called, played an important role in the pietistic concept of building God's Kingdom, for it was their responsibility not only to hear confessions but also lead exemplary spiritual lives, to uphold all spiritual rules and regulations, and initiate new groups and prayer meetings. Many went on to become lay evangelists and missionaries.[123]

The matrix of the *ecclesiola* thus became the source for the actual, practical expansion of Christian ministry beyond the clergy; the priesthood of believers being given concrete expression beyond mere theory or an exclusively "spiritual" sense.

The profusion and informal networking of such *ecclesiola* groups across Germany and on into Scandinavia and among New

World Lutherans formed, to a large degree, the basis for the impact of the Halle Pietist institutions. The growth of Pietism gave Francke an audience and constituency; his Halle institutions gave him the resources of people, money, and literature for his reform crusade; and the favor of the Prussian court opened strategic doors. The base Francke built at Halle, extending well beyond his role as pastor and university professor, was impressive. His large orphan house, where some 3,000 people lived and worked, was one of the biggest buildings in Germany; his dispensary was the first to commercially produce standardized medicines on a large scale. Gary Sattler notes: "As of 1697 the Halle institutions were granted tax-free status by the Elector. From the 1709 edition of 'Footsteps' (*Fusstapfen*) we learn that in a four-year period beginning in 1697 the Elector Friedrich III granted royal privilege to the *Stiftungen* for the manufacture and selling of goods, exemptions from excise taxes . . . , permission to have a bookstore, printshop, bookbindery, and public pharmacy, the right of first purchase of local land, bakery and brewery permits, and other similar advantages."[124] And W. R. Ward adds,

> His institutions received royal privileges which had a cash value; there were charitable collections all over Europe; but the whole organization turned on commercial ventures on an enormous scale, Francke's spiritual agents tapping the markets for a wide range of products all the way from Venice to the Far East. But the great business of Halle lay in the supply of medicaments and Bibles and other religious literature. The press speedily became one of the chief in Germany, publishing not only in German and Greek and Russian Cyrillic type, but in a whole range of Slavonic languages where nothing of the kind had been available before. . . . Francke . . . began with Utopian aims of setting to rights, and supported them by a gigantic correspondence, by establishing his agents in all the key points of central and eastern Europe, and by alliances with a number of important imperial courts outside Prussia. . . . [125]

The foundation for these far-flung endeavors was the interdependent, interlocking set of institutions at Halle and the internal life of discipline, instruction, and division of responsibilities within these institutions. Francke proved himself a visionary, promoter and propagandist, and able administrator, all in one. As the number and size of the Halle institutions grew, he held an organizational meeting each morning after breakfast with his various "department heads"—the orphan house administrator, the supervisor of the schools, the doctor who directed the pharmacy, the bookstore supervisor, and so forth. "Although clearly the dominant figure in the Halle institutions, Francke was inclined to a very relaxed form of absolutism and was obviously wise enough to surround himself with capable administrators and assistants."[126]

In 1701 Francke outlined his vision for a *Seminarium universale,* which he brought into existence as the *Collegium orientale* the following year. Francke's proposal reveals much about his reform vision. He intended the new school as "a botanical garden of God-fearing men who as pastors, teachers, politicians, lawyers, missionaries, doctors, pharmacists, booksellers, etc., would employ everything for God's glory and God's domain in the world."[127] The school would send out "better shepherds" into "all classes in and outside of Germany, yea, in Europe and all other parts of the world" and would include an "institute for the education of youth of noble and lesser condition, rich and poor, and for both sexes. . . "[128]

As the parish-based *collegia pietatis* were the basis for Pietist vitality across Germany, so in Halle the gathered life in the network of educational and philanthropic institutions was the basis for the extension of Pietist influence not only in Germany but around the world. Life within the Halle orphanage and schools was in effect a close-knit, controlled institutional community existing for educational and missionary purposes. Literature, correspondence, and a flow of graduates from the Pietist schools extended the influence of the movement.

If Francke gave relatively little theological prominence to the priesthood of believers, his vision for equipping a whole generation of artisans and professionals for social service and Christian witness was a practical application of this doctrine. Francke had a high view of the worth of individuals and of the impact disciplined, dedicated Christians could make at all levels of society.

ISSUES OF RENEWAL

Visser 't Hooft evaluated Pietism as follows:

> There is no doubt that this second reformation had a great and often beneficial effect on the life of the churches. . . . But we cannot say that it has resulted in a renewal of the life of the churches as such. Why did it not succeed? There would seem to be two reasons. First of all the new reformers were so preoccupied with "life" that they did in fact shift the whole emphasis to the new, the reborn man. In reaction against a false objectivism they fell into a false subjectivism. . . .

> The second reason follows from the first. Although the movement began in the Reformation churches and intended at first to work for the renewal of those churches, the majority began soon to despair of such a renewal of the whole. The resistance of orthodoxy and institutionalism combined seemed to make such renewal a hopeless affair. The individualistic orientation led to a weakening of the sense of responsibility for the total Church. It is typical that it was in this milieu that the biblical concept of "edification" which means the building up of the life of the Church acquired a different meaning, namely the building up on the inner life of the individual. And so this movement resulted in creating groups of consecrated Christians in the churches or in the formation of new movements outside the churches, but not in a renewal of the churches as a whole.[129]

Despite the obvious positive impact of Pietism, this seems on balance a fair critique—particularly of second-stage Pietism, less so of early Pietism under Spener. Yet while Pietism never fully reformed the churches, and certainly fell short of Francke's lofty goals, it did bring about a significant and long-lasting renewal of the internal vitality of the church. It failed to turn the church as fully outward toward the world and the transformation of society as some might wish, nor did it overcome "the Lutheran acceptance of the political society as 'given' and to be endured.''[130] Rather Pietism perpetuated, for the most part, the relative passivity of Lutheranism toward the state, despite much social welfare work and concern for the poor.

As to the ecclesiology and internal dynamics of German Pietism, and the broader question of church renewal and renewal movements, three issues may be noted:

1. The doctrine of the priesthood of believers and the way this was actually worked out in Pietism are especially significant. Spener clearly advocated this teaching and called for its practical implementation through personal mutual edification, the *collegia pietatis,* and the institution of a congregational council of elders. Though less explicitly acknowledging the doctrine, Francke worked for its practical implementation through designing educational programs for believers from all walks of life.

Pietism placed more emphasis on the doctrine of the priesthood of believers (picked up of course from Luther) than did Moravianism, Methodism, or most other movements of renewal. For the broader question of church renewal in general, the issue is both the elaboration of the doctrine and the degree to which it is actually worked out in practice.

2. A second issue concerns the internal structure of Pietism. This structure seems to have been grounded in a variety of forms of *collegia* or *ecclesiolae* but clearly was supplemented by wide-ranging personal, political, and at times even military contacts, especially among people of social and political influence. Literature also played an important role. Nonetheless, the evidence points to the significance and dynamic of *ecclesiola* structures themselves in releasing and sustaining the life of the movement.

3. The experience of Spener, but even more of Francke, raises the question of the place of discipline, rules, practical instruction in godliness, and personal discipleship within a movement such as Pietism. To what degree must *koinonia* be buttressed by discipline and instruction? How do such discipline and instruction fit into the experience of rebirth or spiritual awakening?

We will return to such questions in chapter 7.

NOTES

[1] Theodore G. Tappert, "Orthodoxism, Pietism, and Rationalism 1580–1830," in Harold C. Letts, ed., *Christian Social Responsibility* (Philadelphia: Muhlenberg, 1957), 2:47.

[2] Ibid., 42–43.

[3] On Arndt, see especially Peter Erb, ed. and trans., *Johann Arndt: True Christianity* (New York: Paulist, 1979); F. Ernest Stoeffler, *The Rise of Evangelical Pietism,* (Leiden: E. J. Brill, 1965), 202–12; and Wilhelm Koepp, *Johann Arndt: Eine Untersuchung über die Mystik im Luthertum* (Berlin, 1912).

[4] Stoeffler, *Evangelical Pietism,* 204.

[5] Erb, *Johann Arndt,* 5. Near the end of his life two additional books were included consisting of miscellaneous tracts and letters and Arndt's two prefaces to the *Theologia Germanica.* Stoeffler calls chapter 21 the "central chapter" of Book 1 and chapter 11 the heart of Book 2. In the latter chapter Arndt argues that a Christian is by faith made a lord *over* all, and by love a servant *under* all, and that Christ's life is the Christian's pattern and mirror.

[6] Stoeffler, *Evangelical Pietism,* 209.

[7] John Arndt, *Of True Christianity: Four Books,* trans. Anthony William Boehm (London: Joseph Downing, 1712), 1:2–3. Volume 2, containing Book 2, part 2, and books 3 and 4, was published in 1714. This is the English edition John Wesley would have used and the one through which Cotton Mather became acquainted with Arndt.

[8] Ibid., 370.

[9] Ibid., 2, 300–301.

[10] Bengt Hoffman, Introduction, in Bengt Hoffman ed. and trans., *The Theologia Germanica of Martin Luther* (New York: Paulist, 1980), 30.

[11] Erb, *Johann Arndt,* 16.

[12] Stoeffler, *Evangelical Pietism,* 211.

[13] Koepp, *Arndt,* 19.

[14] Stoeffler, *Evangelical Pietism,* 228. On Spener, see especially K. James Stein, *Philipp Jakob Spener: Pietist Patriarch* (Chicago: Covenant Press, 1986).

[15] August Tholuck, "Philip Jacob Spener," trans. F.A. Muhlenberg, *Evangelical Quarterly Review* 14:53 (1862): 69.

[16]"In his boyhood Spener . . . read several English books which he found in German translation in his father's library and which for some time enjoyed a wide circulation on the continent," including the ones just mentioned. Theodore G. Tappert, Introduction, in Philip Jacob Spener, *Pia Desideria,* trans. by Theodore G. Tappert (Philadelphia: Fortress, 1964, 1977), 9.

[17]Stoeffler, *Evangelical Pietism,* 231.

[18]Tappert, Introduction to *Pia Desideria,* 9.

[19]Stoeffler, *Evangelical Pietism,* 228–29.

[20]Tholuck, "Spener," 70.

[21]Stoeffler, *Evangelical Pietism,* 164.

[22]Tholuck, "Spener," 73.

[23]Spener, *Erbauliche Evangelisch—und Epistolische Sonntags— Andachten* (Frankfurt, 1716), 638, quoted in Tappert, Introduction to *Pia Desideria,* 13.

[24]Tappert, Introduction to *Pia Desideria,* 15.

[25]Richard F. Lovelace, *The American Pietism of Cotton Mather* (Washington, D.C.: Christian University Press; Grand Rapids: Eerdmans, 1979), 220.

[26]Spener, *Pia Desideria,* 87–122.

[27]Stoeffler, *Evangelical Pietism,* 236.

[28]F. Ernest Stoeffler, *German Pietism during the Eighteenth Century* (Leiden: E. J. Brill, 1973), 2.

[29]Ibid., 3.

[30]Erich Beyreuther, *Geschichte des Pietismus* (Stuttgart: J. F. Steinkopf, 1978), 130.

[31]Dale W. Brown, "The Problem of Subjectivism in Pietism: A Redefinition with Special Reference to the Theology of Philipp Jakob Spener and August Hermann Francke" (Ph.D. diss., Northwestern University, 1962), 86, from Johann Arndt, et al., *Der deutsche Pietismus: Eine Auswahl von Zeugnissen, Urkunden und Bekenntnissen aus dem 17. 18. und 19. Jahrhundert* (Berlin: Furche, 1921), 109.

[32]Beyreuther, *Geschichte,* 132; Stoeffler, *Evangelical Pietism,* 4. Francke apparently had earlier encountered the practice of small study groups meeting to pursue particular topics while he was in Kiel (Brown, "The Problem of Subjectivism," 85).

[33]Stoeffler, *Evangelical Pietism,* 4.

[34]Ibid., 12.

[35]Ibid., 6.

[36]Brown, "The Problem of Subjectivism," 2, 88.

[37]Ibid.

[38] Ibid., 91.

[39] Ibid., 92.

[40] Beyreuther, *Geschichte,* 147.

[41] Tappert, "Orthodoxism, Pietism, and Rationalism," 73.

[42] Stoeffler, *Evangelical Pietism,* 34–35; Ernst Benz, "Pietist and Puritan Sources of Early Protestant World Missions (Cotton Mather and A. H. Francke)," trans. by Luise Jockers, *Church History* 20:2 (June 1951): 28–55. See Lovelace, *The American Pietism of Cotton Mather.*

[43] Benz, "Pietist and Puritan Sources," 29–35; Martin Schmidt, "Ecumenical Activity on the Continent of Europe in the Seventeenth and Eighteenth Centuries," in Ruth Rouse and Stephen C. Neill, eds., *A History of the Ecumenical Movement 1517–1948,* 2d ed. (Philadelphia: Westminster, 1967), 100; James S. M. Anderson, *The History of the Church of England in the Colonies and Foreign Dependencies of the British Empire,* 3 vols. (London: Francis and John Rivington, 1848–56), 2:71, 629. The influence of Spener is seen here also, in that the request for missionaries came to Francke through Franz Julius Lutkens, a former student and friend of Spener serving as court preacher in Copenhagen. "At Lutkens' request Francke selected the first two missionaries." Geoffrey F. N. Nuttall, "Continental Pietism and the Evangelical Movement in Britain," in J. Van Den Berg and J. P. Van Dooren, eds., *Pietismus und Reveil,* Kerkhistorische Bijdragen, 7 (Leiden: E. J. Brill, 1978), 216.

[44] Stoeffler, *Evangelical Pietism,* 35.

[45] Ibid., 31.

[46] John Weborg, "Spener's Doctrine of the Church" (B.D. thesis, North Park Theological Seminary, 1961), 38.

[47] Spener, *Pia Desideria,* 67.

[48] Ibid., 76.

[49] Spener, "Of the Christian Church," unpublished translation by K. James Stein, p. 2. The sermon was originally published in *Die Evangelische Glaubenlehre* (Frankfurt am Main: Zunner, 1688).

[50] Ibid., 10.

[51] Ibid., 2.

[52] Ibid., 3.

[53] Ibid., 4.

[54] Ibid.

[55] Ibid., 9.

[56] Ibid., 5.

[57] Ibid., 10. Compare Weborg, "Spener's Doctrine of the Church," 36.

[58] Ibid., 15, 16.

[59] Allen C. Deeter, "An Historical and Theological Introduction to Philipp Jakob Spener's *Pia Desideria: A Study in Early German Pietism*" (Ph.D. diss., Princeton University, 1963), xii.

[60] Ibid., 41.

[61] Ibid., x, 74; Arthur W. Nagler, *Pietism and Methodism or The Significance of German Pietism in the Origin and Early Development of Methodism* (Nashville: M. E. Church, South, 1918), 18.

[62] See especially Martin Schmidt, *Wiedergeburt und Neuer Mensch* (Witten: Luther-Verlag, 1969); Johannes Wallmann, "Wiedergeburt und Erneuerung bei Philipp Jakob Spener," *Pietismus und Neuzeit, Jahrbuch 1976 zur Geschichte des Neueren Protestantismus,* ed. Andreas Lindt and Klaus Deppermann (Bielefeld: Luther-Verlag, 1977), 7–31; Beyreuther, *Geschichte,* 16–19; Manfred W. Kohl, "*Wiedergeburt* as the Central Theme in Pietism," *The Covenant Quarterly* 32:4 (November 1974): 15–35.

[63] Kohl, "*Wiedergerburt,*" 16.

[64] Schmidt, *Wiedergeburt und Neuer Mensch,* 24.

[65] Weborg, "Spener's Doctrine of the Church," 49.

[66] Outlined by Spener in the Introduction to *Der Hockwichtige Articul* and elsewhere. See Kohl, "*Wiedergeburt,*" 16; Wallmann "Wiedergeburt und Erneuerung," 22.

[67] Wallmann, "Wiedergeburt und Erneuerung," 24.

[68] Spener, *Pia Desideria,* 76–81. Cf. Johannes Wallmann, "Pietismus und Chiliasmus. Zur Kontroverse um Philipp Jakob Speners 'Hoffnung besserer Zeiten,'" *Zeitschrift fur Theologie und Kirche* 78:2 (1981): p. 235ff.

[69] Spener, *Pia Desideria,* 81.

[70] Kohl, "*Wiedergeburt,*" 18.

[71] Wallmann points out (in "Wiedergeburt und Erneuerung") that Spener distinguished between "rebirth" and "renewal"; the two are "clearly different concepts" (p. 13). While his point is well taken, it remains true that rebirth and renewal are parallel ideas, both presuming an organic rather than primarily institutional legal view of the church. "Renewal" as Spener understood it appears to mean the renewed vitality (figuratively, the rebirth) of the church based in large measure on the spiritual renewal of her individual members.

[72] Spener, *Pia Desideria,* 92, 93.

[73] Spener, "Of the Christian Church," 6.

[74] John C. Weborg, "Philipp Jacob Spener: Heartfelt Desires for Reform of the True Evangelical Church," *The Covenant Quarterly* 25:1 (February 1967): 21; Stoeffler, *Evangelical Pietism,* 244.

[75] Spener, *Das Gestliche Preistertum* (1677) translated by A. G. Voight, *The Spiritual Priesthood,* (Philadelphia: The Lutheran Publication Society, 1917), 15. As biblical basis Spener cites Rev. 1:6, 5:10; 1 Peter 2:9.

[76] Ibid., 15–16. The joining of 1 Peter 2:9 with Gal. 3:28 is noteworthy.

[77] Ibid., 17.

[78] Ibid., 20–23.

[79] Ibid., 27.

[80] Ibid., 29.

[81] Ibid.

[82] Ibid., 29. Spener adds the duty to admonish, reprove, and, in the unavailability of an ordained minister, to "impute the comfort of the forgiveness of sins or absolution" (Ibid., 30).

[83] Ibid., 30.

[84] Ibid., 31.

[85] "For Spener, as for Luther, baptism was the entrance into the royal priesthood." "In the sacrament of baptism the individual is incorporated into the priesthood and at the same time embarks on a covenantal life" (Weborg, "Spener's Doctrine of the Church," 19, 22).

[86] Spener, *The Spiritual Priesthood,* 29.

[87] Weborg, "Spener's Doctrine of the Church," 33.

[88] Ibid., 29. Compare Spener, *Hauptschriften,* ed. Paul Grunberg (Gotha: Friedrich Andreas Perthos, 1889), 3:163.

[89] Spener, *Pia Desideria,* 89.

[90] Ibid., 91.

[91] Spener, *The Spiritual Priesthood,* 31–32.

[92] Weborg, "Spener's Doctrine of the Church," 52.

[93] Stoeffler, *Evangelical Pietism,* 238–39. According to Stoeffler, Spener was influenced by Reformed practice at this point and "consciously regarded the Reformed congregations of France as models" (Ibid., 237).

[94] See Stoeffler, *Evangelical Pietism,* 236–37; Deeter, "Historical and Theological Introduction," 220; Weborg, "Spener's Doctrine of the Church," 33.

[95] On Francke's ecclesiology, see Stoeffler, *Evangelical Pietism,* 22–23.

[96] Gary R. Sattler, *God's Glory, Neighbor's Good* (Chicago: Covenant Press, 1982), 108.

[97] Dale W. Brown, *Understanding Pietism* (Grand Rapids: Eerdmans, 1978), 116–18; Kohl, "*Wiedergeburt,*" 20–24; Stoeffler, *Evangelical Pietism,* 22–23.

[98] See Martin Schmidt, *John Wesley: A Theological Biography,* 2 vols., trans. Norman Goldhawk (New York: Abingdon, 1962), 1:141.

[99]Ibid., 142–43. Schmidt finds "a similar primitivist motif" in Francke as compared with Spener (p. 141).

[100]Kohl, "*Wiedergeburt*," 21.

[101]See Sattler, *God's Glory,* 102.

[102]Ibid., 103.

[103]August Hermann Francke, "The Doctrine of our Lord Jesus Christ concerning Rebirth" (1697), translated from *Sonn-Fest-und Apostle-Tags-Predigten* (Halle: Waysenhause, 1704), in Sattler, *God's Glory,* 135.

[104]Brown, *Understanding Pietism,* 118.

[105]See, for example, Francke's "Scriptural Rules of Life" (1695), reproduced in Sattler, *God's Glory,* 199–237.

[106]Kohl, "*Wiedergeburt*," 21.

[107]Ibid., 21–22.

[108]Ibid., 23. One can see here the reasons for Barth's early antagonism toward Pietism.

[109]Ibid., 25.

[110]Manfred Waldemar Kohl, "Pietism as a Movement of Revival," *The Covenant Quarterly* 33:3 (August 1975): 6.

[111]John T. McNeill, *Modern Christian Movements* (Philadelphia: Westminster, 1954), 72.

[112]For an excellent overview of the political and economic context within which Pietism gained influence, see W. R. Ward, "Power and Piety: The Origins of Religious Revival in the Early Eighteenth Century," *Bulletin of the John Rylands University Library* 63:1 (Autumn 1980): 231–52.

[113]Deeter, "Historical and Theological Introduction," xxi.

[114]Ibid., 147–48.

[115]Ibid., 148. See John T. McNeill, *A History of the Cure of Souls* (New York: Harper and Brothers, 1951), 182–83.

[116]Spener, *Erzehlung vom Pietismo,* 47f., as quoted in Deeter, "Historical and Theological Introduction," 149.

[117]Ibid.

[118]Deeter, "Historical and Theological Introduction," 150–51.

[119]Ibid., 151.

[120]Kohl, "Pietism as a Movement of Revival," 8.

[121]Ibid., 9.

[122]Tappert, "Orthodoxy, Pietism, and Rationalism," 72.

[123]Kohl, "Pietism as a Movement of Revival," 9.

[124]Sattler, *God's Glory,* 63.

[125]Ward, "Power and Piety," 237.

[126]Sattler, *God's Glory,* 62.

[127]Ibid., 63.

[128] Ibid.

[129] W. A. Visser 't Hooft, *The Renewal of the Church* (London: SCM Press, 1956), 83–84.

[130] McNeill, *Modern Christian Movements,* 72–73. The substantial world missionary thrust engendered by Halle Pietism must be remembered here, however.

Chapter Four

Moravian Sisters and Brothers

Chapter Four

Moravian Sisters and Brothers

Count Nikolaus von Zinzendorf was one of the great enigmatic, appealing, controversial, totally spontaneous and yet contradictory figures of the Christian church. Some found his exuberance overwhelming; others, irresistible. Typical of his whole religious experience is this statement from one of his children's discourses near the end of his life:

> I have had the happiness of knowing the Saviour by experience from my youngest years. It was at Herrnsdorf when I was a child that I learnt to love Him. . . . I have carried on a friendship with Him, quite in a childlike way, sometimes talking with Him for whole hours, as we talk with a friend, going in and out of the room quite lost in my meditations. I have enjoyed this close personal intercourse with Jesus for fifty years, and I feel the happiness of it more and more every day I live.[1]

Zinzendorf sprang from that sector of the German nobility which had been influenced by Spenerian Pietism. He was born in

Dresden, Saxony, on May 26, 1700, into a Lutheran family. His father, who died six weeks after Zinzendorf was born, had been "much attached" to Spener, who had served as a sponsor at the child's baptism.[2]

When Zinzendorf was four, his mother remarried and the young count was put in the care of his widowed maternal grandmother, Henrietta von Gerstorff. He went to live with her at the family estate at Grosshennersdorf, near Zittau in Upper Lusatia, Saxony, not far from the Bohemian border. In this environment the young count absorbed the Lutheran-Arndtian spirituality of Pietism and came early to the spontaneous childlike faith in Christ that marked his whole life. At Grosshennersdorf "he absorbed not only the refined tastes, the self-assurance, the imperious temper, and the great variety of interests of the grandmother he loved and admired, but the simplicity and depth of her religious devotion as well."[3] His whole career would be marked not only by his religious experience but also by the fact that he was a count. Before he was ten he determined to preach the Gospel as widely as he could.

Given his close family ties with Halle, it was natural that Zinzendorf should be sent to Francke's *Paedagogium regium* at the age of ten. He studied there from 1710 to 1716. Even at this young age he made both friends and enemies. He sought out students who, like him, were earnest to follow Christ and formed several close-knit groups. Some of these, he said later, "continued without interruption from 1710 to 1716, so that I left behind to the blessed Prof. Francke a list of seven such societies that I had started."[4] During these years he already demonstrated gifts of spiritual leadership and organization and a missionary and ecumenical vision that reached out to the whole world.

These were difficult years for him, however. He seems to have been treated rather harshly—perhaps as a corrective to his exuberance and independence—and was jeered at by some of the other students who thought him too religious. His biographer and successor, August Spangenberg, says of Zinzendorf at this time: "I know many worthy individuals, and even great men, who became acquainted with him in Halle; and the impression which his tender love to Jesus then made upon them, caused them to honour and love him till his death; whilst it cannot be denied that the opposition the Count met with from others, which was continued as long as he lived, originated also at Halle."[5]

From childhood Zinzendorf had shown an interest in theology and the ministerial office, but it appears that his guardian, Count Otto Christian, sought to discourage this. The church's ministry was not generally considered a suitable profession for nobility. So in 1716 Zinzendorf was sent to the University of Wittenberg, the center of orthodox Lutheranism and the place where Luther had drawn up his Ninety-five Theses a century earlier, to study law and prepare for a diplomatic career. During his three years there he used his spare time to write poetry and theological treatises. While continuing to prepare for public service, he decided in 1717 that the church's ministry was where he ultimately belonged.

The years at Wittenberg were unhappy ones for Zinzendorf. He was confirmed in his Pietist convictions and practices but was caught between pro- and anti-Pietist sentiment. He defended Spener, Francke, and the Halle institutions against widespread criticism; yet many of his Pietist acquaintance were displeased that he went to Wittenberg instead of remaining at Halle. Typically, he tried to work out a reconciliation between the theological leaders of Halle and Wittenberg, but without success.[6]

Zinzendorf began his academic tour in the spring of 1719. He went through Germany and then on to Holland and France, Strassburg, and Basel. On the tour he studied English and other subjects, including Spener's writings. He became familiar with Reformed Church practice and theology in Holland and in several months at Paris became well acquainted with Cardinal Louis Antoine de Noailles (1651–1729) and other Roman Catholic leaders. These contacts increased his ecumenical vision and his desire to build Christian fellowship across confessional lines.

Zinzendorf himself said he was "quite in my element" in Paris because of the sincere "bishops and religious persons" he was able to fellowship with. Yet, he added, "The world knew not what to make of me; because I was externally not different from others, except that I did not dance at court, nor played cards in Paris. Many who knew me, thought I had preserved my baptismal covenant; those who were unable to discriminate, reported me to be a Pietist; whereby they, to whom this name was given, would not let me pass for one."[7]

Due to sickness, Zinzendorf spent several months at the castle of his maternal aunt, the Countess of Castell. Here he fell in love first with one then with another of his cousins, but discovered that his affection was not reciprocated. Later (September 7, 1722) he married Countess Erdmuth Dorothea von Reuss-Ebersdorf.[8]

About this time Zinzendorf, following the wishes of his family, took a position as legal counsel with the government of Augustus the Strong, king of Saxony, at Dresden. He had visited Halle "with the intention of offering his services there," and in May 1721, Francke offered him work with his institutions, subject to the approval of the count's family.[9] According to Spangenberg, Zinzendorf's failure to take this position due to "the refusal of the Count's friends and relatives, who had marked out a very different career for him," was later "the cause of a temporary misunderstanding and estrangement between the count and Francke."[10]

While employed at Dresden, Zinzendorf bought the estate of Berthelsdorf, near Grosshennersdorf, from his grandmother, appointing his friend Johann Andreas Rothe as Lutheran pastor of the village church on the estate. He began building a house on the estate where he hoped eventually to settle.

Zinzendorf remained officially in government service at Dresden until March of 1732, but did little government business, devoting as much time as possible to religious work and his estate at Berthelsdorf. He obtained permission in 1727 for a prolonged absence from the court and finally tendered his resignation, in September 1731. The king accepted his resignation and Zinzendorf officially terminated his government service on March 8, 1732. Thereafter Zinzendorf was free to devote all his attention to the renewal of the church and the spread of the Gospel.

Zinzendorf appears to have purchased the Berthelsdorf estate in part for the purpose of turning it into a center of religious renewal, more or less after the model of Halle. Jesus' words, "the poor have the gospel preached unto them," and the statement in 1 Corinthians 1:16–28 that "Not many wise men after the flesh, not many mighty, not many noble are called" had deeply impressed him. With the background of the spiritual dynamic and perspective of Pietism and the success of Francke's institutions at Halle, and with his own zeal, independence, and creativity, Zinzendorf resolved "Faithfully to take charge of poor souls, for whom Christ has shed his Blood, and especially to collect together and protect those that were oppressed and persecuted."[11]

THE FOUNDING OF HERRNHUT

The conjunction of several events and personalities in 1722 led to the fulfillment of Zinzendorf's vision in ways he could not have imagined—and to the rise or "renewal" of the Moravian Church. Two of the key figures were Johann Andreas Rothe (1688–1758) and Christian David (1690–1751).

Christian David, a carpenter by trade, was born on December 31, 1690, at Senftleben in Moravia. He was raised a Roman Catholic. Through some Protestant contacts he came to doubt the truth of the Catholic faith, prompting several years of spiritual struggle. He studied the Bible intensively on his own and became convinced of the authority of Scripture, but still had no peace of soul. He went to Hungary intending to join the Lutherans but, because of the danger of persecution there for those who converted to Protestantism, was advised to go to Saxony. After visiting Berlin and other places, he eventually came to Gorlitz in 1717, where he remained for some months due to illness. There he had a clear conversion experience under Pietist influence and made the acquaintance of Rothe. During his illness he was visited daily by a Pastor Schwedler of nearby Niederwiese, he reports, "and from him it was that the gospel of Christ came first with power to my soul."[12] David married in Gorlitz and stayed there for five years, from 1717 to 1722. During this period he made three trips to Moravia in order to "preach Christ to my relatives there."[13]

In Moravia, Christian David discovered that a spiritual awakening and the hope of a more general revival were already stirring in some areas. It was essentially a secret, underground movement, principally among the persecuted remnants of the United Brethren, or *Unitas Fratrum,* tracing back to the "Czech Reformation" and the influence of John Hus (c. 1372–1415) and Peter Chelcicky (c. 1390–1460).[14] His contacts and preaching in Moravia excited great interest among these people.

In 1722 Rothe introduced Christian David to Count Zinzendorf. The young count was intensely interested in David's story of the awakening and oppression in Moravia. "Let as many as will of your friends come hither," he said; "I will give them land to build on, and Christ will give them rest."[15] David immediately returned to Moravia and in May 1722 led the first group of ten persons secretly across the border into Saxony. The group arrived at Zinzendorf's estate at Berthelsdorf on June 8. A week later David and the other Moravians started felling trees and building the first houses for a settlement along the main road of the Berthelsdorf estate and about a mile from the village of Berthelsdorf. Zinzendorf's steward, Johann Heitz, gave the settlement the name Herrnhut, "Watched by the Lord." Toward the end of December 1722 Zinzendorf visited Berthelsdorf with his wife and for the first time made the acquaintance of the Moravian émigrés.

Christian David made several more trips to Moravia and led additional families to Herrnhut. Others came on their own. Within two years some 150 people had settled at Herrnhut. By 1727 the community numbered about 200 Moravian émigrés, plus an assortment of other people who wished to join the community.[16] This was the inauspicious beginning of the Herrnhut community, soon to become both model and nerve center for a far-flung missionary and renewal movement under Zinzendorf's leadership.

Because of his position as lord of the Berthelsdorf estate (including the village, where Rothe was pastor) and his vision for renewal, Zinzendorf considered himself responsible for the new community at Herrnhut. He and his wife soon moved to their newly built home on the Berthelsdorf estate, and the count began to take an active role in affairs both at Herrnhut and in the village church. Rothe's powerful preaching and various innovations attracted increasing attention and interest. Music was used extensively in the village church, and following the sermon Rothe conducted a general conversation with his hearers, based on the sermon. On Sunday afternoons at Zinzendorf's house Rothe led another gathering. There Zinzendorf (or, in his absence, Rothe) summarized the morning's sermon.

Zinzendorf set about establishing several institutions at Berthelsdorf, more or less on the Halle model, to help the poor and provide assistance to the new refugees. These included a printing press for publishing cheap editions of the Bible and other religious literature, a bookshop, a dispensary, and a school. Zinzendorf sought Francke's approval for these projects in a visit to Halle in 1724, but unsuccessfully: "The old master and his former disciple held different ideas as to the degree of dependence of the local centers of revival upon the fountain-head at Halle."[17] From this point on, especially after Francke's death in 1727, increasing misunderstanding and tension grew up between Halle and the new center at Berthelsdorf.

The period from 1723 to 1727 was an unsettled time at Herrnhut. Word spread that Herrnhut provided both haven from persecution and freedom to pursue the New Testament ideal of the church. An assortment of refugees and others from Moravia and Bohemia, of Lutheran, Reformed, Separatist, Anabaptist, and even Roman Catholic backgrounds, arrived at Herrnhut, bringing a variety of ideas and expectations and inevitably disputes and discord. There were, in addition, differences between Rothe and

Zinzendorf's Calvinist estate steward, Heitz, and conflicts between Rothe and the Herrnhuters over Rothe's insistence that all the refugees confess themselves Lutherans and follow Lutheran liturgical practices. Zinzendorf stepped in personally to restore harmony in the fall of 1724. He "opened to us the Scriptures, and gave us direction to understand them aright," said Christian David. This was "the first great change and unification of the Brethren."[18]

Some degree of structure was introduced into the Herrnhut community in 1725, including a system of helpers, teachers, and exhorters. These steps were not wholly adequate, however, and Zinzendorf increasingly spent time at Berthelsdorf, away from Dresden, going daily to Herrnhut to work with the community. Finally he decided to move from his own house on the estate to a residence at Herrnhut itself. He moved into an apartment of the orphan house, then under construction, in June 1727. With this began a most remarkable period of renewal, creativity, and growth in the life of the Herrnhut community. Spangenberg notes,

> The count now entered upon a new period of his life. He devoted himself entirely to the service of the poor exiles, and to the promotion of their temporal and spiritual welfare. Nothing was too mean or difficult, if he could, by its means, do them any good. Instead of deriving any outward advantage from it, he was obliged to assist, on every occasion, with his own property. Nor could he expect fame and honour; since, from the very beginning, disgrace was heaped upon him.[19]

On May 12, 1727, Zinzendorf called together the Herrnhut community. After a three-hour address and exhortation he read out a document, "Manorial Injunctions and Prohibitions" (*Herrschaftliche Gebote und Verbote*). This the people were asked to sign, and they willingly did. The document was essentially a civil instrument which "simply inaugurated a village constitution differing little from that obtaining on many another Saxon noble's estate."[20] The significance however was also spiritual, for in this agreement Zinzendorf committed himself to care for the Herrnhuters in a very active way. This date became a day, says Spangenberg, "particularly memorable to the brethren" as "the first voluntary reformation of life and doctrine at Herrnhut" in which the Brethren "sincerely renounced self-love, self-will, disobedience, and free-thinking."[21] In other words, this agreement firmly established Zinzendorf's authority at Herrnhut.

This document was followed on July 4 by the "Brotherly Union and Compact" (*Bruderlicher Verein und Willkur*), a voluntary covenant, which in effect constituted the Herrnhuters (including some who did not actually reside in Herrnhut) as a distinct religious society. "The Brotherly Union went no further than the creation of a voluntary society of persons who, as individuals, added an agreed mode of communal life to their precedent obligations of loyalty to the greater society; in this case, the Lutheran Landeskirche."[22] Stoeffler adds, "Thus the count had now joined the company of those people of his day who meant to transform Spener's *ecclesiolae in ecclesia* into communal settlements, the whole life of which was dominated by a given religious ideal."[23]

On May 12 and at subsequent meetings, the Herrnhut community was further organized. Zinzendorf was appointed as warden or superintendent, and twelve elders were elected. Four of these, including Christian David, were chosen by lot on May 20 as "chief elders." Several other kinds of workers were appointed: teachers, overseers, monitors (charged with exhortation and discipline), visitors of the sick, almoners to care for the poor, and overseers of trades responsible "to provide every one, as far as it was practicable, with work, but also to take care that good work was delivered at a moderate rate."[24]

Zinzendorf met regularly with the elders and supervised the whole life of the community with great attention to detail and a seemingly endless round of meetings and conferences. Helpers, for example, met on Tuesdays, teachers on Wednesdays, overseers on Thursdays, and monitors on Fridays. Zinzendorf's intention seems to have been not only order and the minute spiritual and temporal oversight of the community but also the productive and meaningful involvement of every able person. According to Spangenberg, the count "considered how every brother might be appointed to that particular station in the church, for which he appeared to have received the necessary gifts from God. After this was done, he took care that every one duly attended to the duties incumbent upon him, and in particular, that every thing should be done at a proper time, and in a proper measure."[25]

In his travels between 1727 and 1732, Zinzendorf visited the universities at Halle and Jena, where he found much curiosity about the developments at Herrnhut. At Jena in 1727 he encountered Professor Johann Buddeus (1667–1729), the Pietist scholar, and a group of students and professors who met in his home, among whom was August Spangenberg (1704–92). The count visited Jena again in 1728, going from there to Halle, and in both places found about 100 students who had been spiritually awakened and wanted to learn more about the movement at Herrnhut. Through these contacts both Spangenberg and Peter Böhler (1712–75), a student at Jena who had been converted in part under Spangenberg's influence, cast their lot with the Moravian Brethren.

The Revival of 1727

The developments at Herrnhut were not simply the result of Zinzendorf's leadership and force of personality. They sprang also from a significant spiritual awakening which swept the Herrnhut community in August of the critical year of 1727. This awakening has ever since been commemorated by the Moravian Church as the birthday of the Renewed Church of the United Brethren. The events of the previous several weeks, particularly Zinzendorf's extensive personal work among the Herrnhuters and the ratification of the "Brotherly Union and Compact," seem to have paved the way for this awakening.

The Herrnhut community experienced a Pentecostal outpouring of the Holy Spirit at the celebration of the Lord's Supper on August 13. The Swede Arvid Gradin, who became a Moravian, gave this account:

> On the 13th day of August 1727, all the members of this flock in general were touched in a singular manner by the efficacy of the Word of reconciliation through the Blood of Christ, and were so convinced and affected that their hearts were set on fire with new faith and love towards the Saviour, and likewise with burning love towards one another, which moved them so far that of their own accord they embraced one another in tears, and grew together into an holy union among themselves, so raising again as it were out of the ashes, that ancient Unity of the Moravian Brethren.[26]

Zinzendorf described this day as "a day of the outpouring of the Holy Spirit upon the Congregation" and "its Pentecost." Spangenberg said, "Then were we baptized by the Holy Spirit Himself to one love." Christian David commented, "It is truly a miracle of God that out of so many kinds and sects as Catholics, Lutheran, Reformed, Separatist, Gichtelian and the like, we could have been melted together into one."[27]

What happened at Herrnhut in 1727 and in the decade that followed could properly be called a charismatic renewal, although glossolalia apparently was not a part of the community's experience. Various kinds of manifestations of the Spirit, and particularly miraculous cures, were in evidence about 1731. Zinzendorf welcomed such manifestations but was careful not to give them undue attention. According to Spangenberg, the count

> did not wish that the brethren and sisters should regard such things as extraordinary, and thus attach themselves to them; but whenever they occurred, as, for instance, when any one experienced an instantaneous cure, . . . he regarded it as a thing that was known, and spoke little about it. He also frequently asserted . . . that wonder working faith was a gift, which did not make its possessor a better child of God, but that he might even be inferior to others who did not possess such gifts, . . .

that to love Christ, be resigned to him in all things, and submit every thing to his will, was a much safer way.[28]

Particularly significant was the organization of "bands" and other small groups within the Herrnhut community about this time. Other innovations included night watches and prayer vigils. Soon a continuous volume of prayer was being offered up around the clock, seven days a week, either in groups or in private prayer vigils arranged in a continuous chain. This prayer vigil continued uninterrupted for over a century—the famous "one-hundred-year prayer meeting."

The bands (*Banden* or, later, *Kleine Gesellschaften*) were first organized at Herrnhut in July of 1727. They were small groups, usually of only two or three persons. Segregated by sex and marital status, they met once or twice weekly, usually in the evening. While these were an innovation at Herrnhut and were considerably smaller and more intense than typical Pietist *collegia pietatis,* they were actually the renewal of an ancient Moravian tradition.[29] Zinzendorf divided virtually the whole community into bands, appointing one person as the leader (*Bandhalter*) of each group. The count had spent many hours over several months talking with the Herrnhuters so that these divisions were not totally arbitrary; he grouped the people with some sensitivity to their personalities and needs. In addition, he arranged that the composition of the groups might change periodically. Groups that were not productive were discontinued or restructured. Martin Schmidt observes, "As everything was so personal and intimate the bands were of a charismatic rather than an institutional character."[30]

The band system was soon operating throughout the Herrnhut community and was instituted wherever the Moravians went. The pattern spread as well to some neighboring towns and villages and was instituted to some degree by professors and students at the universities of Jena and Tübingen.[31] In 1732, when the Herrnhut community had grown to about 500 persons, the number of bands was reportedly about eighty.[32] These figures would indicate that the great majority of the adult members of the community were probably meeting in bands. When John Wesley visited Herrnhut in 1738 he found "about ninety bands, each of which meets twice at least, but most of them three times a week, to 'confess their faults one to another, and pray for one another, that they may be healed.' "[33]

Over a period of time from 1728 to 1736 the community was gradually organized into divisions called "choirs" (*Chore*) by age, sex, and marital status. The bands then became subdivisions of the larger choir groupings. Most of these choirs were in effect separate households with their own internal organization (with the exception of the choirs of small children). The ten groups were (1) the married choir, (2) the widowers, (3) the widows, (4) the single brothers, (5) the single sisters, (6) the big boys, (7) the big girls, (8) the little boys, (9) the little girls, and (10) the infants in arms. Due to the sensitivity and oversight of Zinzendorf and the elders, this rather elaborate organization seems initially to have worked with considerable success.

Essentially this same structure of community continued for many years with only minor modifications. While women were fully involved in many of the responsibilities at Herrnhut, the functions of the community were strictly divided by sex, with general oversight solely in the hands of men.

This intense community life and extensive structure show that the Herrnhut community, and the movement which grew from it, were something much more radical than Spenerian Pietism or even the institutionalized Pietism of Halle. Here was a total community organized as a Christian fellowship and household where the personal, economic, social, and religious dimensions of life were integrated into one common system. Although there was no general community of goods, the level of shared life was very intense. Zinzendorf himself had a genius for creating and sustaining community; he said, "I acknowledge no Christianity without fellowship."[34]

The Herrnhut regime seems impossibly strenuous by today's standards. The whole community met for singing and praise at 5:00 A.M. in winter, 4:00 A.M. in summer. General meetings for praise, worship, and instruction were usually held three times daily during the week. Special meetings were held for children, the aged, and the infirm. Several services were held on Sunday, beginning at 5:00 A.M. and ending about 9:00 P.M., including the worship service at Berthelsdorf and a visitors' service at 3:00 P.M. Whenever he was at Herrnhut, Zinzendorf set aside four hours on Saturdays to counsel with individuals. He also set up a system of visitation whereby every member of the community was visited at least once every two weeks.

All work at Herrnhut was considered as service for the Lamb, whether farm labor or missionary work. "It is very important," said Zinzendorf, "that the Brethren should labour everywhere in the true spirit of community, not seeking their own advantage, but that of the whole Church. To consult our own ease at the very time that we are sending hundreds of brethren into all parts of the world, in the midst of poverty and distress, and while the Church altogether is so poor, would be an affront to the Cross of Jesus."[35]

A number of trades and businesses were started and were strictly regulated by a board of arbitrators. As Lewis notes:

> The wool-spinning of the Single Brethren prospered; the weaving and delicate embroidery of the Single Sisters came to be renowned in the courts of Europe; the firm of Durninger achieved an international reputation; the Congregation's farm and bakery became models for the whole area, and all the profits were put into a common fund—the Treasury of the Lamb.[36]

Lutherans or Moravians?

As community life was developing at Herrnhut, however, Zinzendorf ran into two serious problems, one internal and one external. The internal problem concerned the relationship between

Herrnhut and the Lutheran Church, and the sense in which the community was to be in fact a renewal of the ancient *Unitas Fratrum*. The external problem concerned the mounting controversy in Saxony, Bohemia, and beyond, in both ecclesiastical and political circles, over the Herrnhut experiment.

Both Zinzendorf and Rothe felt the Herrnhut community should be a Lutheran congregation and part of the church at Berthelsdorf. In July of 1727 Zinzendorf discovered in the Zittau library a copy of the *Ratio Disciplinae* of the *Unitas Fratrum* (1616) in the Latin edition of John Amos Comenius (1592–1670). Here he learned for the first time of the original character and structure of the United Brethren. He was struck by the similarity between this document and the "Brotherly Union," ratified at Herrnhut just a few weeks earlier.

Zinzendorf circulated a German extract of the *Ratio Disciplinae* among the Moravian émigrés at Herrnhut. The Herrnhuters were encouraged to discover that their church was being renewed in substantial fidelity to the ancient discipline. Later when Zinzendorf tried to persuade the Herrnhuters to become more fully Lutheran, the Moravians resisted, insisting that the ancient form and constitution be retained and pointing out that the more intensive internal discipline of the *Unitas Fratrum,* which had in fact been commended by Luther himself, was obviously lacking in the Lutheran Church. The Moravians said they would leave Herrnhut and go elsewhere rather than abandon their identity as United Brethren.

Zinzendorf at first disagreed with this Moravian insistence but, typically, considered the matter with an open mind. He came to several conclusions: that there were no legitimate grounds for compelling the Moravians to abandon their ancient constitution; that in fact the Lutheran Church would do well to adopt such a discipline; that restricting the Moravians' freedom in this matter would have harmful consequences; and that the Lord had some particular providence in this matter. "I should certainly have been no friend to Luther," he said, "if I had let this opportunity slip, of uniting the brethren with us."[37]

In 1731 the decision whether the Herrnhuters should abandon the Moravian constitution in favor of simply being Lutherans was submitted to lot. The decision was to continue with the Moravian constitution. This was a new confirmation, in Zinzendorf's mind, that God had revived the Moravian Brethren for a special purpose. It deepened his own sense of commitment to the oversight of the growing movement.

Zinzendorf at this time believed, however, that the ancient *Unitas Fratrum* was never strictly an independent church but only a society within the church. He could therefore defend his support of the Moravians on the basis of *ecclesiola in ecclesia* and the vision of being a leaven of love and union among all the churches. As William Addison comments, Zinzendorf's aim "was *not* to set up an independent Moravian Church but to forward the ideal of gathering all Christians as into one wide and open and equal 'Community of Jesus.' "[38]

About this time Zinzendorf determined to seek Lutheran ordination, in part to silence criticism of his leading role among the Moravians. He was successfully examined as to his Lutheran orthodoxy and was ordained in 1734. Meanwhile the larger question of a fully Moravian ministerial office was arising at Herrnhut, especially since Moravian missionaries were now being sent to non-Lutheran lands. The Herrnhuters decided that the Moravian Brethren should take over the episcopal succession of the *Unitas Fratrum,* still surviving in two bishops, Daniel Ernst Jablonski (1660–1741), grandson of Comenius and at the time serving as Reformed court preacher in Berlin; and Christian Sitkovius of Poland, who had been consecrated a *Unitas* bishop in 1734. The Herrnhuters selected David Nitschmann (a carpenter and a descendant of a *Unitas* family in Moravia), who was accordingly consecrated as Moravian bishop by Jablonski at his home in Berlin on Sunday, March 13, 1735, with the written concurrence of Sitkovius. Two years later, Zinzendorf was himself consecrated a Moravian bishop by Jablonski and Nitschmann, again with the concurrence of Sitkovius. This rather unique ordination was carried out with the approval of both King Frederick William of Prussia and of the archbishop-elect of Canterbury, John Potter, thus paving the way for the recognition of the Moravian Church in Prussia and for Moravian work in England. From this point on Zinzendorf was officially the bishop or *ordinarius* of the Moravian Brethren and their undisputed ecclesiastical leader. Zinzendorf carried out his first ordination on December 15, 1737, when he ordained Peter Böhler to the Moravian ministry.[39]

Controversy and Growth

The more external problems facing Zinzendorf at this time arose from the notoriety and controversy the events at Herrnhut were provoking far and near. Government inquiries were held in 1732 and 1736. Although these absolved the Moravian community of doctrinal errors or of soliciting further immigration from Moravia, controversy continued. After 1732 Zinzendorf permitted no more émigrés from Moravia or Bohemia to settle on his estates. When at the instigation of his enemies Zinzendorf was ordered to sell his estates in 1732, he transferred the legal title to his wife. He was banished from Saxony by King Frederick Augustus III of Saxony in March of 1736, and from then until October, 1747, with the exception of a few months in 1737–38, he was in exile from Herrnhut. He traveled extensively during this period, accompanied by a varying band of Moravian Brethren that he called the Pilgrim Congregation. Eventually the Saxon king changed his mind, visited Herrnhut, and lifted his ban. In 1749 he issued a decree granting full liberty of conscience and worship to the Brethren in Saxony.

During his banishment Zinzendorf supervised the expanding Moravian missionary work while maintaining close contact with Herrnhut. Leonard Dober had been sent as a Moravian missionary to the slaves in the Danish possessions in the West Indies in 1732. In January of 1733, Christian David and two other brethren went as missionaries to Greenland. By this time the Brethren had extensive contacts in England and several places on the continent. In 1734 several Brethren, including August Spangenberg, were sent to Georgia in North America to establish a community and to seek to convert the Indians. A larger group, including several families, went to Georgia via England in 1735, and it was this contingent that John and Charles Wesley encountered on their voyage to America.

The Moravians had contacts in England from about 1727 on. In time a strong Moravian movement emerged in England, with many interrelationships with early Methodism. Zinzendorf himself visited London in 1737, in part to consult with authorities concerning Moravian work in the New World and in part to secure Anglican recognition of the Moravian episcopacy. He conferred with the archbishop-elect of Canterbury, John Potter, and also became acquainted with Charles Wesley, recently returned from Georgia. (John Wesley was still in Georgia at this time.)

While in London, Zinzendorf also consulted with General James Oglethorpe and established a Moravian Diaspora society. The count later made his headquarters in England from 1749 to 1755, returning to Herrnhut in March, 1755. He died on May 9, 1760, at Herrnhut.

Meanwhile, August Spangenberg increasingly emerged as a key Moravian leader. He was appointed Zinzendorf's successor when the count died and became, in effect, the apologist and domesticator of the Moravian Church. With his evenhanded administration and the publication in 1779 of his *Brief Idea of Christian Doctrine,* Spangenberg, as Stoeffler notes, "succeeded in bringing the Zinzendorfian movement back under the roof of an essentially pietistic understanding of the Lutheran confessions. By the same token, however, some of the early dynamic had gone out of the movement, so that in terms of numerical expansion its successes henceforth remained modest."[40]

Moravianism under Zinzendorf had considerable impact beyond Germany. Herrnhut became the model for many similar Moravian communities established elsewhere on the Continent, in England, and at places such as Bethlehem and Nazareth, Pennsylvania, in the New World. These settlements became the bases for extensive preaching and other missionary activity. In this and several other respects the Moravians of this period exhibit many similarities to such groups today as Youth With a Mission (YWAM), said now to be the largest missionary organization in the world.[41] As Addison notes, the typical Moravian settlement

> was a disciplinary system at once economic, social and religious. In a manner not unlike the medieval monastic settlements, groups of Brethren congregated at such quiet solitudes, remote from the greater centres of population as Niesky, Herrnhaag, Pilgerruh, and Marienborn. There, as a few years later in England, a township would arise wherein the civil regulations, the economic occupations and the round of religious observances might subserve the Moravian devotional ideal. Social life and public amusements were so regulated as to promote fellowship and innocence. Suitable business enterprises and occupations were fostered, the sick and aged cared for by the community, hostels provided for the various "Choirs."[42]

ZINZENDORF'S VIEW OF THE CHURCH

To Zinzendorf, the church was the congregation of God in the Spirit and the little flock of the wounded Lamb.[43] Zinzendorf often described the church as "a congregation of God in the Spirit." However, his language about the church and Christian experience so centered in the suffering and wounds of Christ and in the imagery of a flock that the phrase "little flock of the wounded Lamb" well captures his basic conception. One may say that, in general, he saw the local congregation as the little flock of

Christ, while on a more universal scale the church was the "Congregation of God in the Spirit."[44]

Like Spener and Francke, Zinzendorf accepted the orthodox Lutheran creeds but stressed the living, organic nature of the church rather than its institutional side. Expounding the Augsburg Confession before Moravian seminary students at Marienborn in the 1740s, Zinzendorf said the term Christian Church "properly imports no other than the general *Assembly of such Men, who are true Believers, and Saints.*"[45] This is "synonymous," he said, with stating that the church consists "of such who are poor Sinners, and thro' the Blood of Jesus Christ have obtained Forgiveness of their Sin."[46]

Zinzendorf was keenly interested in church history and hoped eventually to write a more adequate history than was then available, one which "treated about something else than Heretic-Making."[47] The focal point of Zinzendorf's ecclesiology is typically represented in the following quotation: "Has there been *at all Times* a holy Christian-Church? then she must needs have always kept to the *Doctrine* of the SUFFERINGS OF JESUS: there must at all Times have been a Society laying for their Foundation, the Lord's Passion, the Martyrology of Jesus Christ, the . . . Bonds and cruel Scourging which he sustained for the Sin of our Soul."[48]

One of the most characteristic and remarkable features of Zinzendorf's ecclesiology was the way in which he combined a persistent emphasis on the church as a close-knit community (the "little flock") with a strong stress on the universal church. On this point, as on several others, Zinzendorf's ecclesiology shows some affinity with the Anabaptist or Radical Protestant tradition. He saw the invisible church as consisting of the "People of God in every Nation," even among "erroneous Sects and in the darkest Ages," where "Souls belonging to the Saviour are still preserv'd right in what is essential to Salvation," despite, perhaps, some false doctrines.[49] As to the unity of the church, Zinzendorf noted:

The Church of Christ is as yet scatter'd abroad, and not existing in any one Seat, so as to be circumscrib'd there. Hence arise three Kinds of Union. 1. I cannot conclude I am not united in Spirit with anyone in the whole World who calls himself a Christian, until I have closer Knowledge of him. 2. The being join'd in one Soul I extend to all, who explicitly hold the same principal Truths, and stand on the same Foundation with me. But indeed 3. in one body I am joined only to those, who are some way Members with me of the same Constitution.[50]

Zinzendorf recognized both wheat and tares in the visible church, even among the Moravians. "Tho' there are not many in our Congregation who do not believe," he said, "yet we are never quite without such . . . thus there is a Mixture of Faith and Unbelief," even as was true with Jesus' disciples.[51]

The dual focus on the Christian community and on the broader, universal church was central to Zinzendorf's vision of renewal and of the Moravians' place within it. This was really the vision of Spener and Francke in an expanded form, for it offered a more intensive experience of community than the earlier Pietists espoused and called for a more comprehensive and thoroughgoing renewal of the entire church. Within this vision Zinzendorf felt that the Moravian Brethren were divinely called to play a key role: "He saw the new Brotherhood as a tiny rivulet making its way to join the great ocean of the one wide *Gemeine Christi,* the one Holy Catholic Church"[52] — not merely as a tributary stream but as a key catalyst in bringing about the church's unity. As A. J. Lewis notes, Zinzendorf felt "It was the glorious task of the *Unitas Fratrum,* as renewed in the Moravian Church, to exist as an example of such unity, bearing more and more 'the signature of a congregation and people of Christ,' seeking a qualitative and not a quantitative character, serving the cause of unity in all denominations, and then being ready and willing to disappear from the scene."[53]

Ecclesiola, Tropus, and Diaspora

An understanding of Zinzendorf's *Tropus* idea is essential in order to comprehend his view of the church, church renewal, and the peculiar role (as Zinzendorf saw it) of the Moravians.

Zinzendorf's *Tropus* theory is really an expansion and adaptation of the idea of *ecclesiola in ecclesia*. It is hard to see in fact how Zinzendorf ever could have come to the *Tropus* theory without the background of the Pietist development of the *ecclesiola* concept.

From childhood, especially through the influence of Spener and his circle, Zinzendorf was exposed to the idea of *ecclesiolae in ecclesia*. Zinzendorf's idea, once Herrnhut began to develop, was that the *Unitas Fratrum* would be an *ecclesiola* within the German Lutheran church. He thought initially that this was consistent with the original self-identity of the ancient *Unitas Fratrum*. Soon the growing size of the community and the Moravian self-consciousness of the Herrnhut settlers, coupled with the count's missionary concern, led to the idea that the Moravians could and should be an *ecclesiola* in a larger sense, within the whole church, for the triple purpose of renewal, unity, and missions. Such a vision presupposed not only the divine hand in the Moravian renewal but also a conception of the distinct denominations as each having positive value but none having all the truth. Each denomination was a *Tropus;* a unique member in the larger body of Christ. The Moravian historians J. Taylor and Kenneth G. Hamilton note,

> During the Synod of Marienborn, from May 12 to June 15, 1744, Zinzendorf developed his *Tropen* concept. The term is derived from the Greek *tropoi paideias* ("methods of training"). He believed that the evangelical churches were one in essentials but that each possessed its own special talent for training souls in accordance with its traditions. Hence there should properly be a Lutheran, a Reformed, and a Moravian "trope"—later even a Methodist—within the Unity of Brethren, so that souls would be educated for eternity in conformity with the peculiar

emphasis of each. For no one church alone had the exclusively correct method in the cure of souls. . . .[54]

Zinzendorf attempted to put his plan into operation, actually naming leaders of the various *Tropoi*. "Here at last, thought Zinzendorf, was the instrument to gather in one all the 'christed ones' of God while yet preserving the heritage of all denominations."[55]

Zinzendorf's belief in the unique contribution of each denominational tradition seems to have been prompted by a sincere appreciation for "the manifoldness of life and revelation," and not by mere pragmatic or political considerations.[56] "Nature is full of different creatures of different inclinations," wrote Zinzendorf; "it is the same in the spiritual world; we must regard variety of thought as something beautiful."[57] In each *Tropus*—Lutheran, Calvinist, Anglican, even Roman Catholic—the Lamb was preparing his flock for full participation in the one universal church. Lewis notes, "Zinzendorf would have none of these Tropuses destroyed, although none of these was an end in itself."[58]

Within the array of denominational families, Zinzendorf perceived a unique role for the Moravians. "'Tis not properly our Business to enlarge the Knowledge of Christians of whatever Denomination, or correct their Principles; but to refresh to them the Image of Jesus, the tormented Form of our suffering God, which in all those Denominations is acknowledg'd, and esteem'd reverent."[59] Thus the Moravians had a special calling within the various denominational families.[60]

Uncharacteristic of his age, Zinzendorf saw both validity and value in the variety of denominations and traditions—even though he saw them as transitory, intended to lead the people of God to a greater unity. Zinzendorf radically relativized the claims of all denominations, while also affirming their value, when he said the denominational confession of a Lutheran or Calvinist "gives neither the one or the other the least right to salvation; it only distinguishes them as honest Persons among the Faithful according to their Manner of Conception."[61] He said in 1747:

> The different establish'd Religions among Christians, are rather a divine than Human Invention; . . . There is Ground to think, that there are National Religions; I mean that some Nations will never prosper, but under such or such an Ecclesiastical Constitution; . . .
>
> Yea, each Denomination is generally possess'd of some Jewel (a Clearness of Truth, or valuable Temper) peculiar to itself [though often obscured] . . . As to the Ancient *Brethren,* being prior to the Distinctions between Protestants, they maintain a general Connexion with all; and 'tis the Principle of these plain Servants of Christ, . . . on the one hand indeed to preserve their Jewel, (viz. that they have ever asserted the Possibility of some stricter New-Testament-Church) but yet, at the same time, to acknowledge whatever is laudable in other Denominations.[62]

Zinzendorf said similarly in 1758, just two years before his death, that "in the plurality and multiplicity of the various schools of Christ's religion lies one of the deepest intentions of God, whereby His spiritual Empire and Unity are not dissipated but where there may afresh arise a universal political Church-Empire."[63]

Ever the tireless optimist, Zinzendorf thought the Moravian Brethren would fulfill their missionary ecumenical role and pass from the scene within fifty years. The various Tropuses would themselves disappear when the church reached its full unity in Jesus Christ.[64]

Zinzendorf's *Tropus* idea lay behind many of his contacts and conferences with leaders in various communions, including his successful efforts to gain Anglican recognition of Moravianism as a valid episcopal church in England. As a matter of fact, however, the system never worked. Whether it could have under other circumstances is an open question. Zinzendorf's proposal was too bold and controversial to be generally appreciated. In attempting to gain entrée for the Moravians, Zinzendorf was often suspected of opportunism and insincerity when he professed to seek the universal unity of the church. Further, many of the Moravians themselves failed to comprehend, or were not in sympathy with, the *Tropus* scheme.[65] Zinzendorf claimed in 1749 that Lutheran, Reformed, Moravian, Mennonite, and Anglican Tropuses had been formed, as well as Tropuses of "Neophytes" (converts from among the heathen) and of members of the Pilgrim Congregation. Lewis notes however that by 1789 "any vestige of a claim to the continuance of the Tropuses had disappeared: from that year the heads of the respective Tropuses were no longer appointed."[66]

Linked to the *Tropus* idea was Zinzendorf's conception of the Moravian *Diaspora* and the Pilgrim Congregation (*Pilgergemeine* or *Pilgerhaus*). These ideas were also expansions of the *ecclesiola* concept in that they were ways of viewing the role of the Moravians within, and for the sake of, the larger church.[67]

The Moravian *Diaspora* (based on 1 Peter 1:1) was the dispersion of teams of Moravians throughout Christendom as agents of unity and renewal, while the Pilgrim Congregation was an itinerant Moravian minicommunity, usually based in Zinzendorf's own household, which served as the nerve center of Moravian communications and travels.

Though Zinzendorf did not use the term *Diaspora* until 1749, the actual scattering abroad of Herrnhuters throughout Christian lands began with "the pentecostal experience of unity" at Herrnhut in August 1727.[68] Moravian teams were to organize "Diaspora Societies" of Christians for prayer and fellowship wherever they could. The emphasis was to be on simplicity and informality. "The people," said Zinzendorf, "should only sing, pray and talk with one another. What goes beyond the discussion of Christian experience is offensive."[69] Members of Diaspora Societies remained within their own Christian communions but were in close fellowship with the Moravian Brethren and shared Moravian literature and hymns (but not the Moravian Lord's Supper).[70] This explains, in large measure, the original nature and intention of the

Fetter Lane Society in London, of which the Wesleys were a part from 1738 to 1740 (to be discussed in the next chapter).

The Diaspora societies were in some ways similar to charismatic fellowships and prayer groups within Catholic and Protestant communions today (for instance, in the use of literature and music and in the function of the Lord's Supper as a primary point of identification with one's own tradition or denomination). This pattern was actually rooted in Spenerian Pietism; the Diaspora Societies were to work much as Spener intended the *collegia pietatis* to function. The common ingredients were fellowship and mutual edification free of doctrinal disputations; the major difference was the ecumenical reach and intent of the Moravian pattern. Lewis notes: "It was through the network of meetings and societies established by the Diaspora in the various denominations that the Moravians quickened the life and unity of Christendom."[71] Reportedly some 159 such societies had been formed by 1745 (eighty-eight Lutheran, thirty-eight Reformed, thirty Moravian, and three others).[72]

The Pilgrim Congregation, growing out of Zinzendorf's banishment in 1735 and first instituted in 1743, was essentially a "mission module"[73] — "the itinerant headquarters, training, organizing, and manning a vast campaign of evangelism and ecumenical witness."[74] It functioned as an intentional community with a common purse, but with most expenses being met by Zinzendorf himself, supplemented by gifts and loans from others.[75] "The Pilgrim Congregation was made up from all ranks of society, but everyone shared the common hardships, the same food, the same few necessities. None received any wages; if a Pilgrim had private means he contributed to the common needs."[76] The Pilgrim Congregation traveled with Zinzendorf around the Continent and the British Isles, being based for some time in the 1750s in London at Lindsey House, which he had purchased as a headquarters.[77]

Any conception of *ecclesiola in ecclesia* involves some degree of tension between the two levels of church life. In Moravianism the tension was between the Brethren as a renewing community within the churches and as a separate denomination (which they increasingly became). Lewis observes, "Zinzendorf was never able to reconcile this conception" of an ecumenical Moravian *Diaspora* "with the establishment of a fully organized Moravian Church. . . . This unresolved tension between the Diaspora-idea and the Church-idea plagued Zinzendorf to the end, as it did most of the Moravian leaders throughout the eighteenth century."[78]

The Church as Community

Zinzendorf's ecclesiology was both highly Christological (the flock of the wounded Savior) and highly pneumatological (the community of the Spirit). Both aspects reinforced the conceptions of the church as a community.

In his sense of the church as community Zinzendorf was building on Spener's organic image of the church but taking it much further. The experience of community at Herrnhut shows what Zinzendorf had in mind. He clearly was thinking of Herrnhut when he spoke of Jesus at times appearing (but in a way "which many thousand Children of God have no opportunity to share in") to "a Congregation, or little Flock of his. A particular Breath from Him moves amongst them at times; and whenever this happens in Congregations of God, they advance and become quite alter'd, from that very Date."[79]

Like Spener, Zinzendorf saw confession as essential to Christian growth, and the communal life of the church as its proper place. It was for this purpose, especially, that bands were useful. Zinzendorf argued that it should be normal practice

> for People to tell one another sometimes how it stands with their Heart. For that is the only Way to get an upright and honest Flock, *viz.* to habituate them to express the true and proper Sense of their Mind; or at least, certainly not to pretend such a Thing, if it be not indeed so.[80]

149

Zinzendorf saw an intense, visible expression of community as especially important for evangelism and witness. We must establish the principle, he said,

> that the happy, fruitful, and almost irresistible calling in of many thousand of Souls, supposes a little Flock in the House, cleaving to our Saviour with Body and Soul, Souls who are already there, united to our Saviour, in such a Manner, that we may as it were point to such People with the Finger, when we are inviting others; that it is an Advantage, a Blessing, a preaching of the Gospel to Purpose, if we can say, Come, all Things are ready, I can shew you the Persons, who are already there, do but come and see. . . . then a Preaching of the Gospel from this little Flock must be done, in this Manner, *Come, for all Things are ready, . . . This is simply that Thing which is called preaching the Gospel.*[81]

In such a community the rich and powerful are no more worthy than the poor. While the rich are not excluded, in the community's witness "one must not be detained by them principally"; rather one should seek "the wretched, the poor Creatures, who have nothing at all to value themselves upon, them into whose Heads it could never enter, that much pains will be taken about them, call such, they will come, to them you will be welcome."[82]

This stress on the integrity of community meant that Zinzendorf saw growth more as a danger than as success. "All denominations and sects strive to grow larger and stronger," he noted, "but our rule must remain that of keeping the door open for everyone to leave us, yet of being more cautious in admitting them." He added, "It is to be feared that in our time our Church may sicken due to its largeness rather than its smallness."[83] Here Zinzendorf was reflecting on the experience of the Herrnhaag community which, "because of the large number of those competing for admission to it at present, has announced publicly that it would accept no one as an additional member without the Saviour's approval" (presumably to be determined by lot).[84]

Zinzendorf's particular conception of the Holy Spirit is relevant here. With a good deal of consistency and deliberateness, he employed feminine imagery when referring to the Holy Spirit. This was really part of his view of the church as a community and family. Thus Zinzendorf would speak of the Spirit as "Our Mother that bare us" (i.e., the regenerate, born by the Spirit through the wounds of Jesus);[85] "the Nurse of Mankind";[86] or refer to "the Motherlike Work of the Holy Ghost."[87] Jesus, the Spirit, and the community were often bound together through such imagery. He saw "the Holy Ghost our heavenly Mother, and Christ our everlasting *Husband,*" as interceding for the church.[88] The Holy Spirit works for the Savior's sake, "who is the Holy Ghost's Bosom-Darling, his own Jesus."[89] (Such language was common in Moravian correspondence as well.)

Zinzendorf was often attacked by orthodox Lutherans for using such language. It is clear he was speaking metaphorically, however, and that the imagery functioned especially to reinforce his communal understanding of the church. Thus Zinzendorf wrote that the fellowship of the Holy Spirit "is attended with a childlike and ready Discernment of this our Mother's Will; and likewise with a Resemblance of her Nature, so that it may be seen what Spirit's Children we are. The whole blessed Trinity must shine forth in the Countenance of each; . . . "[90] Zinzendorf (reflecting his experience with his maternal grandmother?) said the Holy Spirit "our Mother will comfort, warn, break us of all unseemly Habits, and make us well bred."[91] He said the Spirit's "Effect on our Heart justifies" the name "Mother" for the Holy Spirit, "Tho' otherwise we don't pretend at all to determine the Deity's intrinsic Mode of Existence."[92] In defense of such language, commenting on the phrase "as a mother comforts" in Isaiah 66:13, he said,

> Now if in treating of this Passage, we should interpret the Word *comfort* of the Holy Ghost, no Divine would find Fault, for He is stiled the Comforter; but if we should take the Word *Mother,* and apply it to Him, People would make a great Outcry. I can

151

see no reason for such peevish Prejudices; for if an Action or Function belongs to the Holy Ghost, the corresponding Title belongs to him too. . . . [So] our Congregation has ventur'd, in the Simplicity of the Gospel, after several Intimations from holy Writ, to characterize Him, as well as the other Divine Persons, by the relative Names in a human Family. Christ is our Husband, his Father our Father, and the Holy Ghost our Mother: This is round and natural, and thus the domestic Ideas, which among all human ones are the eldest, most venerable and endearing are affix'd to the Holy Trinity as consider'd in its Relation to *us*.[93]

The Moravians commonly applied maternal imagery as well to the whole Moravian Church and to the mother community at Herrnhut.[94] This underscores the communal significance of such language. In this application of family imagery to Christian community Zinzendorf was taking Spener's organic imagery and applying it up to and beyond the limits acceptable in his day.

Church Order and Discipline

Zinzendorf's view of the church as community was closely linked with his practical concern for church discipline and structure. Here two emphases are especially noteworthy: the need for *structure* in order to build and sustain community, and the need for *flexibility* in order to prevent structures from leading to institutionalism and dead orthodoxy.

Zinzendorf summarized his basic approach to structure as follows: "When they [Moravians] see that such or such a Meeting is of Service, they keep it up duly; but when it does not rightly edify, they lay it aside for a time, or entirely."[95]

Zinzendorf recognized discipline and order as necessary for community, but as potentially counterproductive if not employed with sensitivity to the Holy Spirit and the human spirit. "Church-Discipline, the completer it is, is very apt to make the more refin'd Hypocrites. Our best Discipline, with respect to Hearts where Grace really rules, is the Merit of Jesus, since none of us can forget at what an Expence he was redeem'd; . . ."[96] It must be a "principle Rule," therefore, "to preserve to every one an un-clogg'd Liberty of going away" in the assurance that a "Heart truly laid hold of by the Wounds of Jesus, will not go."[97]

This approach to order, combining functionality with attention to detail, is seen in the organization of Herrnhut and other Moravian communities. Zinzendorf did not always follow his own principles, however. The Moravian movement quickly became so large and far-scattered that he could not adequately supervise it himself. At times his insistence that Moravian communities proceed in a particular manner brought confusion, conflict, and in some cases decline. The excesses of the so-called Sifting Time (1738–52) at Herrnhut and Herrnhaag, when Zinzendorf's sensual imagery was taken to an extreme, was due in large measure to the count's absence. Also, the failure of the Moravian community at Fulneck, England, seems primarily due to Zinzendorf's ill-advised interference and insistence that the group follow his notions. According to Joseph Hutton, Zinzendorf's insistence that the Moravians at Fulneck "build a settlement on the Herrnhut or Herrnhaag model" with a close centralization of all the Moravian work in the area under the Fulneck settlement "was German rather than English in conception" and "was the road, not to Church extension, but to Church extinction."[98]

In the areas of ordination, ministry, and sacraments, Zinzendorf accepted orthodox Lutheran views, blending with them the Moravian episcopal polity as contained in the *Ratio Disciplinae* of the *Unitas Fratrum* and bending them toward his conception of the church as a missionary community. He held to no particular theory of episcopacy, seeing it, according to Lewis, "simply as the historically developed means and symbol of the unity and continuity of the Christian Church," useful especially in facilitating ecumenical relationships.[99] Zinzendorf stated at the Synod of Ebersdorf in 1739 that "our bishops are subordinate to the Elders, and have no function except to ordain."[100] Thus the Moravian conception of the bishop's office has been that of purely spiritual leadership. It was inevitable of course that during Zinzendorf's lifetime he himself would exercise the dominant leadership role among the Brethren, regardless of official structures.

Zinzendorf, like Francke, put little stress theoretically on the priesthood of believers. His conception of the Brethren as a missionary community and of all Moravians as "soldiers of the Lamb," the many leadership and service functions within the Moravian communities, and the broad opportunities for missionary service, however, provided great openness to various kinds of "lay" leadership and ministry. Virtually every Moravian was given some ministry or service assignment, so that the priesthood of believers (in the form of ministry and of mutual edification) was probably applied much more extensively among the Moravians than among Lutheran Pietists generally. Many young Lutherans, spiritually awakened through Pietism, were in fact attracted to the Moravians precisely because of the ministry and missionary opportunities the Brethren provided, much as young people today affiliate with missionary societies or orders as a means of ministry. Böhler and Spangenberg are outstanding examples of the move from Lutheran Pietism to Moravianism.

Reflecting his "wounds theology" and ecumenical interests, Zinzendorf's sacramental views also were formally orthodox but somewhat singular. While "properly there are but *two Sacraments only*," he noted, yet in a broader sense others may be comprehended under these two, since no Protestant council has ever settled the issue of the exact number.[101] Marriage, in fact, meets the accepted definition of a sacrament and is a "mystery" in the sense of Ephesians 5.[102] With regard to the Lord's Supper (of special significance among the Moravians) Zinzendorf said, "We demand of our Communicants, Faith in the real, substantial Presence," but he denied transubstantiation.[103] Baptism is being buried in the blood flowing from Jesus' side: "to be baptized out of the Side of Jesus" is "to pour that entire Stream . . . and Heart's Blood of Jesus Christ, upon a Soul, making her so to swim on in the Ocean of the Wounds. . . . "[104] One of Zinzendorf's sacramental hymns is now widely used in Protestant hymnody: "Jesus, Thy Blood and Righteousness."

In light of his missionary and ecumenical goals, Zinzendorf felt it was counterproductive to focus much on questions of eschatology. For him the biblical record seemed contradictory, and speculation was unedifying, distracting from the "general Heart-Truths."[105] "I wish from my Heart," he said, "that my Brethren . . . may never meddle at all" with "this Subject of Things to come."[106] Yet he saw a millennial age coming, more or less secretly; a "Thousand Years Oeconomy."[107] This would be a flowering of the vision for a renewed, united church:

> But how he will bring his People together again from all the four Winds of the Earth, and assemble . . . scattered Children of God, He knows best; He will not make Use of us to this End, least of all will He need an Army for it or pull down a single Potentate from his Throne upon this Score, or . . . make an Alteration in the Constitution of any one Kingdom of the World. But . . . Satan will not be permitted at that Time to despise the Kingdom of our Saviour, much less to disturb it, and impede the Course of the Gospel among the Nations; but there will be a Kind of general inclination for the spiritual Kingdom of Christ.[108]

This will be a time of universal liberty of religion and conscience. "And thus Men will rule humanly, they will follow reasonable human Influences, and not satanical ones."[109]

The present economy or dispensation is the kingdom of the Cross, which leads to a new, eternal economy and kingdom, already partly begun, which "will be then fully manifested, when all those shall be brought into it, who are still sweating in the Kingdom of the Cross."[110] The kingdom of God, which is "Righteousness, Peace, and Joy in the Holy Ghost" (Rom. 14:17), "appears most glorious in those Souls, that are of a spiritual Mind, and have a spiritual Taste."[111]

Perhaps most remarkable in Zinzendorf's eschatology are his optimism as to the possibilities of grace in the present order and his conception of the eternal kingdom of God as not highly disjunctive from present reality but rather as the free course of the Gospel among the nations. God's "preventing Grace" is now at work in the world.[112] Jesus died for all; he says "all Souls are mine; shew my Children and the Work of my Hands to *me*."[113] Thus "no human Creature is existing, let it live as it will, . . . who may not, through the sovereign Power of *Jesus Christ,* the Creator of the World, be delivered from its Sins, snatched and plucked out of its Misery."[114] Zinzendorf believed that "no sooner has [a sinner] a mind to be saved, but he can be saved," and thus there is not "a single soul, whom we may not behold with brotherly Eyes."[115] He reconciled this view with predestination and election by holding that while some people *must* be saved, because of election, "the Son, as the Sovereign Lord of all Souls, has still Power to save whomsoever he will; he is not tied to Election, neither are we to suppose that no more Men will be saved" than the elect, who are merely the first fruits.[116]

In summary, Zinzendorf's ecclesiology was built on the foundation of Lutheran Pietism but was developed more fully in the directions of community and mission due to his particular gifts, his personality, and the influence of the Moravian–Bohemian remnant. In comparison with Spener and Francke specifically, the following points may be noted:

1. Though Zinzendorf stressed community more intensely than did either Francke or Spener, his fundamental ecclesiology seems closer to Spener's than Francke's in terms of its basic organic imagery. Virtually all the distinctive notes of Spener's ecclesiology were found in Zinzendorf.

2. Zinzendorf did not emphasize *Wiedergeburt* as strongly as did Spener and reacted against the Halle emphasis on the penitential struggle (*Busskampf*), presumably because this was not part of his own experience. His spiritual pilgrimage was more like that of Spener, though with a stronger emotional exuberance. Kohl suggests that "when Zinzendorf left Halle, he also left behind him the pietistic concept of *Busskampf.* For him, the sovereignty

and the absolute love of Christ became increasingly important, and he came to realize that one can come to the Savior without fulfilling any prerequisites."[117] For Zinzendorf, Christian faith centered less in *Wiedergeburt* (though that was important) than in a social experience of the faith in close community. Zinzendorf and the Moravians had, as Gillian Gollin notes, a profound sense of "the social character of religious experience."[118]

3. Zinzendorf's stress on training and discipline finds parallels in Spener and especially Francke. As we have seen, Zinzendorf saw the various Christian traditions as training schools for God's people. But whereas Spener saw discipline and training happening primarily in local parishes through *collegia,* and Francke promoted the same through educational and philanthropic institutions and agencies, Zinzendorf's more comprehensive (and perhaps less realistic) vision was of God working freely through the various Tropuses to nurture a renewed, united church of God. Within Moravianism, of course, Zinzendorf also relied heavily on small-group structures and educational agencies.

4. In his more intense conception of community, Zinzendorf put greater stress than did Spener and Francke on reaching and incorporating the poor (though this emphasis was not totally lacking in Zinzendorf's Pietist forebears).

5. Zinzendorf's ecclesiology was generally more irenic and ecumenical than Spener or Francke's, with more openness to Roman Catholicism. Here again, however, he was merely traveling further down the road marked out by Francke in his ecumenical contacts and by Spener in the *Pia Desideria.*

6. One finds in all three men a strong optimism of grace and of the present possibilities of church renewal and reform. Spener's "hope for better times" was matched by Zinzendorf's optimism regarding the growth of Christ's kingdom and the uniting in fellowship of all Christians in the world. All three felt that renewal was worth working for and was being divinely assisted.

THE INTERNAL DYNAMICS
OF MORAVIANISM

The first impression one has in comparing Moravianism with Pietism is the much greater complexity of Moravian organization. This was due to the rather total community life at Herrnhut and other Moravian settlements and to the extensive Moravian missionary enterprise. In essence Moravianism under Zinzendorf became an intense but highly mobile missionary order, settling later under Spangenberg into more traditional denominational patterns.

The personality and genius of Zinzendorf obviously were key factors in the dynamics of Moravianism. But an adequate understanding of the movement requires noting in more detail how the movement itself actually functioned. We must examine more closely the Moravian band and choir system, note how the Moravian settlements functioned as communities, and observe the Moravian missionary enterprise in action.

The Band and Choir System

As noted earlier, the cell groups formed at Herrnhut in 1727, called bands or classes, developed over a period of about ten years into the choir system, which was then used extensively throughout Moravian settlements. Gollin notes, "Although these bands constituted an important antecedent of the choirs, they were not synonymous with them. The degree of stratification was less rigid; moreover, membership in these bands was voluntary, whereas membership in the choir organizations became obligatory for every member of the community."[119]

The choir system provided, in effect, quasi-celibate suborders of men and women (marriage was not discountenanced) within the larger Moravian community, which itself functioned much like a Protestant missionary order. Married couples generally lived together,[120] but childcare was provided for the children collectively through the system of children's choirs. This freed parents for work in the community or for missionary service elsewhere. Sociologically, the choir system was in this sense actually "a family surrogate . . . which, by explicitly subordinating a Moravian's familial obligation to his religious duties, would maximize the individual's loyalty to the religious goals of the community."[121]

The choir system was thus admirably suited to the dual purpose of intimate community and missionary outreach. For married couples it provided flexibility, freedom, and mobility akin to that of singles; for singles it provided a sense of family akin to that of married persons; and for widows and the elderly it provided community and economic security.

The development from band to choir was in part a transition from a primarily religious structure to one which was intentionally social and economic as well. The transition may be seen, in fact, as the gradual adaptation of the *collegia pietatis* to the ideal and exigencies of a more or less totally communal existence. *Collegia pietatis* presuppose a parish situation where believers mix with the world socially and economically, so that the *collegium* becomes a temporary periodic withdrawal from the world (a coming-apart and coming-together) for spiritual nurture. But in the Moravian settlements the believers were for the most part in contact only with one another. The people one prayed and worshiped with were the same ones a believer ate, worked, and often lived with. Why not, then, organize the total community, and the total life of the community, into consistent smaller groups according to age and marital status? This was done in the Moravian settlements. The practice of piety was the central but no longer the only basis upon which groups were organized and functioned.[122]

The gradual transition from band to choir at Herrnhut seems to have been fairly natural and is quite understandable. Many single men and women, Lutheran university students and others, were attracted to Herrnhut during and following the revival of 1727. Religious life was bound together through the system of small bands, as well as by the constant round of larger-group services. As the single men, and similarly the single women, began to share a total communal life together, it was natural that the cell organization of the community should be carried out primarily within these divisions. And thus in fact the choir system began among the single men, spread to the single women, and finally extended to the whole community. John Sessler, commenting on the beginning of the choir system first in Herrnhut and then at Bethlehem in America, notes that the system

> at first was used only with respect to the single men and single women, but later applied to all classes. Large houses were erected for them in Herrnhut, where the young men and the young women lived, segregated and under strict supervision. Each house had sleeping quarters, a place for worship, a kitchen, and a dining-room. In connection with these institutions there were workshops where the men, who were mostly mechanics, carried on their trades, and the women their weaving and needle-work. Each retained his earnings (except in the years of the General Economy in America [1741–62]) and paid for his room and board. The exclusive village system of Herrnhut and the pioneer conditions in America compelled them to adopt some such arrangement.[123]

We see in this development a community gathered for religious purposes struggling with the physical, social, and economic aspects of a total shared life; the emergence, in effect, of an alternative socioeconomic system. Sessler notes:

> The community was arranged so that the physical needs made the least possible demand on their time and money, which were the Lord's. The economic advantages of an efficient economy were regarded as secondary. But the fact remained that both their religion and their physical environment demanded an efficient community organization. The Choir arrangement adequately served this end. Under this system food and clothing could be bought in large quantities; and one roof over many heads simplified the lodging problem.[124]

At Herrnhut the formation of the Single Brethren's Choir in 1728 was followed by that of the Single Sisters' Choir in the spring of 1730.[125] The Single Brethren's Choir initially consisted of twenty-six men, comprising about 8 percent of the Herrnhut population. By 1733 it had grown to ninety, constituting about 15 percent of the community. The Single Sisters' Choir began with eighteen in 1730 and by 1734 totaled sixty-two (about 10 percent of the total population). By 1742 Herrnhut had approximately 120 Single Sisters, but about one-third were still living with their families rather than in the Single Sisters' Choir, as a separate Single Sisters' choir house had not yet been built.[126]

Understandably, the choir system was extended more slowly to married persons and children, but apparently by the late 1740s it included nearly all the people in the community.

The small band groups were principally for mutual confession, encouragement, and prayer. They were but one element in a daily and weekly pattern of many meetings, singing, special liturgies, and the mundane activities of community life. Each choir had its own special hymns and liturgies. Bost notes,

> The *bands* . . . , which were subdivisions of the *choirs,* were a means of great blessing to the church, inasmuch as they accustomed the brethren to the greatest frankness and mutual confidence. They met on certain fixed days in the week. Even the children had their meetings of this kind, and derived great benefit from them. The brethren who presided over these bands usually met together on the Lord's day, to communicate the observations they had made.[127]

The band and choir system was thus well integrated into the total pastoral structure of the community. The elders were able to monitor the progress of the various groups, making changes or modifications as need required.

The Moravian Communities

The band and choir system was actually the proliferation of the *ecclesiola* pattern into several different levels. The Brethren themselves were, in Zinzendorf's mind, an *ecclesiola* within the universal church. Each Moravian settlement was in turn a congregation subdivided into sex-and-age-differentiated choirs, constituting an *ecclesiola* system within the local community of believers. The choirs were in turn divided into smaller cells for spiritual nurture.

In addition to these levels of *ecclesiolae* there was, at Herrnhut and elsewhere, a wide range of officers and ministry functions (as noted earlier). These in turn required other groupings gathered around the various functions of the social, religious, and economic life of the community. Zinzendorf's concern was not only to regulate community life in an orderly and spiritually edifying fashion but also to provide for the exercise of a wide range of gifts.

Showing his sensitivity to the organic imagery of 1 Corinthians 12, Zinzendorf said:

> That we ought not to lay all the duties of the church on one person, no more needs proof, than we need to demonstrate that the foot is not to eat, the hand to run, or the eyes to hear. "God hath set the members every one them in the body, as it hath pleased him," 1 Cor. xii. 18. If, for example, we were to set a man naturally mild and gentle in his character, to watch over and detect the various deceits of the human heart, he would be distressed, and a thousand times deceived. If, on the other hand, a man of keen mind and harsh disposition were charged with the duty of exhortation, there would be no end of disputes, and his exhortation would either have no effect, or a very bad one. But if the former be set to exhort, and the latter to apply himself to the discernment of spirits, truth and love are maintained together.[128]

Under the guidance of the twelve elders or pastors, and of Baron de Watteville and Zinzendorf (when the latter was present), various leaders and helpers functioned. These included "monitors" charged with administering advice and reproof with firmness but compassion; "inspectors" or "overseers" who had "the duty of watching, with strict impartiality, over every occurrence in the church" and reporting secretly to the monitors "any thing inconsistent with the spirit of Christ, and the order of the church"; attendants on the sick; almoners to help the poor; and "serving brethren" to provide for the love feasts and other meetings.[129] Bost notes that to most of these offices "there were corresponding ones among the females, who were in fact excluded from none but public duties," this being necessary since "the separation of the two sexes was a fundamental, and invariable law" among the Moravians.[130]

Gillian Lindt Gollin analyzed sociologically the community dynamics at Herrnhut and Bethlehem in *Moravians in Two Worlds*. She shows how in both communities the choirs took on increasingly central economic and social functions. The story of these communities is not only one of spiritual nurture and experience, she notes, "but also a history of house moving, rental negotiations, and building developments."[131] The communal choir system "offered an ingenious solution to the housing problem" as many people, especially unattached singles, came to Herrnhut. Thus "the choirs of the Single Brethren and Single Sisters provided an ideological and religious rationale for the sharing of quarters that were generally crowded and frequently devoid of privacy."[132] The Moravians at Herrnhut, Bethlehem, and in many other settlements put up with inconveniences, hardships, and often economic difficulties with an ease and graciousness unimaginable but for the depth of spiritual and social meaning they found in these communities.

A 1754 description of the Single Brethren's house at Bethlehem shows how the choirs became social and economic units in the Moravian communities:

> It is similar to a castle; is built of sandstone, has five stories and contains over 70 large and small rooms. In the basement there

are several carpenter's shops. On the first and second floors there are two dining halls, five tables in each, at which twenty people can be seated per table. The whole of the third floor is taken up by sleeping quarters with its 200 beds. On the fourth floor is the silkworm industry, and on the fifth hang the clothes of the Brethren.[133]

This system concentrated and combined social, economic, and religious functions, introducing significant economies of scale in both production and consumption. Gollin suggests, however, that the increasing economic significance of the choir system was a mixed blessing, since each choir functioned as a more-or-less self-contained economic unit and not all the choirs were equally prosperous. The rigid insistence on sexual segregation, in particular, was often an economic disadvantage. This problem might have been solved by a general community of goods. This was, in fact, practiced at Bethlehem from its beginning in 1741 until 1762, but never became general practice at Herrnhut. Anna Nitschmann, leader of the Single Sisters' Choir in Herrnhut at the beginning, later wrote, "We lived at the beginning in a community of goods, but then suspicion and mistrust began to spread among a few, and love was disturbed."[134]

Gollin notes, "As the choirs came to control a larger and larger share of an individual's daily activities the definition of their social functions broadened considerably."[135] They took on increased socializing functions, not only for new arrivals or converts to the community, but especially for children. Young children were transferred to the care of the appropriate choirs when still very small. "The Christening ceremony marked the transfer of responsibility for the child from parent to the community."[136] The supervisor of the children's nursery at Bethlehem wrote Zinzendorf in 1746 that "the mothers plead almost with tears in their eyes, that they [their children] may be placed in the nursery, as soon as they have been weaned."[137]

Zinzendorf initially believed the choirs could train children in godliness more effectively than parents could. In a sense this was taking the model of Francke's Halle institutions one step further, virtually eliminating the traditional family unit. In fact, Francke's orphan house seems clearly to have been the model for Zinzendorf's childcare arrangements at Herrnhut. Zinzendorf founded an orphanage on the Halle model at Herrnhut in 1727, as noted earlier, but after his return from America in 1743 he transformed it into an institution for caring for the children of the Herrnhut community only.[138]

Later Zinzendorf concluded that the choir system was actually overeducating young people for the Moravian missionary task and so insisted that parents should "raise their own children, in order that they may savor the toils of life from childhood on and learn to work. Otherwise we get nothing but princes, priests and officers, and no common soldiers."[139] Nevertheless, for a period of about twenty to forty years (more or less, according to the particular Moravian community) "the choir rather than the family" was "the formal agent of socialization" among the Moravians, notes Gollin.[140]

The seeming success of the choir system eventually brought problems, both socially and economically. Parental authority waned due to the separation of parents and children. Many of the choirs grew too large to be able to maintain sufficient intimacy, in spite of the various smaller subdivisions.[141] Some choirs prospered economically, especially in America, to the extent that economic considerations and the profit motive began to outweigh religious considerations. Hamilton notes, "the industrialization of the Choir establishments" in Bethlehem, though essential, "contained the seeds of its own decay. Inevitably, Choirs began to think in terms of profits rather than of religious growth."[142] On the other hand some of the choirs, particularly of single sisters, were economic failures. According to Gollin, "The history of the Single Sisters' choir, seen from an economic standpoint, is a tale of perpetual woe. The Sisters were unable to find enough remunerative work to support them," despite attempts to introduce new trades.[143] Part of the problem was that economic functions were so subordinated to religious ones that often only a few hours per day were available for productive work.

Increasing numbers of the elderly, the widowed, and children of Moravian missionaries constituted a growing economic burden as well. The frequent comings and goings of the Moravians from one community to another was to some degree economically disruptive. Often the most gifted people were sent off to pioneer missionary work. Gollin argues that "a religious community which cherishes its missionary commitment is inevitably faced with the dilemma of having to decide whether to send its religious elite among the heathen of other lands or to place such leaders among the potential heathen of its own ranks. The Moravians chose the former, without perhaps fully realizing the risks such a choice entailed."[144]

At Herrnhut an increasing infiltration of people from the aristocracy also produced problems. While gifts and bequests from the wealthy helped keep the community afloat economically, they tended to preserve class consciousness and may have weakened some of the community's original missionary zeal.

These varied problems contributed to, or were compounded by, the perennial problem of all religious movements and close-knit communities: maintaining the original zeal and vision in the second and third generations. Gollin notes,

> By 1750 a second generation whose members had all been born into the community was growing up, few of whom had experienced the kinds of personal conversions so instrumental in their parents' affiliation with Herrnhut. This was the generation that had been raised under the auspices of the choir and whose parents had had little to do with them once they had passed out of the infant stage.
>
> Although there must undoubtedly have been some young people whose behavior left little to be criticized, the records tell us almost nothing about them. They are preoccupied with the many persons whose socialization under the choir regime apparently failed to yield the religious and social graces which Zinzendorf had hoped for. The complaints are numerous, but

invariably they center on the same points—namely, that the young men and women had become too worldly and lacked the spirit of religious devotion and enthusiasm which had been the hallmark of their parents' conduct. . . . On the one hand many of the young people had apparently become worldly and had failed to develop a personal sense of religious commitment to the goals of community. On the other, many of those who remained immune to the pull of secular forces still lacked the active and militant *Streitergeist* of their parents.[145]

The result of these various strains was a gradual decline in the authoritarianism of the Moravian communities, a return to traditional family patterns, and the modification of the choir system, making it voluntary. Children's and Married Persons' choirs disappeared completely, while choirs for single persons and the widowed continued on into the nineteenth and in some cases the twentieth century.[146]

It is arguable that none of the problems encountered by the Moravian settlements was inherently insoluble; that ways might have been found to preserve the integrity and intimacy of community, religious zeal, missionary outreach, and economic viability. In most cases the problems were not, however, immediately resolved. Eventually Spangenberg's hand brought social and economic stability, but at the cost of much of the original community and missionary dynamic of the movement.

The Moravian Missionary Enterprise

Moravian communities existed primarily for mission, and especially for foreign missionary outreach. The rapid deployment of many young missionaries around the world in the space of a few short years is one of the most remarkable Moravian achievements. Lewis comments, "Certainly no Protestant Church has ever directed her efforts to so many different races; never had one Protestant Church possessed so varied, so mobile and itinerant a band of missionaries and ministers; and they moved from one field of service to another with often an almost bewildering rapidity."[147]

Sessler links the beginning of Moravian missions to necessity: After 1733 the Saxon government forbade more exiles to settle at Herrnhut, and they had to be sent somewhere.[148] But while assorted exiles and Lutheran students may have provided the human resources for the missionary enterprise, its roots lay in the primal missionary vision of Zinzendorf, a vision he successfully imparted to the whole movement. David Schattschneider notes that when the first Moravian missionaries went to the West Indies in 1732, "it was the first time in Protestantism that missionaries had gone forth with the full support of the entire community which was sending them. Their journey marked the introduction into Protestantism of the concept of 'the whole church as mission.' "[149] This statement needs some qualification, however, since sixteenth-century Anabaptists did see the church as a missionary community, though not particularly in the sense of foreign missions.

By 1760 the Moravians had sent out 226 foreign missionaries. In that year the Brethren reported a total of thirteen mission stations in Greenland, Jamaica, Danish West Indies, Antigua, Surinam and Barbados, and among the North American Indians, with 3,057 baptized, 900 communicants, and 6,125 under Moravian care.[150] This was in addition to the Moravian Diaspora societies and the Moravian settlements in England, North America, and on the continent. In 1800 the Brethren had 161 missionaries active and some 24,000 people connected with their mission posts.[151]

The Moravian missionary enterprise was remarkable for the breadth and extent of its initial pioneering missionary work. The Moravian Church itself never became a large denomination, however. This was due partly to the Moravian goal to seek the benefit of all churches rather than its own growth, and partly to the cooling of the original missionary zeal and the necessary consolidation and retrenchment, partially for financial reasons, after Zinzendorf's death in 1760. The initial missionary outreach (or outburst) was sparked largely by Zinzendorf's own vision, the precedents of the mission work of Halle Pietism, and the spiritual energy released by the renewal in Herrnhut in the 1720s. It was made possible by a relative unconcern with training, finances, or structure. "In the days of Zinzendorf the missionary received from the Church just sufficient money to take him to the port and then worked his passage across the ocean. On the mission field he took up whatever occupation would provide him with the bare amount of food and clothing."[152] This approach produced many heroic and dramatic stories of pioneer mission work and of Moravian faith and zeal.

A large part of the Moravian missionary impact was its catalytic role in sparking missionary vision in other groups through its example and Diaspora witness. Moravian influence may be seen in the founding of the Basel and Leipzig missionary societies in Europe and the London and Baptist missionary societies in England.[153] Moravian Diaspora societies spread a flame of renewal and enlivened thousands of formerly nominal Christians throughout Europe through the work of itinerant Moravians sent out from Herrnhut in twos and threes beginning in late 1727. "Within three years the Diaspora seed had been sown over a wide area of Europe—in Sweden, the Baltic Provinces, Austria, Berlin, Württemberg, Pomerania, the Palatinate, and Switzerland."[154] A significant awakening was kindled in the Baltic Provinces especially, where within a few years some 45,000 persons were meeting in Moravian-sponsored Diaspora societies.[155]

From the beginning of the renewal, music accompanied the Moravians wherever they went and became a key element in the renewing dynamic and spontaneity of the Brethren. Zinzendorf himself was a prolific poet and hymnwriter, often composing hymns impromptu during Moravian song services (*Singstunden*) and at other times. Lewis notes that "the Moravians sang from a larger collection of hymns and from more diverse sources than any body of Christians of the day, and as they sang their way around the world they broke down many walls of partition."[156] Moravian music had a strong influence on John Wesley, who translated a number of Moravian hymns. Wesley's hymnbook of 1741 (influenced by the Moravian *Gesangbuch* of 1735) and the English Moravian hymnbook of 1742 were, according to Lewis, "the first church hymnals in the English language."[157] Music must thus be reckoned as one of the factors contributing to the dynamic of Moravianism as a movement.

ISSUES OF RENEWAL

The primary period of Moravianism as a renewal movement is marked by the time of Zinzendorf's dominant influence: the thirty-three years from 1727 to 1760. The foregoing analysis of Zinzendorf's theology and of the Brethren under his influence raises a number of renewal issues. We will note especially the following five.

1. It would appear that the Moravians carried the priesthood of believers further, in practice, than did German Pietism generally. While the Moravians gave little attention to the doctrinal development of this theme, both the *Unitas Fratrum* tradition and Zinzendorf conceived of the church as a missionary community. This gave each member a sense of ministry and reduced the significance of the clergy/laity distinction. Moravians appointed many people to a wide range of ministry functions with great freedom, based on discernment of gifts and, often, the decision of the lot. Zinzendorf's dominant imagery of the church as a fellowship or community open to all and of Moravians as "soldiers of the Lamb" tended to reinforce the sense of every believer being a minister.

Under Zinzendorf the Moravians were, in fact, a missionary community and missionary order. To be a Moravian was to be called to the Moravian mission. On the other hand, where Moravians worked principally as renewing agents within established communions they respected the given church structure and patterns, including the clergy. Here Moravianism functioned more like Spenerian Pietism (but with a more ecumenical flavor) than like Moravian communities of the Herrnhut type. The priesthood of believers translated primarily into the affirmation that the pietistic experience of religion was open to all and was manifested in the use of "lay" Christians in leading bands.

It may be argued also that in their openness to music, poetry, and emotional warmth the Moravians made space for a wider range of ministry and self-expression than did mainstream Pietism. Although sexual segregation was strictly enforced and overall authority was firmly in male hands, this very segregation required a wide range of women ministers at all levels of community life.

On balance, then, it would seem that Moravians practiced more fully what Spener preached, and that they carried the priesthood of believers, especially among women, further than did Pietism generally.

2. The Moravian experience highlights the *ecclesiola* question in some new ways. The Moravians both raised the *ecclesiola* concept to a higher level in conceiving of the Brethren themselves as an *ecclesiola* and carried it to new intensity in the bands and choirs of the Moravian settlements.

Theologically, Zinzendorf's whole ecclesiology was built on the *ecclesiola* pattern. *Tropus,* Diaspora society, settlement, band, and choir were all restatements at different levels of the idea of special-function subgroups within the larger *ecclesia.* Zinzendorf in fact used the Pietist *ecclesiola* idea to elaborate a broad ecumenical theology of the church which was unique at that time.

This use of the *ecclesiola* concept meant that the tension inherent between *ecclesiola* and *ecclesia* was very much present at all levels of the Moravian experiment. Zinzendorf's holding the two in tension, it may be argued, was part of the renewal dynamic, both spiritually and sociologically, of Moravianism as a movement.

3. A related issue is the level, or depth of intensity, of community to be experienced in the church. Zinzendorf had a very

lofty ideal of Christian community and pushed this ideal as far as he could. While he did not advocate a total community of goods for all Christians, a high level of economic sharing was often present among the Moravians, and Zinzendorf exhausted his own personal fortune in behalf of the movement.

The issue here is really twofold: (1) what degree of shared life together should be seen as normative (either biblically or pragmatically) for a Christian congregation, and (2) whether fairly total, intense forms of Christian community can function peaceably, with mutual acceptance and respect, as *ecclesiolae* within the larger church. These questions may be raised at several levels: intentional communities or shared households within a particular congregation; some congregations or other groups leading a quasi-communal existence within a denomination where this is not the normal pattern; or a whole denomination or movement which adheres to a high ideal and practice of community existing as an *ecclesiola* within the universal church. Both the Moravians and the contemporary church scene provide examples of these various levels of community.

A thesis to be explored further is that while the church is by definition a community, and therefore some level of shared community must always be found in the church, yet there may be a wide range of possible and acceptable forms of community, up to and including total community of goods. Community is normative, but acceptable forms of community may be ranged along a continuum and may vary according to social context, the needs and ideals of the persons involved, and other factors. The question then arises: By what criteria may one discern faithful Christian community in a given context?

4. The Moravian experience poignantly raises the question of passing on the original renewal impulse and vision to succeeding generations. Sociologically, this is the question of the religious socialization of the second and third generations. While this is a problem of all religions (and indeed of culture in general), it is particularly acute in movements of renewal which flow against

dominant currents and which usually arise out of circumstances which in the nature of the case are not repeatable.

Theologically, this may be viewed in part as the question of the renewal of the church versus the normative vitality of the church. Can renewal movements translate their discoveries into normative patterns of church life so as to make a subsequent renewal either unnecessary or more or less "automatic"? Or are cycles of renewal and decline inevitable?

5. The strong missionary thrust of the Moravians raises the general issue of mission in the life and renewal of the church. Moravianism was more missionary-oriented than was Pietism generally, although Pietism saw itself as having a mission to renew the church. The question is to what degree a strong sense of mission to society generally, beyond the church, affects the vitality, effectiveness, and endurance of a renewal movement itself and of smaller *ecclesiola* structures within it.

NOTES

[1] F. Bovet, *The Banished Count* (London: E. T. J. Gill, 1865), 16.

[2] August Gottlieb Spangenberg, *The Life of Nicholas Lewis Count Zinzendorf, Bishop and Ordinary of the United (or Moravian) Brethren,* trans. Samuel Jackson (London: Samuel Holdsworth, 1838), 1–2.

[3] F. Ernest Stoeffler, *German Pietism during the Eighteenth Century* (Leiden: E. J. Brill, 1973), 132–33.

[4] Hans-Christolph Hahn and Hellmut Reichel, eds., *Zinzendorf und die Herrnhuter Bruder: Quellen zur Geschichte der Bruder-Unitat von 1722 bis 1760* (Hamburg: Wittig, 1977), 21.

[5] Spangenberg, *Life of Nicholas,* 10.

[6] A. J. Lewis, *Zinzendorf the Ecumenical Pioneer* (Philadelphia: Westminister, 1962), 27.

[7] Ibid., 18–19.

[8] Ibid., 31–32; Stoeffler, *German Pietism,* 135–37; Spangenberg, *Life of Nicholas,* 31–32, 36–37.

[9] Spangenberg, *Life of Nicholas,* 27–28.

[10] Ibid., 28.

[11] Ibid., 36.

[12]Christian David's account of his life as recorded by John Wesley in *The Journal of the Rev. John Wesley, A.M.*, ed. by Nehemiah Curnock, 8 vols. (London: Epworth, 1909–16; repr. 1938), 2:30. (Hereafter cited as Wesley, *Journal*).

[13]Ibid.

[14]The *Jednota Bratrska*, or *Unitas Fratrum*, was founded as, in effect, a renewal community within the Roman Catholic Church in Bohemia in 1457. They viewed themselves as a community living in fellowship with Christ, and in their first synod in 1464 committed themselves to a covenant relationship, mutual correction and reproof, and the ban. They were severely persecuted, but until 1467 considered themselves as a reforming movement within the Roman Catholic Church, bent on purging the church from corruption and superstition. In 1467 they became an independent church, establishing their own priesthood and securing episcopal ordination for their leadership through the Waldensians. The group modified its structure in the *Ratio Disciplinae* of 1616. The *Unitas Fratrum* reportedly had over 300 churches and some 100,000 members in Bohemia alone by 1500. In the sixteenth century some of the *Unitas Fratrum* leaders had contact with the major reformers, notably Luther, Bucer, Capito, and Calvin (1520–22). Under persecution in the sixteenth and seventeenth centuries, many members of the *Unitas Fratrum* went to Poland. Lewis says, "in matters of faith, the Brethren were closer to Luther; in matters of order, close to Calvin; and they still maintained a window to Catholicism" (ibid., 41). See Lewis, *Zinzendorf*, 35–44; Donald F. Durnbaugh, *The Believers' Church: The History and Character of Radical Protestantism* (New York: Macmillan, 1968), 51–63; E. R. Hasse, *The Moravians*, 2d ed. (London: National Council of Evangelical Free Churches, 1913), 10–13.

[15]Christian David in Wesley's *Journal*, 2:31.

[16]Edward Langton, *History of the Moravian Church: The Story of the First International Protestant Church* (London: George Allen and Unwin, 1956), 55–62; Spangenberg, *Life of Nicholas*, 39–41; Wesley, *Journal*, 2:28–32; Stoeffler, *German Pietism*, 137–38.

[17]William George Addison, *The Renewed Church of the United Brethren 1722–1930* (London: Society for the Promoting of Christian Knowledge, 1932), 22.

[18]Lewis, *Zinzendorf*, 49.

[19]Spangenberg, *Life of Nicholas*, 79.

[20]Addison, *Renewed Church*, 41.

[21]Spangenberg, *Life of Nicholas*, 83.

[22]Addison, *Renewed Church*, 41.

[23] Stoeffler, *German Pietism,* 139.

[24] Spangenberg, *Life of Nicholas,* 90–91.

[25] Ibid., 84.

[26] Arvid Gradin, *A Short History of the Bohemian/Moravian Protestant Church of the United Brethren* (London, 1743), 43. Quoted in Lewis, *Zinzendorf,* 59. On Gradin, see Wesley, *Journal,* 2:47–49.

[27] Lewis, *Zinzendorf,* 59.

[28] Spangenberg, *Life of Nicholas,* 136.

[29] Martin Schmidt, *John Wesley: A Theological Biography,* 2 vols., trans. Norman Goldhawk (New York: Abingdon, 1972; German ed., 1966), 2:267.

[30] Schmidt, *John Wesley,* 1:232–33.

[31] Addison, *Renewed Church,* 61–62.

[32] Schmidt, *Wesley,* 1:232.

[33] Wesley, *Journal,* 2:50.

[34] *The Moravian Magazine,* 1 (London, 1854): 337. See Lewis, *Zinzendorf,* 67.

[35] Lewis, *Zinzendorf,* 76.

[36] Ibid., 77.

[37] Spangenberg, *Life of Nicholas,* 82.

[38] Addison, *Renewed Church,* 56.

[39] Spangenberg, *Life of Nicholas,* 232–33; Lewis, *Zinzendorf,* 111–14.

[40] Stoeffler, *German Pietism,* 165.

[41] See Charles J. Mellis, *Committed Communities: Fresh Streams for World Missions* (South Pasadena, Calif.: William Carey Library, 1976), 96ff.

[42] Addison, *Renewed Church,* 59.

[43] The rather exclusive focus here on Zinzendorf's ecclesiology is not intended to slight the significant role played by the administrative and theological leadership of August Gottlieb Spangenberg following Zinzendorf's death in 1760. Much of what Moravianism later became was due to Spangenberg's leadership. But the initial theological vision which sparked the renewal of the Moravian Brethren, and gave it shape as a renewal movement, clearly came from Zinzendorf. So far as the renewal-movement dynamics are concerned, Spangenberg's was a conserving, stabilizing role, which, however much needed, tended to transform Moravianism into a settled denomination rather than a missionary crusade. For Spangenberg's theology, see his *Exposition of Christian Doctrine, as Taught in the Protestant Church of the United Brethren, or, Unitas Fratrum,* 3d English ed. (Winston-Salem, N.C.: Board of Christian Education of the Southern Province of the Moravian Church, 1959).

[44]See Lewis, *Zinzendorf,* 138–39.

[45]Nikolaus von Zinzendorf, *Twenty One Discourses or Dissertations upon the Augsburg Confession, Which is also the Brethren's Confession of Faith,* trans. F. Okeley (London: W. Bowyer, 1753), 246.

[46]Ibid.

[47]Ibid., 237.

[48]Ibid., 237–38.

[49]Nikolaus von Zinzendorf, *Maxims, Theological Ideas and Sentences, out of the Present Ordinary of the Brethren's Churches. Extracted by J. Gambold* (London: J. Beecroft, 1751), 210–11. (Hereafter cited as Zinzendorf, *Maxims*).

[50]Ibid., 139.

[51]Ibid., 183.

[52]Addison, *Renewed Church,* 64.

[53]Lewis, *Zinzendorf,* 17.

[54]J. Taylor Hamilton and Kenneth G. Hamilton, *History of the Moravian Church* (Bethlehem, Pa.: Interprovincial Board of Christian Education, Moravian Church in America, 1967), 101–02.

[55]Lewis, *Zinzendorf,* 152.

[56]Ibid., 140.

[57]Ibid., 102.

[58]Ibid.

[59]Zinzendorf, *Maxims,* 93.

[60]Zinzendorf often spoke of "the economy of God," connecting this with Christ's kingdom. See Zinzendorf, *Sixteen Discourses upon Important Subjects in Religion, Preached in Fetter-Lane-Chapel at London, in the Year MDCCXLVI* (London: James Hutton, 1748), 23. He was, according to Lewis, the first to use the word *oikoumenē* to mean the worldwide Christian church. Lewis, *Zinzendorf,* 13.

[61]Zinzendorf, *Maxims,* 205.

[62]Ibid., 332–33.

[63]Addison, *Renewed Church,* 35–36.

[64]Lewis, *Zinzendorf,* 141; Addison, *Renewed Church,* 34.

[65]Addison, *Renewed Church,* 69–70.

[66]Lewis, *Zinzendorf,* 159.

[67]See Lewis, *Zinzendorf,* 117–20.

[68]Ibid., 119.

[69]Ibid.

[70]Ibid., 121.

[71]Ibid.

[72]Ibid., 120.

[73] Addison, *Renewed Church,* 56, 57; Hamilton, *Moravian Church,* 73.

[74] Lewis, *Zinzendorf,* 116.

[75] Ibid., 116–17. Zinzendorf himself, though a man of some wealth, was frequently in financial difficulty because of the heavy expenses of the Moravian enterprise. His own finances were deeply intertwined with those of the Moravians so that the two were practically indistinguishable. At his death in 1760 Zinzendorf left the Moravian Church 150,000 pounds in debt; it took the Moravians over forty years to liquidate this encumbrance. See Lewis, *Zinzendorf,* 36–37.

[76] Ibid., 117.

[77] See Spangenberg, *Life of Nicholas,* 428.

[78] Lewis, *Zinzendorf,* 130.

[79] Zinzendorf, *Maxims,* 73.

[80] Zinzendorf, *Twenty One Discourses,* 243–44. Zinzendorf refers here to Gal. 6:1–2 and James 5:16.

[81] Nikolaus Zinzendorf, *Nine Publick Discourses upon Important Subjects in Religion, Preached in Fetter-Lane Chapel at London, in the Year MDCCXLVI* (London: James Hutton, 1748). Republished as *Zinzendorf: Nine Public Lectures on Important Subjects in Religion,* ed. and trans. George Forell (Iowa City: University of Iowa Press, 1973), 43. Quotations here are from the 1748 edition, which was a translation of Zinzendorf's original German.

[82] Ibid., 45.

[83] Zinzendorf as quoted in the original Bethlehem Diary for 1742, in Kenneth G. Hamilton, ed. and trans., *The Bethlehem Diary, 1:1742–1744* (Bethlehem, Pa.: The Archives of the Moravian Church, 1971), 106.

[84] Ibid.

[85] Zinzendorf, *Maxims,* 301.

[86] Ibid., 275.

[87] Zinzendorf, *Twenty One Discourses,* 111.

[88] Ibid., 257.

[89] Ibid., 111.

[90] Zinzendorf, *Maxims,* 97.

[91] Ibid., 215.

[92] Ibid.

[93] Ibid., 212–13.

[94] Valdis Mezezers, *The Herrnhuterian Pietism in the Baltic and Its Outreach into America and Elsewhere in the World* (North Quincy, Mass.: Christopher, 1975), 90–100.

[95] Zinzendorf, *Maxims,* 144.

[96] Ibid., 91.

[97] Ibid., 91–92.

[98] J. E. Hutton, *A History of the Moravian Church,* 2d ed., rev. (London: Moravian Publication Office, 1909), 308, 314.

[99] Lewis, *Zinzendorf,* 179–81.

[100] Ibid., 181.

[101] Zinzendorf, *Twenty One Discourses,* 229.

[102] Ibid.

[103] Ibid., 227.

[104] Ibid., 230.

[105] Ibid., 152.

[106] Ibid.

[107] Ibid., 147.

[108] Ibid.

[109] Ibid.

[110] Zinzendorf, *Sixteen Discourses,* 158.

[111] Ibid., 157.

[112] Ibid., 26.

[113] Zinzendorf, *Nine Publick Discourses,* 24.

[114] Ibid., 25.

[115] Ibid., 25, 26.

[116] Ibid., 24.

[117] Manfred W. Kohl, "Wiedergeburt as the Central Theme in Pietism," *The Covenant Quarterly* 32:4 (November 1974): 25.

[118] Gillian Lindt Gollin, *Moravians in Two Worlds* (New York: Columbia University Press, 1967), 18.

[119] Ibid., 68.

[120] In the early days at Bethlehem married couples generally did *not* live together but could meet privately once a week. This was apparently not true at Herrnhut (ibid., 85); Beverly Prior Smaby, *The Transformation of Moravian Bethlehem From Communal Mission to Family Economy* (Philadelphia: University of Pennsylvania Press, 1988), 101–03.

[121] Ibid., 67.

[122] Gollin comments that "The early development of the choir system, although primarily the outgrowth of religious enthusiasm, can also be seen as an organizational response to Zinzendorf's insistence on the segregation of the sexes. This motive is clearly an important one in the formation of the first choir, that of the Single Brethren" in 1728 (p. 70).

[123] John Jacob Sessler, *Communal Pietism Among Early American Moravians* (New York: Henry Holt, 1933), 93.

[124] Ibid., 84.

[125]See Anna Nitschmann's first-person account of the formation of the Single Sisters' Choir at Herrnhut in Elizabeth Lahman Myers, *A Century of Moravian Sisters: A Record of Christian Life* (New York: Fleming H. Revell, 1918), 35–36. Nitschmann became a key leader in the early Bethlehem community following her arrival there in late 1740.

[126]Gollin, *Moravians*, 71–72.

[127]A. Bost, *History of the Bohemian and Moravian Brethren*. Trans. from the French, abridged, with appendix (London: Religious Tract Society, 1834; 2d ed., 1838), 237.

[128]Ibid., 234.

[129]Ibid., 235–36; Spangenberg, *Life of Nicholas*, 90–91.

[130]Bost, *Moravian Brethren*, 236.

[131]Gollin, *Moravians*, 76.

[132]Ibid.

[133]P. J. Acrelius, "A Visit to the American Cloister at Bethlehem, June, 1754," *A History of Sweden*, 403–04. Quoted in Gollin, *Moravians*, 77.

[134]Ibid., 79; see Smaby *Transformation*, passim.

[135]Gollin *Moravians*, 80.

[136]Ibid., 81.

[137]Ibid.

[138]Sessler, *Communal Pietism*, 194.

[139]Gollin, *Moravians*, 82.

[140]Ibid., 88.

[141]Ibid., 89.

[142]Kenneth G. Hamilton, "John Ettwein and the Moravian Church During the Revolutionary Period," *Transactions of the Moravian Historical Society* 12 (Nazareth, Pa.: Whitefield House, 1940), 141.

[143]Gollin, *Moravians*, 101.

[144]Ibid., 97.

[145]Ibid., 104–05. One wonders about possible connections between these trends and the excesses of the "Sifting Time" of the 1740s.

[146]Ibid., 108–09.

[147]Lewis, *Zinzendorf*, 91. It would appear that in the present generation the Moravian achievement has been surpassed in all these respects by some of the new youth-oriented missionary movements arising out of, or benefiting from, the Jesus Movement of the 1970s—for example, Operation Mobilization and Youth With a Mission. See Mellis, *Committed Communities*, 93–104.

[148]Sessler, *Communal Pietism*, 72.

[149]David Allen Schattschneider, " 'Souls for the Lamb': A Theology for the Christian Mission According to Count Nicholaus Ludwig von Zinzendorf and Bishop Augustus Gottlieb Spangenberg" (Ph.D. dissertation, Chicago Divinity School, 1975), 1.

[150]Ibid., 50–52.

[151]Ibid. Total communicants stood at 15,819 in 1832 and 188,700 in 1973. In 1973 the Moravians had 710 congregations worldwide (including 108 in Nicaragua) and a total membership of 413,932 (ibid., 56–58).

[152]Lewis, *Zinzendorf,* 92.

[153]Ibid., 94.

[154]Ibid., 120.

[155]Ibid.; Mezezers, *Herrnhuterian Pietism,* 61–75.

[156]Lewis, *Zinzendorf,* 169.

[157]Ibid., 164.

Chapter Five

The Methodist Revolution

Chapter Two

The Methodist Revolution

Chapter Five

The Methodist Revolution

In the late 1720s and early 1730s when Moravianism was coalescing into a movement at Herrnhut, John Wesley was an Oxford scholar and a newly ordained Anglican priest. Wesley had begun intimate meetings with a small circle of like-minded friends at Oxford University in a quest for a well-ordered life of piety and good works. Contact with the Moravians was still some years away, but already Wesley had been influenced by Continental Pietism. This influence came partly through Pietist writings and partly through the religious society movement which had begun in England some decades earlier.

John Wesley was aware of Francke at least by the 1730s and probably, through his parents, much earlier. He had read Francke's *Pietas Hallensis* en route to Georgia in 1735.[1] Wesley regarded Arndt's *True Christianity* highly and later condensed the work in the first volume of his *Christian Library*. He was reading Arndt (presumably *True Christianity*, though the title is not specified) in Georgia in 1736.[2] He must have been aware of Arndt for some time previous to this, but for how long is unclear.[3] In addition, Wesley knew and regarded highly the writings of Richard Baxter and other English writers who were read among Pietist and pre-Pietist German Lutherans.

THE RELIGIOUS SOCIETIES

Particularly significant in this connection was the religious society movement—although here the links with Pietism are somewhat indirect.

The key figure in the rise of the "religious societies" in England, according to most accounts, was Dr. Anthony Horneck (1641–97), preacher at the Savoy Chapel in London from 1671 until his death. Horneck became a noted and influential preacher, as well as a conscientious pastor. About 1675 he preached a number of "awakening sermons," as he called them, prompting the first of what became a small but significant movement of religious societies.

Though an influential Anglican preacher, Horneck was German by birth. He was born at Bacharach in the Palatinate and grew up in Reformed Pietist circles.[4] After studying at the University of Heidelberg, he emigrated to England in 1661, at the age of about nineteen, becoming an Anglican. He entered Queen's College, Oxford, in 1663, where he excelled in Oriental languages. He made a visit to Germany in 1669, before beginning his ministry at the Savoy in 1671.[5] According to Stoeffler, Horneck had known Spener in Germany, and like Spener had had contact (both directly and indirectly) with Jean de Labadie.[6]

The religious societies began in London primarily under Horneck's influence, and about the same time as the *collegia pietatis* emerged in Germany under Spener.[7] While these societies were clearly and avowedly Anglican in character, some of the inspiration and models for the groups may well trace back to Continental Pietism through Horneck and, in a more general way, to the contacts between England and the Continent. Horneck himself, according to his contemporary biographer, Bishop Richard Kidder, "had great correspondencies with learned Men beyond the Seas, and was often visited by them."[8]

Anthony Horneck seems to have been a conscientious pastor in the Pietist mold. According to Kidder, "He took great pains at Catechising and instructing the Youth, in visiting the sick, and directing and satisfying the doubtful and scrupulous, and encouraging all good beginnings, and promoting worthy designs, and provoking those he conversed with to love and good works."[9] He kept a diary and conducted a spiritual self-examination each night. He showed particular concern for the poor and for the reformation of church life, meeting with considerable success. Large crowds attended his preaching. Kidder notes that Horneck "encouraged Piety where-ever he came," particularly among the young, and "had the care of several Societies of Young Men, whom he directed and encouraged," and to whom he gave rules for the functioning of the societies.[10]

The religious societies inspired by Horneck were strictly Anglican in character and design, whatever the source of their inspiration. They breathed the spirit of Anglican sacramental spirituality more than the fervently experience-oriented piety of the Continental *collegia pietatis* but were otherwise quite similar to the groups concurrently springing up in Germany. While the major circles of such groups derived from the influence of Horneck and Richard Smythies of St. Michael's, Cornhill, other similar societies sprang up independently about the same time or a little later.[11]

The religious societies initially were rather strictly organized groups of young Anglican men concerned with pursuing a holy life. The character of these societies is evident from the rules drawn up by Horneck:

I. That all that entered into such a Society should resolve upon a holy and serious Life.

II. That no person shall be admitted into this Society till he arrive at the age of Sixteen, and hath been first confirmed by the Bishop, and solemnly taken on himself his Baptismal Vow.

III. That they chuse a Minister of the Church of *England* to direct them.

IV. That they shall not be allowed in their meetings to discourse on any controverted point of Divinity.

V. Neither shall they discourse of the Government of Church or State.

VI. That in their meetings they use no Prayers but those of the Church, such as the Litany and Collects, and other prescribed Prayers; but still they shall not use any that peculiarly belongs to the Minister, as the Absolution.

VII. That the Minister whom they chuse shall direct what practical Divinity shall be read at these meetings.

VIII. That they may have liberty, after Prayer and Reading, to sing a Psalm.

IX. That after all is done, if there be time left, they may discourse each other about their spiritual concerns; but this shall not be a standing Exercise, which any shall be obliged to attend unto.

X. That one day in the Week be appointed for this meeting, for such as cannot come on the Lord's Day; and that he that absents himself without cause shall pay three Pence to the Box.

XI. Every time they meet, everyone shall give six Pence to the Box.

XII. That on a certain day in the year, *viz. Whitsun-Tuesday,* two Stewards shall be chosen, and a moderate Dinner provided, and a Sermon preached, and the Money distributed (necessary Charges deducted) to the Poor.

XIII. A Book shall be bought, in which these Orders shall be written.

XIV. None shall be admitted into this Society without the consent of the Minister who presides over it; and no Apprentice shall be capable of being chosen.

XV. That if any Case of Conscience arise, it shall be brought before the Minister.

XVI. If any Member think fit to leave the Society, he shall pay five Shillings to the Stock.

XVII. The major par⁺ of the Society to conclude the rest.

XVIII. The following Rules are more especially to be commended to the Members of this Society, *viz.* To love one another: When reviled, not to revile again: To speak evil of no man: To wrong no man: To pray, if possible, seven times a day: To keep close to the Church of *England:* To transact all things peaceably and gently: To be helpful to each other: To use themselves to holy Thoughts in their coming in and going out: To examine themselves every night: To give every one their due: To obey Superiors both Spiritual and Temporal.[12]

While the fortunes of the religious societies varied somewhat according to the political climate, they prospered especially under William and Mary (1689–1702), spreading throughout London, to Oxford and Cambridge, and to other parts of England. Some variety and development in the societies and in the rules they employed are evident over the course of two or three decades.

Josiah Woodward notes, "These young men soon found the benefit of their conferences one with another, by which as some of them have told me with joy, they better discovered their own corruptions, the devil's temptations, and how to countermine his subtle devices; as to which each person communicated his experiences to the rest."[13]

By 1700 some forty religious societies were meeting in London alone. Many more were to be found elsewhere, including a reported nine or ten societies in Dublin, Ireland, involving some 300 persons.[14] Records of sixteen societies in London in 1694 indicate that many society members were lower- and middle-class workers: glaziers, wiredrawers, butchers, silversmiths, etc.[15]

Besides observing strict devotional rules, religious society members "visited the poor at their houses and relieved them, fixed some in a way of trade, set prisoners at liberty, furthered poor scholars at the University," and established scores of charity schools for the poor.[16] Heitzenrater notes that by 1700 "this form of religious organization had established itself with the structure of the Church as a viable expression of Christian piety and social concern"; "the Church of England made a concerted effort to secure such reforming zeal within its own structure" by permitting and encouraging these societies.[17] The societies were, however, controversial from the beginning. Opponents saw them as divisive or potentially schismatic and as "a refining upon a reformed Church." In their defense, Woodward said that society members

> do not well understand what the objector means by refining upon our reformed Church. If it be meant that they pretend to reform her doctrine, or quarrel with her government, they utterly disclaim any practice. But if it be meant that they desire to refine and reform themselves and others so as to come nearer to her purity of doctrine in their practice . . . , they own this, and must adhere to it, not doubting but they shall have the prayers of all good people that they may do so.[18]

Although the relationship between these Anglican societies and Continental Pietism has never been fully investigated, some contacts between German Pietists and Anglicans involved in the religious societies are on record. As early as 1678 Spener was informed of the societies in England through Friedrich Breckling in Amsterdam.[19] This correspondence, dated April 5, 1678, is evidence that some religious societies must have been formed prior to 1678. Spener appears to have prepared his Latin edition of the *Pia Desideria* in part to reach the Anglican societies.[20]

Francke learned of the religious societies through a German edition of Woodward's *Account,* translated by Daniel Jablonski and printed in Berlin about 1699. Francke refers to the societies and to Woodward's *Account* in a letter to "some gentlemen in London" dated January 21, 1700, and Woodward takes note of Francke's work at Halle in the fourth edition of his *Account*. Obviously leaders involved with the religious societies in England and the Pietist *collegia* in Germany were aware of each other and of the affinity of the two movements.

The Anglican societies and the Pietist *collegia* differed, however, in at least two key ways. First, the religious societies do not seem to have had the same fervency and intensity of personal religious experience that marked Pietism. They seem to have lacked, by and large, the central dynamic of Pietism: an intense, conscious sense of the new birth. This may account for the fact that the religious societies never developed into a movement of the proportions of Pietism. It is interesting to note that Horneck's life and theology seem more akin to the spirit of Pietism than to the religious societies and that he personally emphasized conversion and the new birth.[21] In the Anglican context of the day, however, conversion was simply assumed (the religious society members already being baptized churchmen) and therefore apparently not stressed in the quest for holiness. In fact, the subjective meaning of justification by faith had become almost totally eclipsed. It was this virtual loss of the doctrine of regeneration as the foundation for sanctification which in part accounts for John Wesley's years of spiritual struggle leading up to his Aldersgate experience in 1738.

The second difference between the religious societies and the Pietist *collegia* was the greater emphasis in the Anglican context on charitable acts, ministry to the poor, and the "reformation of manners." Although the ethical sensitivity of Continental Pietism can be demonstrated, the Anglican societies were more actively and explicitly committed to practical service to society, and especially the poor. This was seen as an essential part of holy living.

From the religious society movement came the Society for the Reformation of Manners in 1691, the Society for Promoting Christian Knowledge (SPCK) in 1698, and its sister organization, the Society for the Propagation of the Gospel in Foreign Parts (SPG) in 1701.

The SPCK was founded by a group of friends in London who were already active in the religious society movement. The key figures were the Anglican clergyman Thomas Bray (1656–1730) and four Anglican laymen. The society was founded "to promote and encourage the erection of charity schools in all parts of

England and Wales; to disperse, both at home and abroad, Bibles and tracts of religion; and in general to advance the honour of God and the good of mankind, by promoting Christian knowledge both at home and in other parts of the world by the best methods that should offer."[22] The society was soon publishing and distributing many "pious books and catechisms." Within two or three years it had reportedly given away nearly one million Bibles, Common Prayer books, catechisms, and assorted other books of devotion and practical divinity. It was soon involved also (along with the SPG) in supporting the growing missionary movement in North American and elsewhere.[23]

As noted earlier, August Francke was in contact with the SPCK virtually from its beginning and early became a corresponding member of the society. The connection between the SPCK and the Continental Pietists became stronger when the society began supporting the Danish-Halle missionaries to India, Ziegenbalg and Plutschau, in 1711.

The SPCK later became a link between Pietism and John Wesley in a couple of ways. Wesley joined the SPCK as a corresponding member in August 1732, while at Oxford. The society became an important source of books and information on foreign missions for Wesley. John's father, Samuel Wesley, had been an early supporter of the SPCK and in 1702 organized a society for promoting Christian knowledge in his Epworth parish, following the SPCK pattern.[24] Pietist influence on Wesley also came through the missionaries Ziegenbalg and Plutschau. An account of the Danish-Halle mission to India, compiled from the missionaries' letters, was published in London by Anton Bohme in 1709 and went through several editions.[25] Wesley read this account in May 1730, and later published his own edition of it.[26] The book may well have had some influence in awakening John Wesley's own missionary interest which led him to Georgia in 1735.

More significant, perhaps, was the impact which this account had on Susannah Wesley, John's mother, more than twenty years earlier. In a letter written to her husband, dated February 6, 1712,

Susannah speaks of reading "the account of the Danish missionaries":

> I was, I think, never more affected with anything; I could not forbear spending good part of that evening in prayer and adoring the divine goodness for inspiring them with such ardent zeal for His glory. For several days I could think or speak of little else. At last it came into my mind, Though I am not a man, nor a minister, yet if my heart were sincerely devoted to God, and I was inspired with a true zeal for His glory, I might do somewhat more than I do. I thought I may pray more for them, and might speak to those with whom I converse with more warmth of affection. I resolved to begin with my own children, in which I observe the following method: I take such a proportion of time as I can spare every night to discourse with each child apart. On Monday, I talk with Molly; on Tuesday with Hetty; Wednesday with Nancy; Thursday with Jacky [John]; Friday with Patty; Saturday with Charles; and with Emily and Suky together on Sunday.[27]

From this point on Susannah worked more intensely in the spiritual formation of John (then about eight) and the other Wesley children and began holding informal devotional meetings (in effect, a *collegium pietatis*) in the Epworth rectory during her husband's protracted absence in London.[28]

JOHN WESLEY

John Wesley was born at Epworth on June 17, 1703. Born into a devout and well-educated Anglican family with Dissenting roots, Wesley from the first was nurtured in a faith of deep earnestness and a high ideal of holiness. At the age of ten he left Epworth, some 100 miles north of London in Lincolnshire, to enter the Charterhouse School in London. Four years later, in 1720, he matriculated at Christ Church, Oxford University. For most of the next fifteen years Wesley was at Oxford (with frequent trips to Epworth). He was elected to a fellowship at Lincoln College, Oxford, in March 1726, began tutoring at Lincoln later that year, and obtained his master's degree the following February. During the formative years of Oxford Methodism from 1726 to 1735, Wesley held his Oxford fellowship and tutored a small number of students. He thus had considerable freedom to order his life and pursue his religious ideals as he saw best.

Wesley's spiritual quest began in earnest when, in 1725, he heeded his father's urging and began studying for ordination. The direction of his quest was clear from the beginning: "I began to aim at, and pray for, inward holiness."[29] Wesley was ordained a deacon in September 1725 and a priest in July 1728. During this period he read extensively, and was strongly attracted to mysticism. He encountered William Law's *Serious Call to a Devout and Holy Life* some time after it was published in 1728, as well as Law's *Christian Perfection,* first published in 1726. These books "convinced me, more than ever, of the absolute impossibility of being half a Christian, and I determined, through his grace, (the absolute necessity of which I was deeply sensible of,) to be all-devoted to God, to give him all my soul, my body, and my substance."[30]

At Oxford John Wesley and his younger brother Charles devoted themselves to the quest for personal holiness and also sought to enlist others in the same endeavor. John wrote his father in 1734, "My one aim in life is to secure personal holiness, for without being holy myself I cannot promote real holiness in others."[31] To this end the Wesleys soon gathered a small company of like-minded friends around them. The group became known around Oxford as the "Holy Club." From about 1732 on the Wesleys and their friends were commonly called "Methodists" because of their regular disciplines and John Wesley's penchant for applying a method to nearly every significant task.

The Oxford Holy Club was neither a Pietist *collegium pietatis* nor the highly organized, consistent cell that is sometimes pictured. It was like an Anglican religious society in its sacramental and devotional piety, but was also a somewhat amorphous and fluid group which evolved from an academic study group to a more strictly devotional cell over the period of a few years.

Throughout this period the group maintained a consistent and growing ministry to the poor and imprisoned in and about Oxford.

The original Holy Club, consisting of John and Charles Wesley, Bob Kirkham, and William Morgan, began meeting regularly (though with no formal organization or a rigid schedule) in June of 1729. After several weeks back at Epworth, John returned to Oxford on November 21, and from that point on the "four young gentlemen of Oxford" were frequently together. By March of 1730 the four were meeting three times during the week "to read over the classics" (as John later wrote), and also on Sunday evenings for theological and devotional reading. The following year the group began visiting prisoners and poor families, initially at the instigation of Morgan.[32]

By August of 1732 the men were meeting together almost daily, but to some extent in smaller subgroups, with the whole group usually meeting on Sunday evenings. By this time the focus of study had shifted to a concentration on the Greek New Testament, devotional writings (including those of August Francke), and a new interest in the early church. By the end of that year the Oxford Methodists consisted of a core group of seven; a somewhat larger group meeting with less regularity and intensity; and others (in some cases Wesley's pupils) who were more or less associated with the Wesleys or with members of their circle.

Wesley gave a theological rationale for what he was attempting in a sermon on "The Circumcision of the Heart" preached before the university on January 1, 1733. By this time, Heitzenrater notes, there had emerged at Oxford

> what finally can be called (without any hesitation) Methodism. The opponents of John Wesley had denominated it as such, he himself had recognized the term, and a historical and theological rationale had been formulated. The Methodists had received public notice not only throughout Oxford but across the kingdom. Vicious pockets of vocal opposition had been offset to a certain degree by important centers of support. The

movement seemed to be gaining momentum and strength, building upon a small, but strong and active, group of followers.[33]

Although the fortunes and constituency of the Methodists fluctuated some over the next two years, the group continued to grow and become a self-conscious movement. Benjamin Ingham became an intimate part of the group in early 1733, and by the end of that year the group included George Whitefield.[34] A "university-wide network of cell groups, more or less following John Wesley's scheme," had developed, involving by 1734 at least two dozen persons with a core group of about seven.[35]

By the end of 1734 Wesley was meeting with one or another group of Methodists every night.[36] He began his long publishing career by editing and printing prayers and other devotional materials for the group. His first book, published in January 1734, was *A Collection of Forms of Prayer for Every Day in the Week*. It contained prayers gathered from a variety of sources (which Wesley had been collecting and sifting for several years), plus lists of "general" and "particular" questions for self-examination which also had undergone considerable editing and revising over the course of some years.

When Wesley finally left Oxford in 1735, the Oxford Methodists numbered approximately forty-five persons. This was the high water mark of Oxford Methodism. From this point the movement declined until the birth of the Methodist Revival a few years later under the preaching of Whitefield and the Wesley brothers.

C. E. Vulliamy gives this description of the Holy Club of the 1733–34 period:

> The members of the Club spent an hour, morning and evening, in private prayer. At nine, twelve and three o'clock they recited a collect, and at all times they examined themselves closely, watching for signs of grace, and trying to preserve a high degree of religious fervour. They made use of pious ejaculations, they frequently consulted their Bibles, and they noted, in

cipher diaries, all the particulars of their daily employment. One hour each day was set aside for meditation. . . . they fasted twice a week, observed all the feasts of the Church, and received the Sacraments every Sunday. Before going into company they prepared their conversation, so that words might not be spoken without purpose. The Primitive Church, in so far as they had knowledge of it, was to be taken as their pattern.[37]

On a trip to London in 1735 the Wesley brothers met General James Oglethorpe, an adventurer and philanthropist who was organizing a group to help settle his new colony in Georgia. The Wesleys agreed to go along, John as a missionary to the Indians and Charles as Oglethorpe's secretary. In October they set sail on the *Simmonds* for the New World.

John Wesley went to Georgia primarily, he said, to save his own soul and learn the true meaning of the gospel by preaching to the Indians. He was sponsored by the Society for the Propagation of the Gospel in Foreign Parts (SPG) at a salary of fifty pounds per year.[38] Characteristically, he didn't go alone. He joined with Charles and two friends, Benjamin Ingham and Charles Delamotte, to form what amounted to a Methodist Holy Club aboard the ship. Three of the four (all except Delamotte) had been Oxford Methodists, so in effect the Holy Club continued in this small shipboard band. John at thirty-two was the oldest of the four; Ingham and Delamotte were in their early twenties. On leaving England, the four companions made the following covenant:

We, whose names are underwritten, being fully convinced that it is impossible, either to promote the work of God among the heathen, without an entire union among ourselves, or that such a union should subsist, unless each one will give up his single judgment to that of the majority, do agree, by the help of God: —first, that none of us will undertake anything of importance without first proposing it to the other three; —secondly, that whenever our judgments differ, any one shall give up his single judgment or inclination to the other; —thirdly, that in case of an equality, after begging God's direction, the matter shall be decided by lot.[39]

Wesley and the Moravians

The long weeks on board ship to Georgia gave Wesley his first opportunity to observe the Moravian Brethren closely. A small band of Moravian missionaries under the leadership of David Nitschmann was among the passengers. Normally Wesley spent the evening hour from seven to eight with them. He noted in his journal for Sunday, January 25, 1736, "At seven I went to the Germans. I had long before observed the great seriousness of their behaviour. Of their humility they had given a continual proof, by performing those servile offices for the other passengers which none of the English would undertake; . . . If they were pushed, struck, or thrown down, they rose again and went away; but no complaint was found in their mouth."[40]

What impressed Wesley was not only the Moravians' piety and good works but also their calm assurance of faith during storms at sea—something he lacked. During his two years in Georgia he stayed in close contact with the Moravians, including the missionary leader, August Spangenberg.

In Georgia, Wesley's zeal for holiness became "a burning desire to revitalize the church" and to build "a model Christian community in one Anglican parish," as Frank Baker puts it.[41] Understandably, the rigor of his efforts in the lax frontier setting was not universally appreciated. Already, however, Wesley was introducing such innovations as hymn singing in public worship and the use of laymen and laywomen in parish work.[42] Because of his zeal and his innovations, he was accused of "leaving the Church of England by two doors at the same time"—Roman Catholicism and Puritan Separatism. But at heart his experiments simply sprang from his desire to recover the spirit and form of early Christianity.[43]

Wesley thought he saw in the Moravians some genuine elements, at least, of early Christianity, and he tried some of their methods. As Baker notes,

Wesley organized societies for religious fellowship quite apart from ordered public worship. In these gatherings the members spent about an hour in "prayer, singing and mutual exhortation," naturally under the close supervision whenever possible of their spiritual director. . . . Wesley even divided these societies into the "more intimate union" of "bands" after the Moravian pattern. It was this which readily fostered the charge of his having instituted a Roman Catholic confessional, for mutual confession was indeed one of the purposes of these small homogeneous groups.[44]

Here we see Wesley introducing a Moravian element into the religious society pattern he brought from England, and being charged with Romanism!

Wesley's behavior in Georgia, as well as on board the *Simmonds,* should be seen also in light of his sponsorship by the Society for the Propagation of the Gospel. The SPG prescribed detailed rules for missionaries, which Wesley followed to the letter. On board ship, missionaries were to "demean themselves . . . so as to become remarkable examples of piety and virtue to the ship's company." If possible they were to conduct daily morning and evening prayers with preaching and catechizing on Sundays, and they should "instruct, exhort, admonish and reprove as they have occasion and opportunity, with such seriousness and prudence, as may gain them reputation and authority."[45] Richard Butterworth notes that much Wesley did in Georgia, including book distribution, starting schools, visiting outstations and seeking to reach the Indians, was "in direct obedience to the Instructions of the Society."[46]

Wesley spent two frustrating years in Georgia, however. His strictness and zeal, while helping some, made enemies of others. Added to this was the complication of a frustrated romance. He went back to England in early 1738, arriving in London on February 3. He returned amid controversy, considering his missionary efforts a failure. He had been unable to evangelize any Indians; he had stirred up opposition and controversy among the Anglican settlers; and he knew he lacked inward peace.

Back in London, Wesley soon encountered the Moravian missionary, Peter Böhler. Twenty-five when Wesley met him, Böhler was an effective *Bandhalter,* or band organizer, for the Moravians. Wesley must have been impressed with Böhler on two counts: his convincing presentation of instantaneous conversion by faith alone, and his practical organizing skill. In many ways, including his erudition, he was a man much like Wesley. Wesley walked and talked frequently with Böhler from the time of their first encounter until Böhler's departure for America on May 4. Both John and Charles accompanied Böhler to Oxford on February 17, but they were puzzled by his views regarding conversion and justification by faith. Böhler wrote to Zinzendorf, "I travelled with the two brothers, John and Charles Wesley, from London to Oxford. The elder, John, is a good-natured man; he knew he did not properly believe on the Saviour, and was willing to be taught."[47]

Böhler spent some days at Oxford and organized a band there. Wesley had further discussions with him both there and later in London. In March, Wesley recorded, "I was, on *Sunday* the 5th, clearly convinced of unbelief, of the want of that faith whereby alone we are saved."[48]

Wesley began to seek a true understanding and experience of salvation by faith. He reread the New Testament in Greek, discovering that instantaneous conversions did indeed take place in the New Testament church. He walked with Böhler again on April 26, and Böhler later recorded, "He wept bitterly and asked me to pray with him. I can freely affirm, that he is a poor, broken-hearted sinner, hungering after a better righteousness than that which he had thus far had, even the righteousness of Christ."[49] Böhler reported that Wesley was one among several who were seeking a closer fellowship "and want therefore to begin a Band."[50]

On May 1 Wesley records, "This evening our little Society began, which afterwards met in Fetter-lane."[51] This was the beginning of the Fetter Lane Society, organized by Wesley and

Böhler, which played a key role in Wesley's pilgrimage over the next several months.

The Fetter Lane Society was an important structural link between Wesley and the Moravians. Though it bore some resemblance to an Anglican religious society and may have been perceived as such by some of the Anglican participants, it began not as a typical religious society but rather as a Moravian band. This is clear from Böhler's diary:

> At nine in the evening I met the elder Wesley at Hutton's. . . . We now settled the names of the brethren who were of one mind, who wished for fellowship with each other, and who were willing to form a Band:—Hutton, Bray, Edmund, Wolf, Clark, Otlee, Procker, Harphey, Sweetland, Shaw, and the elder Wesley. To these I spoke on the fellowship of the children of God. They listened to me with joy, and desired to remain in that state of mind and to enter into a covenant with each other. They are all people after our own heart. Some of them are full believers, others are still in search of saving faith. It is probable that others will soon join us . . . , and then they will break into groups, and the youths and men will have separate meetings.[52]

Here we see Böhler following the typical Moravian pattern. He was operating consistently with Zinzendorf's dream to organize a network of such societies throughout the main bodies of the church, without separating from them. Perhaps from its beginning some members of the group had conflicting ideas as to just what this society should become. Those most closely associated with the Moravians probably understood and shared Zinzendorf's vision, while others perhaps saw the group simply as another of the many Anglican religious societies.

The Fetter Lane Society's rules included weekly meetings for prayer and confession, division into bands of from five to ten persons each, the right and duty of each person to speak freely, procedures for admitting new members, and provision for a love feast from 7:00 to 10:00 P.M. one night per month. An agreed-to financial contribution was to be collected monthly. Though

Wesley could not have foreseen it, the Fetter Lane Society was to become the "seed-plot of the British Moravian Church, an *ecclesiola* which became an *ecclesia*."[53]

Wesley "broke the faith barrier" (as one has written[54]) on Wednesday, May 24, 1738, about three weeks after Böhler departed for America. This was his famous heart-warming experience during a meeting in Aldersgate Street, an experience which Wesley himself saw as the critical turning point in his spiritual quest. "I felt I did trust in Christ, Christ alone, for my salvation; and an assurance was given me, that He had taken away *my* sins, even *mine,* and saved *me* from the law of sin and death."[55]

Wesley now had a newfound assurance of faith, a supportive group to share his life with, and an expanding preaching ministry. Now, finally, he felt his long-standing dream of a restoration of primitive Christianity within the Church of England was possible. He wanted to learn more, however, from the Moravians and other German Pietists, and so on June 7 he "determined, if God should permit, to retire for a short time into Germany," as he had decided to do even before leaving Georgia.[56]

Wesley went to the Continent in June 1738, in company with several others. He met Zinzendorf at Marienborn, then went on to Herrnhut, where he spent two weeks (August 1–14). He visited other Moravian and Pietist centers, going twice to Halle, where he talked with Professor Gotthilf August Francke (1696–1769), August Francke's son and successor.[57] Wesley also visited Jena, where Böhler, Spangenberg, and other Moravian and Pietist leaders had studied.[58] In his *Journal* Wesley described the Herrnhut community and summarized interviews he had with Christian David and other Moravian leaders.[59]

Revival Begins

Wesley returned to London on September 16 and on the next day recorded, "I began again to declare in my own country the glad tidings of salvation."[60] In October he wrote a letter to "the

Church of God which is in Herrnhut" that reveals both his appreciation for the Moravians and his own growing ministry:

> We are endeavouring here also, by the grace which is given us, to be followers of you, as ye are of Christ. Fourteen were added to us, since our return, so that we have now eight bands of men, consisting of fifty-six persons; all of whom seek for salvation only in the blood of Christ. As yet we have only two small bands of women; the one of three the other of five persons. But here are many others who only wait till we have leisure to instruct them, how they may most effectually build up one another in the faith and love of Him who gave himself for them.
>
> Though my brother and I are not permitted to preach in most of the churches in London, yet (thanks be to God!) there are others left, wherein we have liberty to speak the truth as it is in Jesus. Likewise on every evening, and on set evenings in the week at two several places, we publish the word of reconciliation, sometimes to twenty or thirty, sometimes to fifty or sixty, sometimes to three or four hundred persons, met together to hear it.[61]

Having seen Herrnhut, Wesley had great appreciation for Moravian faith and piety. He was uneasy, however, about the Moravians' "quietism," their tendency toward spiritual complacency, and the "personality cult" which had grown up around Count Zinzendorf.[62] He now threw himself wholeheartedly into itinerant evangelism and care of converts in the London area, and seems to have assumed the primary leadership of the Fetter Lane Society.

Wesley was soon plugging into the existing network of religious societies which were still fairly numerous, even if not very dynamic. John Simon notes, "It is impossible to doubt that into the 'old Societies' certain evils had crept which were weakening their strength as religious organizations."[63] George Whitefield, who at this time was also preaching with great success and setting up societies, wrote that "most of the old Societies in London, I fear, are sunk into a dead formality" and "seldom, if

201

ever, acquaint each other with the operations of God's Spirit upon their souls. . . ."[64] This, Whitefield and the Wesley brothers set out to change.

Whitefield, present at Fetter Lane on January 1, had just returned from preaching in America. Soon barred from London pulpits, he went to Bristol. There on February 17, 1739, he preached for the first time in the open air to about two hundred colliers at Kingswood. Within three weeks the crowds had mushroomed to 10,000.[65]

The busy port city of Bristol, 100 miles west of London, was the second largest city in the kingdom in Wesley's day, numbering about 30,000 inhabitants. It maintained a busy commerce in slaves bound for the New World and was a center of the coal-mining industry, which fed England's emerging industrial revolution.

Rioting had broken out among the coal miners of the Bristol area, particularly at Kingswood. Soldiers were called out and some colliers were arrested. These disturbances were part of a larger pattern of unrest during the period of 1738–40 related to high corn prices, low wages, and the impoverished condition of the emerging class of urban workers.[66]

As Whitefield's crowds increased, he sent for John Wesley, recognizing Wesley's preaching power and organizing skill. Up to this point, however, Wesley had preached only in regular church services while in England. Should he accept Whitefield's appeal to help with the open-air meetings in Bristol? Charles thought not. But John submitted the decision to the Fetter Lane Society, which cast lots and decided he should go.

Wesley arrived in Bristol on March 31. On Sunday evening, April 1, he spoke to a little society about the Sermon on the Mount—"one pretty remarkable precedent of field-preaching," he observed, "though I suppose there were churches at that time also."[67] The next day Wesley reports: "At four in the afternoon, I submitted to be more vile and proclaimed in the highways the glad tidings of salvation, speaking from a little eminence in a ground adjoining the city to about three thousand people. The Scripture on which I spoke was this: . . . 'The Spirit of the Lord is upon me, because he hath anointed me to preach the Gospel to the poor.' "[68]

Characteristically, Wesley immediately began to organize. He formed a number of societies and bands and on May 9 acquired a piece of property where he built his "New Room" as a central meeting place. When Whitefield returned to America in August, Wesley was left totally in charge of the growing work. He divided his time between Bristol and London, concentrating on open-air preaching, organizing bands, and speaking at night to an increasing number of societies. These developments in London and Bristol under Whitefield and Wesley most clearly mark the beginning of the Wesleyan Revival.

Methodist Structure

Within a few months Wesley had set up the basic structure which was to mark Methodism for over a century. The patterns he established formed the infrastructure of the movement and were crucial to its development and growth. They reveal something of Wesley's own understanding of the church and his sense of priorities.[69]

The basic structures of the emerging Methodist Revival were the society, the class, the band, and (a little later) Wesley's corps of traveling preachers. Both Wesley and Whitefield began organizing societies, essentially following the established religious society pattern.

Wesley organized dozens of such societies in the London and Bristol areas. All the groups together he called the United Societies. The main difference between the Methodist societies and the many other religious societies then functioning was that these were directly under the supervision of Wesley and were united chiefly in his person. During these early months Wesley was still meeting with the Fetter Lane Society.

Of all Wesley's innovations, the bands trace most directly to Moravian influence. Wesley had found numerous bands functioning at Herrnhut, and as Baker notes, on his return he "enthusiastically advocated the system of 'bands' for all the religious societies in London, including that in Fetter Lane."[70]

The bands were small cells of either men or women gathered for pastoral care. New converts were beset with temptations and needed both encouragement and opportunity for confession, Wesley noted.

> These, therefore, wanted some means of closer union; they wanted to pour out their hearts without reserve, particularly with regard to the sin which did still easily beset them, and the temptations which were most apt to prevail over them. And they were the more desirous of this, when they observed it was the express advice of an inspired writer: "Confess your faults one to another, and pray for one another, that ye may be healed."
>
> In compliance with their desire, I divided them into smaller companies; putting the married or single men, and married or single women, together.[71]

The Wesleyan class meeting arose in Bristol in early 1742 somewhat by accident. Wesley was increasingly concerned that many Methodists did not live the Gospel; "several grew cold, and gave way to the sins which had long easily beset them." Clearly some mechanism for exercising discipline was needed.

To meet the preaching–house debt in Bristol, the society there (numbering at the time over 1,100) was divided into "classes" of a dozen each. Leaders were appointed to secure weekly contributions toward the debt, and Wesley asked the leaders also to "make a particular inquiry into the behaviour of those whom he saw weekly." This provided the opportunity for exercising discipline. Thus, says Wesley,

> As soon as possible, the same method was used in London and all other places. Evil men were detected, and reproved. They were borne with for a season. If they forsook their sins, we received them gladly; if they obstinately persisted therein, it was openly declared that they were not of us. The rest mourned and

prayed for them, and yet rejoiced, that, as far as in us lay, the scandal was rolled away from the society.[72]

At first the class leaders visited the members in their homes, but this proved to be too time consuming and somewhat complicated for several reasons, in part because of the poor and crowded conditions where many of the people lived. Wesley says, "Upon all these considerations it was agreed, that those of each class should meet together. And by this means, a more full inquiry was made into the behaviour of each person. . . . Advice or reproof was given as need required, quarrels made up, misunderstandings removed: and after an hour or two spent in this labour of love, they concluded with prayer and thanksgiving."[73] And Wesley reflects,

> It can scarce be conceived what advantages have been reaped from this little prudential regulation. Many now happily experienced that Christian fellowship of which they had not so much as an idea before. They began to "bear one another's burdens," and naturally to "care for each other." As they had daily a more intimate acquaintance with, so they had a more endeared affection for, each other. And "speaking the truth in love, they grew up into Him in all things, who is the Head, even Christ. . . . "[74]

The class meetings were not designed merely as Christian growth groups, however, or primarily as cells for *koinonia*— although in fact they did serve that function. Their primary purpose was discipline. The band had already been instituted as the primary spiritual cell of Methodism. As Skevington Wood observes, "The class was the disciplinary unit of the society" and was "the keystone of the entire Methodist edifice," while the band was the confessional unit.[75]

All band and class members met together quarterly for the love feast, another Moravian contribution. A system of membership tickets was used, and only persons with tickets were admitted to the love feasts.[76]

Wesley soon extended his efforts by appointing lay preachers and helpers. Workers in the Methodist movement thus included preachers and assistants, class and band leaders, stewards, visitors of the sick, and schoolmasters.

As Wesley attended to the demands of a growing popular movement, tensions began to develop in the Fetter Lane Society. These were due in part to the arrival in October 1739 of the young Moravian leader, Philip Henry Molther (1714–80). Molther taught a doctrine of "stillness" and stressed a strongly Lutheran understanding of faith which, in Wesley's view, undercut the valid use of the means of grace. Molther began telling the people at Fetter Lane that they did not truly have saving faith if they still had any doubt or fear. Therefore they should abstain from all the ordinances, particularly the Lord's Supper, and "be still" before the Lord until they received true faith. The ordinances are not really means of grace, he taught, for Christ is the only means. Charles Wesley commented, "He expressly denies that grace, or the Spirit, is transmitted through the means, particularly through the sacrament."[77]

John Wesley tried to dissuade the Fetter Lane people from Molther's "stillness" doctrine, but with the strong German Moravian influence in the society and Wesley's frequent absence because of the work at Bristol, he was largely unsuccessful. After several sessions where the issues were joined, Wesley was barred from speaking further to the society. A break occurred finally on Sunday, July 20, 1740, ironically at the society's love feast. Forbidden to preach, Wesley read a short paper stating his points of disagreement with Molther. Then he and about eighteen of the sixty or so present walked out of the meeting.[78] From that point on the Fetter Lane Society evolved from an Anglican-Moravian hybrid into a Moravian congregation.

Even as the crisis at Fetter Lane was deepening, Wesley's personal ministry in London was expanding. For some time Wesley had been preaching to large crowds in Moorfields, a popular park and recreation area. Nearby stood the abandoned Royal Foundry, unused since an explosion and fire some thirty-three years earlier. At the end of 1739 Wesley leased the building and remodeled it. He opened it as his headquarters early in 1740.[79] By June of 1740 the Methodist Society at the Foundry had 300 members.[80]

Wesley was now employed full-time in preaching, writing, and organizing the growing Methodist work in London, Bristol, and elsewhere. The Foundry was a beehive of activity. In remodeling the old building Wesley had built a galleried chapel to hold 1,500 people, a large room which would accommodate 300, a dispensary, and a book room for the sale of his books and pamphlets. Here Wesley opened a free school for sixty children, an almshouse for widows, and the first free dispensary in London since the dissolution of the monasteries.[81] Wesley had an apartment for himself on the second floor. As the movement grew, some sixty-six class meetings met at the Foundry weekly. Two weekly prayer meetings were held, and Wesley or one of his preachers preached daily at 5:00 A.M.[82]

The events from Wesley's return to England in 1738 to his separation from the Moravians in 1740 show that he both benefited from and reacted against the Moravians. The two great Moravian contributions to Wesley came in clarifying for him, and subsequently leading him into, the experience of saving faith, and in providing him models of Christian life-in-community. That he actually saw the Moravian Brethren as an adequate model for renewal within the larger established church, as an *ecclesiola in ecclesia,* is questionable, for Wesley knew the Moravians had in fact become a separate church, despite Zinzendorf's vision. The Pietist institutions at Halle may have appealed more to him as models of what could happen within the established church.

The more Wesley got to know the Moravians, however, the more he felt two distinctly different visions of the church were at stake, despite profound similarities at the level of spiritual experience and *koinonia*. The Moravians were right, he felt, to teach justification by faith and regeneration solely through the merits of the blood of the Lamb. But Wesley believed the

Moravians were weak at two crucial points. They did not take seriously enough the sacramental side of the church, and their inward spirituality was not balanced by a proper emphasis on the ethical side of Christian life—disciplined living, good works, and preaching the Gospel to the poor. The life of Christian holiness as both an inward and an outward reality was still Wesley's goal.

From the Moravians Wesley learned the inwardness of faith, but he insisted on balancing this with that stream of Anglican piety that stressed holy living. Wesley was convinced that this balance was biblical. Throughout his life he would insist that the biblical ideal was "faith working by love." Ironically, Wesley's position was both more Anglican and more truly Moravian (in the historical sense) than was the Lutheran Moravianism he reacted against. Wesley's spirituality was to a large degree the spirituality of Arndt, Spener, and Francke, but in attempting to build renewed Christian communities within the Anglican faith and structure he was prepared to form more radically distinct and committed groups than were the Lutheran Pietists. And here, at the level of actual Christian community life, Wesley was clearly more impressed by the Herrnhuterian Moravians than by the Lutheran Pietists.

Wesley continued building on the foundation he laid in 1738–40 with great consistency over the course of more than fifty years. He gradually extended the Methodist work outward from its main centers to the whole of England, into Ireland, and especially to North America. At his death in 1791 Wesley left 72,000 Methodists in Great Britain and Ireland and a fledgling Methodist denomination in America of some 57,000 members.[83]

Wesley's Doctrine of the Church

John Wesley was sufficiently steeped in church history and Anglican ecclesiology to understand that the concept of the church was at stake in his reforming mission. From early in his ministry he pondered basic questions as to the nature, form, and function of the Christian church, and eventually he developed a fairly comprehensive ecclesiology.

The major sources of Wesley's ecclesiology were the Catholic tradition mediated through Anglicanism and the Believers' Church tradition mediated mainly through the Moravian Brethren. Baker notes that Wesley "firmly accepted the *via media* of the Church of England as incorporated in Cranmer's *Book of Common Prayer,* expounded in turn by Jewel as the fulfillment of Scripture and the Fathers and by Hooker as the crown of human reasoning."[84] The Church of England—which Wesley always considered, over all, the best church in Christendom—was the middle way between Catholicism and Protestantism.

In his *Explanatory Notes upon the New Testament,* completed in 1754 and based largely on the work of the Württemberg Pietist, J. A. Bengel, Wesley gives some of his most succinct descriptions of the church. It is "the believers in Christ," "the whole body of Christian believers," "the whole body of true believers, whether on earth or in paradise."[85] Commenting on Acts 5:11, Wesley describes the New Testament church as "a company of men, called by the gospel, grafted into Christ by baptism, animated by love, united by all kind of fellowship, and disciplined by the death of Ananias and Sapphira."[86]

In his sermon "Of the Church" Wesley said the church is, in the proper sense, "a congregation, or body of people, united together in the service of God."[87] Even two or three united in Christ's name, or a Christian family, may therefore be called a church.[88] The primary expression of the church is the visible, gathered local congregation. But in a broader sense "church" means "the catholic or universal church; that is, all the Christians under heaven," made up of all the local congregations in the world.[89]

Wesley felt he could reconcile the New Testament understanding of the church with Article Nineteen of the Anglican Thirty-nine Articles. He wrote,

> A visible Church (as our Article defines it) is "a company of faithful (or believing) people: *Coetus credentium*." This is the essence of a Church, and the properties thereof are (as they are described in the words that follow), "that the pure word of God be preached therein, and the sacraments duly administered." Now, then, according to this authentic account, what is the Church of England? What is it, indeed, but the *faithful people, the true believers* of England? It is true, if these are scattered abroad they come under another consideration. But when they are visibly joined by assembling together to hear "the pure word of God preached" and to "eat of one bread" and "drink of one cup," they are then properly "the visible Church of England".[90]

Wesley is saying, in other words, that the visibility of the true church consists essentially in its coming together as the Christian community. The visible church is the church assembled; the invisible church is the church scattered and dispersed. Wesley said he did not propose to defend this definition of the church, but he thought it was compatible with Scripture. Actually, he is straining here toward a more biblical and organic interpretation of what is primarily a rather institutional and sacramental formula, based largely on the Lutheran Augsburg Confession of 1530 and earlier precedents.

The words in the Article, "in which the pure word of God is preached, and the sacraments be duly administered" Wesley interpreted more functionally than formally. They meant any congregation where the gospel was not truly preached or the sacraments not duly administered was neither a part of the Church of England nor of the universal church. Yet Wesley was charitable toward improper practices and even wrong doctrines if a congregation gave evidence of the Spirit's genuine presence: "Whoever they are that have 'one Spirit, one hope, one Lord, one faith, one God and Father of all,' I can easily bear with their holding wrong opinions, yea, and superstitious modes of worship; nor would I, on these accounts, scruple still to include them within the pale of the catholic church; neither would I have any objection to receive them, if they desired it, as members of the Church of England."[91]

At heart, Wesley viewed the church as the community of God's people. Defining the church as a congregation of faithful believers does, however, point to some ambivalence and ambiguity, if not inconsistency, in Wesley. On the one hand the Church of England was essentially the "faithful people" or "true believers" visibly assembled together in Word and sacrament. But on the other hand Wesley virtually accused the Church of England of being apostate. There are only a few in England "whose inmost soul is renewed after the image of God," he wrote in 1763, "and as for a Christian *visible* church, or a body of Christians visibly united together, where is this to be seen?"[92]

Wesley considered the Church of England (and the whole Christian church generally) to be in a largely fallen state. In some formal sense the Church of England with its structures and liturgy was still a true church, but in fact and spirit the true church was really the small groups of faithful believers scattered throughout the Anglican and other communions.

Wesley seems to have seen the Methodist societies as comprising, to a large degree, the true visible church within Anglicanism. Yet he recognized that not even all Methodists were "true Believers" or "faithful men," and that as time went on this would become increasingly so.

Outler summarizes Wesley's mature understanding of the church (what he calls "the classical Methodist ecclesiology") as follows:

1. The *unity* of the church is based upon the Christian *koinonia* in the Holy Spirit.

2. The *holiness* of the church is grounded in the discipline of grace which guides and matures the Christian life from its threshold in justifying faith to its [fullness] in sanctification.

3. The *catholicity* of the church is defined by the universal outreach of redemption, the essential community of all true believers.

4. The *apostolicity* of the church is gauged by the succession of apostolic doctrine in those who have been faithful to the apostolic witness.[93]

This is an apt description. The church is *one* because "in all ages and nations it is the one body of Christ," endued with faith working by love.[94] Its *holiness* consists in the holiness of its members, "because every member thereof is holy, though in different degrees, as He that called them is holy";[95] "no unholy man can possibly be a member of it."[96] It is *catholic* because it is the people of God "dispersed over the whole earth, in Europe, Asia, Africa, and America."[97] And it is *apostolic,* for there has been an uninterrupted apostolic witness to the Gospel through a faithful community and faithful ministers down through history.[98]

Ministry and Sacrament

Wesley's concern with reform and experience naturally led to the question of how and through whom the church ministers God's grace. The question of orders of ministry arose when Wesley began appointing assistants after 1738 to help Charles and himself in the work of preaching. How was this new body of preachers, most of whom were unordained, to be understood ecclesiologically? In what sense were they ministers, what authority did they have, and what was the meaning of Wesley's act of appointing them? These were inevitable and crucial questions given the rather specific theories and procedures of ordination and ministry within the Church of England.

The Wesleys themselves could claim authority to preach based on their Anglican ordination. Their problem was to justify preaching indiscriminately across England (rather than staying in one parish) and their unorthodox practice of field preaching. John Wesley justified his itinerant ministry on at least two grounds: his Oxford fellowship gave him license to teach anywhere, and the results themselves justified his actions. "I did far more good," he remarked, "by preaching three days on my father's tomb than I did by preaching three years in his pulpit."[99] To critics who said he should stay in one parish only, he responded, "I look upon all the world as my parish; thus far I mean, that in whatever part of it I am I judge it meet, right, and my bounden duty to declare, unto all that are willing to hear, the glad tidings of salvation."[100]

But the case was different for Wesley's preachers, for they were unordained. What right did *they* have to preach, and what right did Wesley have to appoint them? Here as elsewhere, Wesley's problem was to remain faithful to Scripture, the early church, and the Church of England while moving to meet the ministry opportunities opening before him.

Wesley insisted that he was appointing *preachers,* not *pastors,* and that his appointment was not ordination to the priesthood. He saw this as consistent with Anglican church order and early church practice. Underlying his reasoning was his perception of the Methodist societies as an evangelical order within the Church of England, not as churches themselves.

Wesley thought he saw in Scripture and the early church a distinction between two kinds of Christian ministers—corresponding to the difference between Anglican priests and Methodist preachers—that would legitimate both. One order of ministers had responsibility to preach and evangelize; the other to give pastoral care, administer the sacraments, and ordain. Thus Wesley explained in his sermon, "The Ministerial Office,"

> So the great High-Priest of our profession sent Apostles and evangelists to proclaim glad tidings to all the world; and then Pastors, Preachers, and Teachers, to build up in the faith the congregations that should be founded. But I do not find that ever the office of an Evangelist was the same with that of a Pastor, frequently called a Bishop. He presided over the flock, and administered the sacraments: The former assisted him, and preached the word, either in one or more congregations. I cannot prove from any part of the New Testament, or from any author of the first three centuries, that the office of an Evangelist gave any man a right to act as a Pastor or Bishop. I

believe these offices were considered as quite distinct from each other til the time of Constantine.

But with the fall of the church under Constantine, the situation was greatly altered: It soon grew common, for one man to take the whole charge of a congregation in order to engross the whole pay. Hence the same person acted as Priest and Prophet, as Pastor and Evangelist. And this gradually spread more and more throughout the whole Christian Church. Yet even at this day, although the same person usually discharges both these offices, yet the office of an Evangelist or Teacher does not imply that of a Pastor, to whom peculiarly belongs the administration of the sacraments. . . . [101]

Wesley thus saw his innovation as a return to New Testament practice. Methodist preachers were simply *"extraordinary messengers, raised up to provoke the ordinary ones to jealousy."* They were not appointed to "exercise the priestly office" or to administer the sacraments but to preach and evangelize.[102]

One might recognize more than two orders of ministry, Wesley thought, but the fundamental distinction was between pastor-priests and preacher-evangelists—the former being "ordinary" ministers and the latter "extraordinary." In the New Testament and the early church one always finds "if not more, at least two orders distinct from each other, the one having power only to preach and (sometimes) to baptize, the other to ordain also and administer the Lord's Supper."[103]

Wesley saw the pastor-priests as the "ordinary," established, institutional ministers of the church while the preacher-evangelists were the "extraordinary" ministers raised up by more immediate divine inspiration somewhat outside institutional channels—and therefore not having the institutional prerogatives of ordaining and administering the sacraments. Both orders of ministers were constituted such by the Holy Spirit, however, "for no man or number of men upon earth can constitute an overseer, bishop, or any other Christian minister. To do this is the peculiar work of the Holy Ghost."[104]

Wesley's view of ministry may be described as charismatic

since he saw all ministry as springing from the Holy Spirit's work in the church. He used the same ordinary extraordinary distinction in discussing the gifts of the Spirit that he employed in distinguishing different kinds of ministries, which suggests that he saw ministry and spiritual gifts as being closely linked.

While Wesley had no fully developed doctrine of the gifts of the Spirit, he did say enough (mainly in response to charges that he himself pretended to extraordinary gifts or inspirations) for one to determine his general perspective. His view is complicated by the distinction he made between extraordinary and ordinary gifts, which is not precisely biblical. Among the "extraordinary gifts" he included healing, miracles, prophecy (in the sense of foretelling), discernment of gifts, tongues, and the interpretation of tongues. Apostles, prophets, and evangelists he listed as "extraordinary officers." The "ordinary gifts" included "convincing speech," persuasion, knowledge, faith, "easy elocution," and pastors and teachers as "ordinary officers."[105]

Wesley felt the ordinary gifts were operative in the church in all ages and should appropriately be desired by Christians— though, of course, as secondary to love.[106] All the gifts including the extraordinary ones had been part of the experience of the church during the first three centuries, he believed, but "even in the infancy of the church, God divided them with a sparing hand," and gave them principally to those in leadership.[107]

Did Wesley believe the extraordinary gifts could be expected in the church in his day? He writes:

It does not appear that these extraordinary gifts of the Holy Ghost were common in the church for more than two centuries. We seldom hear of them after that fatal period when the Emperor Constantine called himself a Christian. . . . From this time they almost totally ceased; very few instances of the kind were found. The cause of this was not, . . . "because there was no more occasion for them," because all the world was become Christians. . . . The real cause was, "the love of many," almost of all Christians, so called, was "waxed cold." . . . This was the

real cause why the extraordinary gifts of the Holy Ghost were
no longer to be found in the Christian Church.[108]

This did not mean, however, that extraordinary gifts had
ceased for all time. God was doing a renewing work through
Methodism in his own day, Wesley believed. Thus he nowhere
ruled out the possibility of new manifestations of the extraordinary
gifts. He felt such gifts either "were designed to remain in the
church throughout all ages," or else "they will be restored at the
nearer approach of 'the restitution of all things.' "[109] Wesley had a
fundamental, though somewhat hidden, optimism regarding such
gifts. He advised Christians that the best gifts "are worth your
pursuit, though but few of you can attain them."[110] "Perfecting
the saints" in Ephesians 4:12 involves "the completing them both
in number and their various gifts and graces." Gifts are given for
their usefulness, by which "alone are we to estimate all our gifts
and talents."[111]

Wesley thus believed that if the extraordinary gifts of the
Spirit had practically vanished in his day, this was because of the
fallen state of the church and represented a less than ideal situation.
In fact God's power was still at work, though in a hindered way.
Wesley certainly did not disparage the gifts. Despite his reticence
concerning so-called extraordinary gifts, he valued all gifts and felt
that in a truly restored, spiritual church they all would be in
evidence.

Within the "ordinary" ministry of the church, Wesley
accepted the traditional threefold distinction of bishops, presbyters
(or priests), and deacons, but saw no essential difference between
bishops and presbyters. In 1747 he suggested that "the three orders
of Bishops, Priests, and Deacons" were plainly evident in the New
Testament, but not prescribed for all ages. Rather, there must be
"numberless accidental varieties in the government of various
churches." "As God variously dispenses His gifts of nature,
providence, and grace, both the offices themselves and the officers
in each ought to be varied from time to time." Thus Scripture

prescribes "no determinate plan of church-government," and there would never have been "any thought of uniformity in the government of all churches" had church leaders "consulted the word of God only."[112] But Wesley still believed "the threefold order of ministers . . . is not only authorized by its apostolical institution, but also by the written Word."[113]

Wesley saw bishops and priests as constituting an "outward priesthood" in the church. This view of Christian ministry—an ordinary, "outward priesthood" empowered to ordain and administer the sacraments and an order of "extraordinary ministers" empowered to preach and evangelize—functioned for Wesley in two ways. On the one hand, it was his justification before Anglican critics for appointing Methodist "lay" preachers. On the other hand, it was his argument before his preachers for refusing to allow them to give the sacraments or assume other powers of the Anglican clergy. Wesley wanted at all costs to keep this distinction clear and permanent, for it was the key to Methodism's remaining a movement *within* the Church of England rather than becoming a separate sect. As long as Methodist preachers could not give the sacraments, Methodists would have to go to the Anglican service; as long as they could not ordain, there could be no Methodist preachers except those whom Wesley himself appointed. This is precisely what Wesley wanted.

Since Wesley saw no real difference between a bishop and a priest, he felt that, biblically, he had as much right to ordain as did anyone—although for the sake of order, and to prevent Methodist separation, he was very reluctant to do this. In letters to Charles in later years he said he was convinced he was "a scriptural *episkopos* as much as any man in England or in Europe,"[114] and that he had as much right to ordain as to administer the sacrament. "But I see abundance of reasons why I should not use the right, unless I was turned out of the church."[115]

But Wesley did in fact finally ordain ministers for American Methodism. This of course caused sharp controversy and required explanation. As early as 1755 Wesley admitted that in appointing preachers he had already in some sense ordained. Later he justified his ordinations for America on the two grounds of biblical authority and practical necessity. He could earlier have ordained the Methodist preachers in England, but this was unnecessary and would have separated Methodists from the Church of England. "But the case is widely different between England and America," he said. In America there was no one to administer the sacraments to Methodist converts. "Here, therefore, my scruples are at an end; and I conceive myself at full liberty, as I violate no order and invade no man's right by appointing and sending labourers into the harvest."[116]

With this approach, Wesley thought he was being at once faithful to Scripture and early church tradition, consistent with a proper understanding of Anglican doctrine, and above all obedient to the gospel in seeing to it that the Word was preached as freely and widely as possible. He thought he had found a way to justify both Methodism with its preachers and the institution of the Church of England with its clergy. This was a crucial point for Wesley; it was his way of mediating between two views of the church, holding together church and sect without denying the validity of either.

F. Ernest Stoeffler believes Wesley's view of ministry is best explained against the background of his contacts with Moravianism and the *collegia pietatis* of Continental Pietism. Though Wesley's view might appear ambiguous, Stoeffler argues that the "ambiguities recede into the background if it is remembered that his view of the ministry is related to a conscious adaptation on his part of the *collegia pietatis* arrangement of the church-related Pietists on the Continent, especially as it was observed among the Moravians."[117] I am not convinced that Wesley was consciously imitating or adapting Moravian and Pietist ideas, but he did see Methodism and its ministry as an evangelical order within the Church of England somewhat akin to Pietism within the Lutheran Church. And he was undoubtedly influenced in some measure by what he saw of Moravian and Pietist models on the Continent.

Wesley's view of ministry was related to his understanding of the sacraments. Wesley's sacramentalism is well known, and he seems most Anglican precisely at this point. But his sacramentalism, like other aspects of his theology and practice, was a modified Anglican position, strongly influenced by his evangelical convictions. Stoeffler suggests that Wesley's spiritual renewal in 1738 influenced his understanding of the sacraments less than it did any other aspect of his theology.[118] Yet even here one finds a marked shift of emphasis after Aldersgate.

Wesley believed the sacraments, especially the Lord's Supper, were "means of grace," necessary "if not to the *being,* at least to the *well-being* of a Church."[119] After Aldersgate the ordinances of the church glowed with the living power of the Spirit for Wesley. The interesting thing is that the Lord's Supper took on deeper meaning for Wesley, not less, after his heart-warming experience. Rather than trading off the sacramental means of grace for the direct intimacy of his newfound experience of God, he thrived on them as nourishment for the new life of God in his soul. This is another instance of Wesley's joining the old and new, the institutional and charismatic—and yet keeping the primary accent on life.

Wesley's view of baptism was similar to his view of the Lord's Supper but somewhat more ambiguous due to his adherence to infant baptism. He felt that in baptism a "principle of grace is infused" and was able to say, "Baptism doth now save us, if we live answerable thereto; if we repent, believe, and obey the gospel: Supposing this, as it admits us into the Church here, so into glory hereafter."[120]

Wesley distinguished between infant baptism and adult baptism, coming close to affirming baptismal regeneration in infants but not in adults. He said of his own experience, "I believe, till I was about ten years old I had not sinned away that 'washing of the Holy Ghost' which was given me in baptism."[121] He held that infants should be baptized because they are guilty of original sin. Baptism washes away original sin, and infants can come to

Christ by no other means.[122] He felt that children baptized in infancy were at that time born again, and that this was presupposed in the *Book of Common Prayer*. But in the case of adults, at least, a person might be born of water but not yet, or necessarily, of the Spirit.[123] His view is pungently pictured in a 1739 entry in his *Journal*:

> I baptized John Smith . . . and four other adults at Islington. Of the adults I have known baptized lately, only one was at that time born again, in the full sense of the word; that is, found a thorough, inward change, by the love of God filling her heart. Most of them were only born again in a lower sense; that is, received the remission of their sins. And some (as it has since too plainly appeared) neither in the one sense nor the other.[124]

It will perhaps help in understanding Wesley's view of baptism to recall his dynamic and experiential conception of conversion and the Christian life. Wesley could say "Baptism doth now save us, if we live answerable thereto" because his emphasis was on the present life of God in the soul. Present evidence of the fruit of the Spirit in one's life proved that the new birth had earlier taken place when the believer was baptized. Still, it was not baptism itself, independently, that wrought the change, but the grace of God appropriated by faith.

In sum, Wesley's view of the church, its role in history, its structure, ministry, and sacraments, was an essentially Anglican position modified and enlivened by his own spiritual rebirth at Aldersgate and by his experiences at the front of a rapidly expanding movement of renewal. The striking thing about Wesley's ecclesiology is that it did not undergo radical transformation after the critical years of 1738–39. It changed very little. But the changes were very significant, parallel to his personal appropriation of justifying faith through which doctrines mentally accepted became living realities in his own experience.

The changes in Wesley's ecclesiology were part of a gradual evolution and shift in emphasis which began as early as 1730 and continued through the early years of the revival. Little or no change seems to have occurred after about 1750. By that time he had arrived securely at the mediating synthesis which was the mark of his theology and ministry.

Grounded in the Anglican rather than the Lutheran tradition, Wesley's ecclesiology could be expected to be quite different from that of Spener, Francke, and Zinzendorf. The similarities, however, seem more impressive than the differences.

1. Wesley was like Spener, Francke, and Zinzendorf in stressing that the essence of the church is persons in direct relationship with God and each other, rather than primarily an institutional reality. Wesley saw the church as the community or fellowship of the Spirit in which the key dynamic was "faith working by love." Though his terminology was not that of Spener, he had a similar organic-charismatic concept of the church while still stressing the validity of the church's institutional dimension. He was attracted to the Moravian experiments in community but was closer to Spener and Francke in the way he saw community worked out in practice.

2. Wesley seems to have put less stress on the priesthood of believers but more on the gifts of the Spirit than did Spener. In this respect he was closer to Zinzendorf. One may say that the priesthood of believers simply was not a theme of Wesley's theology, though his ecclesiology is inherently compatible with the emphasis. It is interesting in this connection that Wesley apparently had no firsthand knowledge of Spener (though he knew of him) and apparently never read the *Pia Desideria*. Wesley could have given a stronger logical and theological grounding for his practice by combining the theme of the priesthood of believers with his stress on gifts.

3. Though Wesley did not use the *ecclesiola* terminology or explicitly draw on the Pietist *ecclesiola* model, he in fact viewed Methodism as an *ecclesiola*. His view of "extraordinary" ministers and gifts seems to presuppose some kind of *ecclesiola* concept.

4. The "optimism of grace" found in Spener, Francke, and Zinzendorf was found as well in Wesley, though in a somewhat

different form. Wesley's high ideal of Christian perfection and his stress on prevenient grace are relevant here as evidence of what Wesley saw as possible now, in the present order. Wesley's optimism was similar to, but somewhat less exuberant, than Zinzendorf's; it was more like Francke's. Wesley's eschatological views were postmillennial, and were largely borrowed from Bengel.

THE INTERNAL DYNAMICS OF METHODISM

The story of John Wesley's life and ministry is the story of creating and adapting structures to serve a burgeoning renewal movement. Within a few years of 1738 the Methodist system of societies, classes and bands, traveling preachers, simple preaching houses, and quarterly love feasts had been set up and was functioning well under Wesley's watchful eye.

The emerging patterns composed, above all, a system of discipline-in-community. E. Douglas Bebb in his study of Wesley's social concern notes, "The Methodist church discipline of the eighteenth century has no parallel in modern English ecclesiastical history" and "would be regarded as intolerable by almost all members of any Christian communion in this country today."[125]

This discipline produced a rapidly growing body of earnest adherents. After thirty years, in 1768, Methodism had forty circuits and 27,341 members. Ten years later the numbers had grown to sixty circuits and 40,089 members; in another decade, ninety-nine circuits and 66,375 members. By 1798, seven years after Wesley's death, the totals had jumped to 149 circuits with 101,712 members. By the turn of the century, according to Bebb, about one in every thirty adult Englishmen was a Methodist.[126]

Understanding the internal dynamics of Methodism requires examining in more detail the Methodist class meeting, the band system, and Wesley's provisions for pastoral leadership.

The Class Meeting

As noted earlier, the Methodist societies were divided into "classes" and "bands." More accurately, the societies were the sum total of class and band members, since the primary point of belonging was really the more intimate level of community of the small cell.

The class meeting was in many ways the cornerstone of the whole edifice. The classes were in effect house churches (not classes for instruction as the term *class* might suggest) meeting in the various neighborhoods where people lived. The class leaders (men and women) were the pastors and disciplers. After the fortuitous organization of classes at Bristol, the class system was introduced in London in 1742 and became the established Methodist pattern throughout England by 1746.[127]

The duties of the class leader as given by Wesley were twofold:

(1.) To see each person in his class, once a week at least, in order to inquire how their souls prosper; to advise, reprove, comfort, and exhort, as occasion may require; to receive what they are willing to give, toward the relief of the poor.

(2.) To meet the Minister and the Stewards of the society, in order to inform the Minister of any that are sick, or of any that are disorderly and will not be reproved; to pay the Stewards what they have received of their several classes in the week preceding.[128]

The classes normally met one evening each week for an hour or so. Each person reported on his or her spiritual progress or on particular concerns and received the support and prayers of the others. "Advice or reproof was given as need required, quarrels were made up, misunderstandings removed: And after an hour or two spent in this labour of love, they concluded with prayer and thanksgiving."[129]

Wesley argued for the class meeting on pragmatic and biblical grounds. "There is something not easily explained in the fellowship which we enjoy in a society of living Christians," he noted.[130] He did not claim the class meeting was prescribed in Scripture but saw it as a prudential means of grace consistent with Scripture. The class meeting became the primary means of grace for thousands of Methodists, serving both an evangelistic and a discipling function. "It was in these meetings, rather than in the preaching services, where the great majority of conversions occurred."[131]

The class meeting system tied together the widely scattered Methodist people and became the sustainer of the Methodist renewal over many decades. The movement was, in fact, rather a whole series of sporadic and often geographically localized revivals which were interconnected and spread by the society and class network than one continuous wave of revival which swept the country. Without the class meeting, the scattered fires of renewal might well have burned out long before the movement was able to make a really deep impact on the nation.

Effective discipline could be exercised in such small groups since each person was known intimately by the leader. Wesley issued small cards or tickets to each class member. The card bore the person's name, the date, and the signature of Wesley or one of his preachers. It was the member's proof of Methodist membership and admitted him or her to the quarterly love feast. Thus it was primarily membership in the class that constituted membership in the Methodist society, not vice versa. Unfaithful members could not get their tickets renewed for the next quarter.[132]

Wesley did not permit discipline to grow lax. In his periodic visits he "examined," "regulated," or "purged" the classes and societies as need required. He (or later one of his assistants) would carefully explain the rules and exclude any who were not seeking to follow them. Excluded members would then receive no quarterly membership tickets. Many of these would later be readmitted if they mended their ways.

Some examples show the extent of the discipline and the nature of the offenses. In 1748 Wesley reduced the Bristol society from 900 to 730, while on other occasions he found no expulsions necessary. In port cities he often had to exclude some for smuggling—and found with time that this discipline bore fruit in reduced smuggling in the area. From one society he expelled sixty-four persons: two for cursing, two for habitual Sabbath-breaking, seventeen for drunkenness, two for selling liquor, three for quarreling, one for wife-beating, three for habitual lying, four for evil speaking, one for idleness, and twenty-nine for "lightness and carelessness."[133] Bebb notes, "few were expelled for strictly religious faults, and none for doctrinal differences, while significantly enough, the largest number were excluded for not taking seriously enough their religion, and to take it seriously always involved, in Wesley's view, right conduct to one's neighbour."[134] In exercising discipline "the question is not," said Wesley, "concerning the heart, but the life. And the general tenor of this . . . cannot be hidden without a miracle."[135] Therefore discipline was both possible and necessary.

The pastoral role of the class leaders with their little flocks of a dozen or so was especially important. Wesley's appointed "lay" preachers were constantly on the move from place to place, and in most cases the Anglican clergy took no responsibility for the pastoral care of Methodists within their parishes. The rapid growth of Methodism could never have happened without the traveling preachers, Methodist historian Abel Stevens noted, but these preachers "could never have secured the moral discipline, or even the permanence of its societies, without the pastoral care of the Class-leader, in the absence of the pastor, who at first was scarcely a day at a time in any one place."[136]

Class leaders were not, however, merely a makeshift arrangement so the Methodist societies could get by without full-time pastors. Rather the class leaders were fundamentally pastors themselves. This was the normal system, based in part on Wesley's convictions that spiritual oversight had to be intimate and personal and that plural leadership was the norm in a congregation. He could never be convinced that it "was ever the will of the Lord that any congregation should have one teacher only." "This preacher has one talent, that another," he said. "No one whom I ever yet knew has all the talents which are needful for beginning, continuing, and perfecting the work of grace in a whole congregation."[137] This is part of the reason the Methodist preachers traveled on circuits. What one lacked, the next one might supply.

The Band System

The classes were buttressed by the bands which, like those in Herrnhut, were smaller and generally divided by age, sex, and marital status. Wesley followed the Moravian system but with some modification. In particular he dropped the Moravian pattern of band "monitors" who reported on those who needed spiritual help or appeared to be in error. Wesley felt this undercut the mutual responsibility of each member to the others in the band.

Band members were expected to abstain from doing evil, to be zealous in good works, including giving to the poor, and to use all the means of grace. Wesley drew up the following statement of rules:

> The design of our meeting is, to obey that command of God, "Confess your faults one to another, and pray for one another, that ye may be healed."
>
> To this end, we intend, —
>
> 1. To meet once a week, at the least.
>
> 2. To come punctually at the hour appointed, without some extraordinary reason.
>
> 3. To begin (those of us who are present) exactly at the hour, with singing or prayer.
>
> 4. To speak each of us in order, freely and plainly, the true state of our souls, with the faults we have committed in thought, word, or deed, and the temptations we have felt, since our last meeting.
>
> 5. To end every meeting with prayer, suited to the state of each person present.

6. To desire some person among us to speak his own state first, and then to ask the rest, in order, as many and as searching questions as may be, concerning their state, sins, and temptations.[138]

Questions to be asked each week were: (1) What known sins have you committed since our last meeting? (2) What temptations have you met with? (3) How were you delivered? (4) What have you thought, said, or done, of which you doubt whether it be sin or not?[139]

The bands proved to be a useful means of spiritual growth. Unlike the classes, the bands were not mainly disciplinary but were to aid the spiritual progress of those who were clearly converted. Normally they averaged between five and ten persons in size.

Also, unlike the classes, the bands were restricted to persons who had the assurance of the remission of sins. Wesley's traveling preachers or assistants were to "closely examine" every band member and to "put out two in three, if they find so many in the best of their judgment, Unbelievers."[140] Band tickets were issued quarterly to all band members. These differed from the class or society tickets in various ways, sometimes by the printed word *BAND* or the letter b on the face of the ticket. These tickets functioned much as did the class tickets and admitted the bearers to the love feast, covenant services, and society meetings.[141]

Understandably, with this kind of rigor fewer bands were organized than classes. Judging from the number of band and class tickets printed, it would appear that about 20 percent of the Methodist people met in bands, whereas all were class members.[142] Since the bands averaged about six members and the classes about twelve, this means there were probably about two or three classes for every band.

Wesley provided an even more intimate cell group, the Select Society, for those who appeared to be making marked progress toward inward and outward holiness, and also instituted separate groups for penitents. These group structures were all functioning by 1744. Thus Wesley explained in the 1744 Conference Minutes that the "United Societies," divided into classes, "consist of awakened persons. Part of these, who are supposed to have remission of sins, are more closely united in the Bands. Those in the Bands, who seem to walk in the light of God, compose the Select Societies. Those of them who have made shipwreck of the faith, meet apart as penitents."[143]

Wesley laid down three additional rules (beyond the band rules) for the Select Societies: "1. Let nothing spoken in this Society be spoken again; no, not even to the members of it. 2. Every member agrees absolutely to submit to his Minister in all indifferent things. 3. Every member, till we can have all things common, will bring once a week, *bona fide,* all he can spare toward a common stock."[144] The reference to "all things common" suggests that at this stage Wesley held the ideal of a true community of goods among those who were closest to attaining the life of the kingdom of God.

That Wesley saw community of goods as an ideal is also suggested by his sermon "The Mystery of Iniquity." Noting that the early believers in Acts "had all things in common," Wesley comments: " 'How came they to act thus, to have all things in common, seeing we do not read of any positive command to do this?' I answer, There needed no outward command: the command was written on their hearts. It naturally and necessarily resulted from the degree of love which they enjoyed. . . . And wheresoever the same cause shall prevail, the same effect will naturally follow."[145] Wesley's comment on Acts 2:42 shows that he understood New Testament *koinonia* as meaning community of goods: "So their daily church communion consisted in these four particulars: (1) hearing the word; (2) having all things common; (3) receiving the Lord's Supper; (4) prayer."[146] *This* was the pattern Wesley sought to reproduce.

The system of bands and classes instituted by Wesley continued for over a century, thus proving more durable, in general, than the Moravian choir system. In England the bands disappeared about 1880 (the last band tickets were issued that year) while class meetings in both England and America survived into the twentieth century, at least in some Methodist churches.

Well before 1900 the class system had lost most of its vitality, however, in most of Methodism. Where it survived the classes often became legalistic or moralistic; the life had long since departed. Among British Methodists class attendance was a condition of church membership until 1912 while in the United States, the Methodist Episcopal Church, South dropped the requirement in 1866. A spate of books and some church conventions attempted to revive the class meetings in America after 1850, but without success.

The reasons for the decline of the class and band system are complex, and one cannot with certainty distinguish between cause and effect. These, however, are some of the factors to be considered: The rise of the stationed pastor, who gradually took over the pastoral function of class leader; the growing sophistication and prosperity of Methodists as they rose into the middle class; the decline of the quest for perfection and holiness; the growth of the crisis-centered revivalism mentality (especially in America), which undercut the perception of faith as a continuing growth in holiness; and the tendency at times to allow classes to get too large without subdividing them.

Pastors and Leaders

The society-class-band system would not have held together had it not been for "the itinerancy"—Wesley's system of traveling "lay" preachers. These preachers were under Wesley's direct supervision. If Methodism looked like a quasi-monastic order, his preachers constituted an order *in fact*—a preaching order which, if not celibate, certainly knew about poverty and obedience. "The itinerants were taught to subsist without means, except such as might casually occur on their routes, to rise at four and preach at five o'clock, to scatter books and tracts, to live by rule, and to die without fear."[147] Wesley gave them strict rules, expecting them to preach, study, travel, meet with bands and classes, exercise daily, and eat sparingly.

The extensive system of bands, classes, societies, and preachers, together with other offices and functions, opened the doors wide for leadership in early Methodism. By the time Methodism had reached 100,000 members at the end of the century the movement must have had over 10,000 class and band leaders, with perhaps an equal or larger total of other leaders. Many of these, as well as some of Wesley's preachers, were women, prompting Bebb to call Wesley "the most outstanding feminist of the eighteenth century" because he provided women with opportunities for leadership available nowhere else.[148]

Wesley put one in ten—perhaps one in five—to work in significant ministry and leadership. These were not the educated or the wealthy with time on their hands, but laboring men and women, husbands and wives and young folks with little or no training, but with spiritual gifts and eagerness to serve. Community became the incubator and training camp for Christlike ministry.

All this provoked some disdain and mockery from Wesley's critics. Augustus Toplady, for instance, author of "Rock of Ages," accused Wesley's "lay" preaching system of "prostituting the ministerial function to the lowest and most illiterate mechanics, persons of almost any class but especially common soldiers, who pretended to be pregnant with 'a message from the Lord.'" His advice for Wesley: "Let his cobblers keep to their stalls. Let his tinkers mend their vessels. Let his bakers confine themselves to their kneading-troughs. Let his blacksmiths blow more suitable coals than those of controversy."[149] Wesley saw, however, that such folk were the stuff saints and ministers were made of.

Such was the Methodist system—built, adjusted, and closely monitored by John Wesley. Wesley saw the world as his parish, but he "refused to preach in any place where he could not follow it up by organized Societies with adequate leadership."[150] He was out to make disciples, disciples who would renew the whole church.

ISSUES OF RENEWAL

In conclusion, a few words may be added about some of the issues of renewal raised by Wesley's doctrine and practice of the church.

1. Much of the genius of Methodism and the other movements studied here (and, almost by definition, of any movement) was its success in enlisting a large number of persons in committed participation and in various ministry and leadership functions. We have seen that whereas all three movements, and especially Moravianism and Methodism, did this successfully, the biblical and theological rationale employed by Spener and Francke, Zinzendorf, and Wesley, varied. Spener's primary basis was a renewed emphasis on the priesthood of believers, viewed as an extension of Reformation principles. Zinzendorf assumed this foundation, but because he saw the Moravians as a unique order or army, he created the self-image of every Moravian being a specially called missioner. He also showed some sensitivity to charismatic gifts, though without an elaborated doctrine of such. With Wesley, the rationale was twofold: the Holy Spirit was doing a new thing, beginning a promised restitution or restoration of the church, including a reemergence of New Testament gifts; and Methodist preachers were "extraordinary ministers" based on biblical precedents.

While Wesley's view of spiritual gifts was not fully developed, Wesley was certainly more aware of, and more positive toward, the *charismata* than most churchmen of his day and dealt with the subject more than did the Pietists. His understanding was complicated however by the distinction between ordinary and extraordinary gifts. It may be argued that for this and other reasons he failed to see the full practical significance of the *charismata* for the life and ministry of the Christian community and to self-consciously connect ministry in the church more closely to the gifts.

If the gifts of the Spirit played a somewhat minor role in Wesley's own theological understanding, however, their exercise played a large role in Methodism. Wesley saw his "lay" preachers as exercising a charismatic office. They were persons who demonstrated gifts for ministry, and Wesley put them to work, confirming their gifts.

The early Methodist system gave ample room, in fact, for a broad range of spiritual gifts. While such Methodist functions as class leaders, band leaders, assistants, stewards, visitors of the sick, schoolmasters, and housekeepers do not seem to have been understood primarily on the basis of the *charismata,* the whole Methodist system in fact encouraged the kind of spiritual growth in which useful charisms would spring forth and be put into redemptive service. Methodism thus provided considerably more opportunity for the exercise of gifts than did the Church of England, where ministry was severely hedged about by clericalism. In this sense Methodist ministry was much more charismatic than were Anglican forms of ministry, and provided more avenues for significant service than did Pietism in general.

2. Wesley viewed Methodism as a renewing, evangelical order within the Anglican Church, and in fact even within the church more generally. His thinking was akin to that of Zinzendorf but without Zinzendorf's more elaborate theoretical trappings. This may be due in part to the fact that Wesley was not grounded in the *ecclesiola* conception common to Pietism. Functionally, however, Wesley did view Methodism as, in effect, an *ecclesiola* within the *ecclesia,* and used *ecclesiola* structures within Methodism. As David Watson notes, "Wesley's concept of the church underwent a number of changes, but the underlying principle was always that of *ecclesiola in ecclesia.*"[151]

The *ecclesia/ecclesiola* tension frequently manifests itself in Wesley's ecclesiology. Frank Baker notes,

Throughout his adult life Wesley responded with varying degrees of enthusiasm to two fundamentally different views of the church. One was that of an historical institution, organically linked to the apostolic church by a succession of bishops and inherited customs, served by a priestly caste who duly expounded the Bible and administered the sacraments in such a way as to preserve the ancient traditions on behalf of all who were made members by baptism. According to the other view the church was a fellowship of believers who shared both the apostolic experience of God's living presence and also a desire to bring others into this same personal experience by whatever methods of worship and evangelism seemed most promising to those among them whom the Holy Spirit had endowed with special gifts of prophecy and leadership. The first view saw the church in essence as an ancient institution to be preserved, the second as a faithful few with a mission to the world: the first was a traditional rule, the second a living relationship.[152]

Wesley viewed the established church as being in a fallen condition but as still the locus of God's presence and work. His view of the church's fallenness could lead to a rather negative and escapist outlook toward the church and its future in the world, such as that found, for example, in modern premillennialism. But Wesley's confidence in the present working of grace gave him a dynamic, positive conviction concerning what God could accomplish through his people in the present order.

Looking back over the history of the church, Wesley concluded that except for the days immediately following Pentecost, the present time was the best so far. Even in the first century the "mystery of iniquity" began to work in the church, culminating with the baptism of the Emperor Constantine, "productive of more evil in the Church than all the ten persecutions put together." For at that time "the Church and State, the kingdoms of Christ and the world, were so strangely and unnaturally blended together, . . . that they will hardly ever be divided till Christ comes to reign upon earth."[153]

In contrast, Wesley saw God's grace remarkably at work in his own time. "Benevolence and compassion toward all the forms

233

of human woe have increased in a manner not known before," with the erection of many new hospitals, infirmaries, and "other places of public charity." And then there was the particular phenomenon of Methodism:

> I cannot forbear mentioning one instance more of the goodness of God to us in the present age. He has lifted up his standard in our islands, both against luxury, profaneness, and vice of every kind. He caused, near fifty years ago, as it were, a grain of mustard seed to be sown near London; and it has now grown and put forth great branches, reaching from sea to sea. Two or three poor people met together, in order to help each other be real Christians. They increased to hundreds, to thousands, to myriads, still pursuing their one point, real religion; the love of God and man ruling all their tempers, and words, and actions. Now I will be bold to say, such an event as this, considered in all its circumstances, has not been seen upon earth before, since the time that St. John went to Abraham's bosom.[154]

Wesley concluded that no time since the apostolic age had been better than the present. "We are not born out of due time, but in the day of his power,—a day of glorious salvation, wherein he is hastening to renew the whole race of mankind in righteousness and true holiness."[155]

This dialectic between the fallenness of the church and the renewing work of the Spirit was basic to Wesley's outlook. It kept him from extreme pessimism or naive optimism, for his view was grounded not in "progress" or the goodness and wisdom of people but in the universal mercy and grace of God. And it permitted Wesley to combine his absorption in an *ecclesiola* with hope for the renewal of the entire *ecclesia*.

3. The Methodist experience provides further material for dealing with the question of intensity of community life within the church. Methodist societies were not total, closed communities like the Moravian settlements, yet they were more distinct and separately organized than were most Pietist *collegia*. Methodist bands, classes, and societies were tied together in one movement, under Wesley's direction, in a way that was never true of

Continental Pietism. In this sense, the Methodist experience of community falls roughly midway between the fellowship of the Pietist *collegia* and the Moravian settlements.

The significance of the issue of intensity of community life, of its manifestation in Pietism, Moravianism, and Methodism, and of its relevance for the dynamics of church renewal, will be explored further in chapters 6 and 7.

NOTES

[1]John Wesley, *The Journal of the Rev. John Wesley, A.M.,* ed. Nehemiah Curnock, 8 vols. (London: Epworth, 1909–1916; repr. 1938), 1:116. (Hereafter cited as Wesley, *Journal.*) Wesley read several of Francke's works during the period 1732–34, and some were used in the Holy Club. See Richard Paul Heitzenrater, "John Wesley and the Oxford Methodists, 1725–35" (Ph.D. diss., Duke University,1972), 504.

[2]Wesley, *Journal,* 2:186, 190.

[3]As noted earlier, A. W. Bohme published an English edition of Arndt's *True Christianity* in two volumes in 1712 and 1714. As early as 1734 Wesley mentions Bohme's *Several Discourses and Tracts for Promoting the Common Interest of True Christianity* (Heitzenrater, "John Wesley," 497).

[4]F. Ernest Stoeffler, "Pietism, the Wesleys, and Methodist Beginnings in America," in F. Ernest Stoeffler, ed., *Continental Pietism and Early American Christianity* (Grand Rapids: Eerdmans, 1976), 185.

[5]Richard Kidder, *The Life of the Reverend Anthony Horneck, D.D. Late Preacher at the Savoy* (London: B. Aylmer, 1698), 3–5.

[6]Stoeffler, *Continental Pietism,* 186. Horneck would have been about six years younger than Spener and may have met him during Spener's *peregrinatio academica* (1659–61), during which time Spener was in contact with Labadie in Geneva. Horneck's professor at Heidelberg, Frederick Spanheim (1632–1701), had once been a follower of Labadie. Nagler says Wesley "came personally in contact with the work of Pietism" prior to his trip to Germany through the religious societies tracing from Horneck, "a Pietist from Germany" (Arthur Nagler, *Pietism and Methodism, or The Significance of German Pietism in the Origin and Early Development of Methodism* [Nashville: M. E. Church, South, 1918], 147).

[7]Most accounts report that the religious societies under Horneck and Smythies began in 1678, but there is some reason to believe this date is

imprecise and that they may have begun somewhat earlier. The *World Christian Encyclopedia* reports that in 1671 "Anton Horneck, Pietistic evangelist," founded the "first Vestry Society in England" (David D. Barrett, ed., *World Christian Encyclopedia* [Nairobi: Oxford University Press, 1982], 27). The first religious societies were called vestry societies, and *collegium pietatis* and *religious society* are virtually synonymous terms. Earle Cairns also gives 1671 (*An Endless Line of Splendor* [Wheaton, Ill.: Tyndale House, 1986], 57). If this is correct, Horneck began such societies in his first year at the Savoy.

⁸Kidder, *Horneck,* 42.

⁹Ibid., 10. This pattern was similar to Spener's and in line with the reforms advocated in the *Pia Desideria.*

¹⁰Ibid., 12–13.

¹¹Josiah Woodward, *An Account of the Rise and Progress of the Religious Societies in the City of London, Etc., and of their Endeavours for Reformation of Manners,* 4th ed. (London: J. Downing, 1712), 4. Woodward's is the earliest account of the religious societies. It was first published in 1697, with subsequent editions in 1698, 1701, 1712, 1724, and 1744.

¹²Kidder, *Horneck,* 13–16. These and similar rules have been published in a number of sources, including Woodward's *Account* and John S. Simon, *John Wesley and the Religious Societies* (London: Epworth, 1921; 2d ed., 1955), 10–11.

¹³Simon, *Religious Societies,* 17.

¹⁴Woodward, *Account,* 43, 46, 65.

¹⁵"The Names, Places of Abode, Employments, and Occupations of the Several Societies in and about the Cities of London and Westminster Belonging to the Church of England, 1694," Bodleian Library, Oxford (Rawl. MS. D. 1312), cited in Heitzenrater, "John Wesley," 10–11.

¹⁶Woodward, *Account,* 120.

¹⁷Heitzenrater, "John Wesley," 8–9.

¹⁸Woodward, *Account,* 125.

¹⁹Martin Schmidt, *John Wesley: A Theological Biography,* 2 vols., trans. Norman Goldhawk (New York: Abingdon, 1962), 1:33.

²⁰Richard F. Lovelace, *The American Pietism of Cotton Mather,* (Washington, D.C.: Christian University Press; Grand Rapids: Eerdmans, 1979), 220.

²¹Simon, *Religious Societies,* 19.

²²"S.P.C.K.," in F. L. Cross and E. A. Livingstone, eds., *The Oxford Dictionary of the Christian Church,* 2d ed. (London: Oxford University Press, 1974), 1298.

²³Heitzenrater, "John Wesley," 17–18; Woodward, *Account,* 67–68.

[24]Martin Schmidt, *John Wesley*, 2:175–176; Heitzenrater, "John Wesley," 9, 19–23; John Henry Overton, *Life in the English Church (1660–1714)* (London: Longmans, Green, 1885), 211–12.

[25]*Propagation of the Gospel to the East, being an Account of the Success of Two Danish Missionaries lately Sent to the East Indies for the Conversion of the Heathens in Malabar* (London, 1709). The missionaries were in fact Germans, though sponsored by the Danish king. On their mission, see Kenneth Scott Latourette, *A History of the Expansion of Christianity*, vol. 3, *Three Centuries of Advance* (1939; repr. Grand Rapids: Zondervan, 1970), 278–79, and the references cited there.

[26]Heitzenrater, "John Wesley," 3, 526.

[27]Wesley, *Journal*, 3:33. See Schmidt, *John Wesley*, 1:62.

[28]John Whitehead, *The Life of the Rev. John Wesley, M.A.* (London: Stephen Couchman, 1793; Boston: Dow and Jackson, 1845), 38–42.

[29]Wesley, *Journal*, 1:467.

[30]John Wesley, "A Plain Account of Christian Perfection," *The Works of John Wesley* (London: John Mason, 1829–31), 11:367.

[31]C. E. Vulliamy, *John Wesley* (London: Geoffrey Bles, 1931), 60.

[32]Heitzenrater, "John Wesley," 86–135.

[33]Ibid., 199–200.

[34]See Arnold Dallimore, *George Whitefield: The Life and Times of the Great Evangelists of the Eighteenth-Century Revival*, 2 vols. (London: Banner of Truth Trust, 1970), 1:61–77.

[35]Heitzenrater, "John Wesley," 229, 232.

[36]Ibid., 233.

[37]Vulliamy, *John Wesley*, 55.

[38]R. Denny Urlin, *The Churchman's Life of Wesley* (London: SPCK, 1905), 27; Luke Tyerman, *The Life and Times of Rev. John Wesley, M.A., Founder of the Methodists*, 3 vols., 2d ed. (London: Hodder and Stoughton, 1876), 1:114.

[39]Benjamin Ingham's Journal, quoted in Tyerman, *John Wesley*, 1:121.

[40]Wesley, *Journal*, 2:70.

[41]Frank Baker, *John Wesley and the Church of England* (Nashville: Abingdon, 1970), 52.

[42]Ibid., 51.

[43]Ibid., 44.

[44]Ibid., 51–52.

[45]Richard Butterworth, "Wesley as the Agent of the S.P.G.," *Proceedings of the Wesley Historical Society* 7:5 (March 1910): 101.

[46]Ibid., 102.

[47]John Telford, *The Life of John Wesley* (New York: Phillip and Hunt, 1899), 95–96.

[48]Wesley, *Journal,* 1:442.

[49]William G. Addison, *The Renewed Church of the United Brethren 1722–1930* (London: SPCK, 1932), 62.

[50]Ibid.

[51]Wesley, *Journal,* 1:458.

[52]J. E. Hutton, "Methodist Bands: Their Origin and Nature—A New Discovery," *Wesleyan Methodist Magazine* 134 (March 1911): 200.

[53]Addison, *Renewed Church,* 82.

[54]A. Skevington Wood, *The Burning Heart: John Wesley, Evangelist* (Grand Rapids: Eerdmans, 1967), 67, quoting Dorothy Marshall.

[55]Wesley, *Journal,* 1:476.

[56]Ibid., 482.

[57]It was the younger G. A. Francke, not A. H. Francke, whom Wesley met. The older Francke had died eleven years earlier.

[58]See Wesley's *Journal,* 2:16–17, 57–61.

[59]Ibid., 19–56.

[60]Ibid., 2:70.

[61]Wesley, *Works,* 13:55.

[62]Albert E. Outler, ed., *John Wesley* (New York: Oxford University Press, 1964), 353.

[63]Simon, *Religious Societies,* 194.

[64]Ibid., 195.

[65]Vulliamy, *John Wesley,* 90.

[66]Elie Halévy, *The Birth of Methodism in England,* trans. Bernard Semmel (Chicago: University of Chicago Press, 1971), 69; Bernard Semmel, *The Methodist Revolution* (New York: Basic Books, 1973), 13.

[67]Wesley, *Journal,* 2:168.

[68]Ibid., 172–73.

[69]Wesley later described how these forms originated in a 1748 letter, "A Plain Account of the People Called Methodists" (*Works,* 8:248–68).

[70]Baker, *John Wesley,* 141.

[71]Wesley, *Works,* 8:258.

[72]Ibid., 253.

[73]Ibid.

[74]Ibid., 254.

[75]Wood, *Burning Heart,* 191.

[76]Wesley, *Works,* 8:307.

[77]Charles Wesley, *The Journal of the Rev. Charles Wesley, M.A.* (London: John Mason, 1849; repr. Grand Rapids: Baker, 1980), 1:221.

[78] Wesley, *Journal*, 2:370; Addison, *Renewed Church*, 84; Vulliamy, *John Wesley*, 140.

[79] Vulliamy, *John Wesley*, 102; Tyerman, *John Wesley*, 1:214, 271–73; Wesley, *Journal*, 2:319.

[80] Frank Baker, "The People Called Methodists. 3. Polity," in Rupert Davies and Gordon Rupp, eds. *A History of the Methodist Church in Great Britain* (London: Epworth, 1965), 1:220.

[81] Nolan B. Harmon, ed., *The Encyclopedia of World Methodism* (Nashville: United Methodist Publishing House, 1974), 2:1444.

[82] Frederick C. Gill, *In the Steps of John Wesley* (London: Lutterworth, 1962), 43.

[83] Robert G. Wearmouth, *Methodism and the Common People of the Eighteenth Century* (London: Epworth, 1945), 177–78.

[84] Baker, *John Wesley*, 2.

[85] John Wesley, *Explanatory Notes upon the New Testament* (London: Epworth, Reprint 1958), 680 (Gal. 1:13), 430 (Acts 9:31), 850 (Heb. 12:23). (Hereafter cited as Wesley, *ENNT*.)

[86] Ibid., 411.

[87] Wesley, *Works*, 6:371.

[88] Ibid.

[89] Ibid., 372.

[90] Wesley, "An Earnest Appeal to Men of Reason and Religion," in *The Works of John Wesley*, vol. 11, ed. Gerald R. Cragg (London: Oxford University Press, 1975), 77.

[91] Wesley, *Works*, 6:375.

[92] Wesley, *Works*, (Oxford ed., 1975), 11:518.

[93] Outler in Dow Kirkpatrick, ed. *The Doctrine of the Church* (New York: Abingdon, 1964), 19.

[94] Wesley, *Journal*, 4:436.

[95] Wesley, *Works*, 6:378.

[96] Wesley, *Journal*, 4:436.

[97] Ibid.

[98] Ibid.

[99] John Wesley, *The Letters of the Rev. John Wesley, A.M.*, ed. John Telford (London: Epworth, 1931), 2:96. (Hereafter cited as Wesley, *Letters*.)

[100] Letter to James Hervey, March 20, 1739, Wesley, *Letters*, 1:286.

[101] Wesley, *Works*, 7:275–76.

[102] Ibid., 277.

[103]John Wesley, "Ought We to Separate from the Church of England?" (Printed as appendix in Baker, *John Wesley*, 326–40), 333. (Written by Wesley in 1755.)

[104]Wesley, *ENNT*, 478–79.

[105]Wesley, "Scriptural Christianity," *Works*, 5:38; Sermon, "The More Excellent Way," *Works*, 7:27; *ENNT*, 713 (on Eph. 4:8–11).

[106]Wesley, *Works*, 7:27.

[107]Wesley, *Works*, 5:38.

[108]Wesley, *Works*, 7:26–27.

[109]Wesley, *Works*, 5:38.

[110]Wesley, *ENNT*, 625 (1 Cor. 12:31).

[111]Ibid., 713, 628 (Eph. 4:12; 1 Cor. 14:5).

[112]Minutes of the Conference of 1747, from *John Bennet's Copy of the Minutes of 1744, 1745, 1747, and 1748; with Wesley's Copy of Those for 1746*, Publications of the Wesley Historical Society, 1 (London: Charles H. Kelly, 1896): 48. A similar attitude underlay Zinzendorf's *Tropus* idea.

[113]Wesley, *Journal*, 3:230.

[114]Letter of August 19, 1785, *Letters*, 7:284.

[115]Letter of June 8, 1780, *Letters*, 6:21.

[116]Letter of September 10, 1784, *Letters*, 7:238.

[117]F. Ernest Stoeffler, "Tradition and Renewal in the Ecclesiology of John Wesley," in Bernd Jaspert and Rudolf Mohr, eds., *Traditio–Krisis–Renovatio aus theologischer Sicht* (Marburg: N. G. Elwert, 1976), 310.

[118]Ibid., 312.

[119]Wesley, "An Earnest Appeal to Men of Reason and Religion," *Works* (Oxford), 11:78.

[120]Wesley, "A Treatise on Baptism," *Works*, 10:92.

[121]Wesley, *Journal*, 1:465.

[122]Irwin Reist, "John Wesley's View of the Sacraments: A Study in the Historical Development of a Doctrine," *Wesleyan Theological Journal* 6:1 (Spring 1971): 48.

[123]John Chongnahm Cho, "John Wesley's View on Baptism," *Wesleyan Theological Journal* 7:1 (Spring 1972): 62, 65.

[124]Wesley, *Journal*, 2:135.

[125]E. Douglas Bebb, *Wesley: A Man with a Concern* (London: Epworth, 1950), 123.

[126]Ibid., 121–22.

[127]Ibid., 127; John S. Simon, *John Wesley and the Methodist Societies* (London: Epworth, 1923), 312.

[128]Wesley, *Works*, 8:253.

[129]Ibid., 253–54.

[130] Wesley, *Journal,* 5:84.

[131] William B. Lewis, "The Conduct and Nature of the Methodist Class Meeting," in Samuel Emerick, ed., *Spiritual Renewal for Methodism* (Nashville: Methodist Evangelistic Materials, 1958), 25.

[132] Abel Stevens, *The History of the Religious Movement of the Eighteenth Century, Called Methodism, Considered in Its Different Denominational Forms, and Its Relations to British and American Protestantism,* 3 vols. (New York: Carlton and Porter, 1858), 2:454–55; Schmidt, *John Wesley,* 2:100. Some thirty-eight different types of tickets were used between 1742 and 1765.

[133] Wesley, *Journal,* 3:71, 380; Bebb, *Wesley,* 128–30.

[134] Bebb, *Wesley,* 129.

[135] Wesley, *Journal,* 3:284–85.

[136] Stevens, *History,* 2:454. Stevens' terminology already betrays the perspective of a later generation, since in Wesley's view (as noted earlier) the itinerant preachers were *not* pastors.

[137] Ibid., 461.

[138] Wesley, "Rules of the Band-Societies," *Works,* 8:272.

[139] Ibid., 273.

[140] Minutes of 1758 Conference, in *Minutes of Conference for 1749, 1755, 1758. Reprinted from John Wesley's Ms. Copy.* Supplement to *Proceedings of the Wesley Historical Society,* (1904), 4:72.

[141] Frederick M. Parkinson, "Methodist Class Tickets," *Proceedings of the Wesley Historical Society* 1:5 (1898): 129–35; Joseph G. Wright, "Class and Band Tickets," *Proceedings of the Wesley Historical Society* 5:2 (1905): 33–44.

[142] "The Band tickets were supplied in the proportion of two to ten Society tickets . . . "; "Note by Mr. George Stampe," *Proceedings of the Wesley Historical Society* 1:5 (1898): 135–37.

[143] *John Bennet's Copy of the Minutes of Conference,* 14.

[144] Ibid.

[145] Wesley, *Works,* 6:240. See the sermon "The General Spread of the Gospel," par. 20; *ENNT,* 401–2, 408–9 (on Acts 2 and 4).

[146] Wesley, *ENNT,* 401.

[147] Stevens, *History,* 2:461.

[148] Bebb, *Wesley,* 140. Wesley, however, at first gave women permission to preach only reluctantly. He was convinced by the results that here also God was at work—just as had happened in his initial recognition of the validity of "lay" preaching in general. See Leslie F. Church, *More About the Early Methodist People* (London: Epworth, 1949), chapter 4.

[149]Bebb, *Wesley,* 139.

[150]Sydney G. Dimond, *The Psychology of the Methodist Revival* (London: Oxford University Press, 1926), 112.

[151]David Lowes Watson, "The Origin and Significance of the Early Methodist Class Meeting" (Ph.D. diss., Duke University, 1978), 175.

[152]Baker, *John Wesley,* 137.

[153]Wesley, *Works,* 7:164.

[154]Ibid., 166.

[155]Ibid.

Dynamics of Renewal Movements

Chapter Six

Dynamics of Renewal Movements

What makes renewal movements tick? Do the stories of Pietism, Moravianism, and Methodism help us understand the church and its renewal? In this chapter we turn to a comparative analysis of these movements, seeking insight into the dynamics of church renewal.

ALL ONE MOVEMENT?
THE STRUCTURE OF RENEWAL

When we examine Pietism, Moravianism, and Methodism, are we seeing three distinct movements or rather one broad movement of renewal? Several points are worth noting here.

1. It is clear that *Continental Pietism, the renewed Moravian Brethren, and early Methodism were part of a larger movement of renewal* in a several senses. Broad currents of renewal seemed to be flowing through much of the seventeenth and eighteenth centuries.

As Stoeffler[1] and others have demonstrated, Lutheran Pietism was part of, and grew from, a larger movement of pietism involving English Puritanism and related currents. The story of these movements and currents is the story of many interrelationships, with multiple influences and counterinfluences. The picture in its broadest scope involves the whole range of religious and cultural developments of the period—including Jewish Hasidism and Jansenism within the Roman Catholic Church.[2]

Speaking more narrowly of renewal currents within Protestantism, we may note that the seventeenth- and eighteenth-century renewal involved not only Pietism, Puritanism, Moravianism, and Methodism but also awakenings among remnants of the *Unitas Fratrum* in Bohemia and Moravia and ascetic "High Church pietism"[3] within the Church of England (as earlier, contributory currents); Continental Reformed Pietism; Calvinistic Methodism and, in general, George Whitefield's ministry; evangelical revivalism in Wales; and the widespread influence of Pietism and Pietistic Lutheranism in the United States.[4] The picture also includes the significant impact of Pietism in Scandinavia and elsewhere and Moravian influences in the Baltic and in other places.

2. History shows that undergirding Pietism, Moravianism, and Methodism was a *significant network of relationships* involving both primary and secondary leaders and extending also to other movements of the period. With reference particularly to Continental Pietism and the evangelical awakening in Britain, Geoffrey Nuttall has demonstrated "how interwoven the Revival was: its leaders knew one another, read one another's books, wrote to and visited one another."[5] Some of these interrelationships have been noted in previous chapters.

One may in fact document a kind of "renewal network"—a web of relationships among key figures in Pietism, Moravianism, Methodism, and other movements which fostered the cross-fertilization of ideas, information, and motivation as these movements were developing and spreading. This network could be traced out in some detail by noting the contacts, correspondence, and other links between the leading persons in the various movements.

This renewal network is significant for at least two reasons. First, it shows some of the ways renewal energies were transmitted and extended, thus illuminating the dynamics of these particular movements. Second, it shows how intricate and multifaceted the renewal was, underscoring that in one sense we are dealing with one broad movement, as noted above.

Tracing this network especially suggests the key roles played by August Francke and John Wesley in the overall renewal pattern. Though the two men never knew each other personally (Francke's death occurring during Wesley's student days at Oxford), both men were at the nerve center of informal but vital communications networks which fit into a larger pattern of relationships. The significance of such networks in the dynamics of renewal movements, and parallels with present-day movements and networks, would be worth studying in some depth.

3. The historical survey underscores the fact that *each of these movements was distinct* in important ways, despite significant similarities, mutual influences, and interrelationships. One important difference was the extent to which each movement stressed and embodied fellowship or community as a central element. In general Moravianism focused much more intensely and intentionally on community, in part because of the more Radical Protestant roots of the Moravians and in part because of the interest and personality of Count Zinzendorf. Herrnhut, as we have seen, became a very close-knit and intimate total community, and in turn provided the ideal and model for other Moravian settlements and groups. Pietism, on the other hand, while it experienced some of the dynamic of "more intimate fellowship" through the *collegia pietatis* and similar groups, never stressed community or fellowship as the Moravians did.

The case of Methodism, inheriting influences from both Pietism and Moravianism, is particularly interesting in this regard. Wesley was attracted both to the widespread renewing influence of

Franckean Pietism and the Halle institutions and to the intense community life he found at Herrnhut. The community at Herrnhut seemed to him a significant approximation to the ideal of the primitive Christian community. The fact is that Wesley was impressed by both the Pietists and the Moravians, but for different reasons. Wesley set out to accomplish what both the Pietists and the Moravians had achieved. He wished to see in England the kinds of reforms and redemptive institutions the German Pietists had effectively instituted, but he wanted more. He wanted to see a renewed *people,* an expression of the Christian community which visibly resembled the primitive church. And subsequent history shows that when it came to the press of competing priorities, Wesley gave his primary attention to creating and guiding "the people called Methodists"—though the educational-philanthropic-institutional concern was never far from his heart and mind.

In this respect Wesley was more like Zinzendorf than like Spener and Francke, and Methodism was closer to Moravianism than to Pietism. On the other hand, in Wesley's desire to "hold to the church" and Methodism's success (in Wesley's lifetime) in remaining within the established body, Methodism was closer to Pietism. As Bernard Semmel says, "The Methodists, in the ambiguous position of seeming to be a sect within a church and possessing certain of the characteristics of both, resembled the associations and Conventicles of the Puritan Richard Baxter and of German pietism in the seventeenth century."[6]

On the other hand, the intensity and intimacy of community life were clearly greater in early Methodism than in either Pietism or Puritanism. Thus there is some point to Semmel's observation, in assessing the Moravian impact on Methodism, that "Wesley's genius, in part, consisted in applying a pattern constructed to serve a monastic community to men and women who lived within the sinful world."[7] The particular breadth of interest and range of gifts which Wesley brought to his role as the leader of Methodism were key factors in this regard. To a large degree, Wesley combined the strengths of Spener, Francke, and Zinzendorf. Comparing Wesley's role in Methodism with those of Spener and Francke in Pietism, Nagler comments,

> Spener was the prophet, the "father-confessor" of the movement, but he lacked those qualities which Wesley possessed in a preeminent degree—energy, aggressiveness, and administrative talent. These deficiencies in Spener's character found extraordinary expression in the personality of Francke. With certain reservations . . . , the conclusion may justly be drawn that Spener and Francke together were to Pietism what Wesley was to Methodism.[8]

Focusing on the aspect of intensity of community (which might be considered a sort of index of sectness), we may see two varieties of renewal movements illustrated in Pietism, Moravianism, and Methodism—one type in which, like Moravianism and early Methodism, fellowship is a primary focal point around which other concerns are organized; and the other, illustrated by Pietism and to some extent by the Anglican religious societies, in which fellowship or community may have played a significant role but received little or no explicit attention. The New Prophecy (Montanism) would seem to have been closer to the former type.

4. Surveying the history of Pietism, Moravianism, and Methodism reveals that *all three movements made use of small cell groups (collegia,* bands, classes, etc.), and all made provision, in varying ways and degrees, for *some practical expression of the priesthood of believers.* The significance of this will be analyzed in the next chapter.

In addition to these factors and points of comparison, three other observations are worth noting in the history of Pietism, Methodism, and Moravianism.

5. *Education and educational institutions played a key role in all three movements.* To a remarkable degree, universities were the seedbed of renewal, even though the movements were in part a reaction against university conditions and soon spread beyond the universities. Spener, Francke, Zinzendorf, the Wesleys, Horneck, and several of their colleagues were all university trained. In fact all

showed marked interest in and talent for biblical studies and (with the possible exception of Zinzendorf) the biblical languages. Pietism developed its chief center at the University of Halle, with significant centers at other German universities. The community at Herrnhut became the chief center of Moravianism, but Spangenberg, Böhler, and many other Moravian leaders came directly from the German universities where they were spiritually awakened and had initial contact with the Moravians. And the experience of the Wesleys and their colleagues at Oxford University in the early 1730s was, as Wesley himself later said, "the first rise of Methodism."

Montanism, the early Franciscans, and other movements not discussed here do not, of course, fit this pattern. So this is a variable among renewal movements. Some modern revivals and renewal movements, including the Catholic Charismatic Renewal, first emerged on college or university campuses.

Why do renewal movements sometimes arise on college campuses? Perhaps the answer, in part, is that the atmosphere of intellectual inquiry and greater personal and academic freedom in university settings, combined with the idealism and mobility of youth, provide a more congenial environment for the initial rise of a spiritual renewal movement than does the church or society generally. One may recall that historically many significant social movements, both religious and political, have sprung up in university settings or among university students.

6. *The significant role played by the written word in all three movements and in their interrelationships is striking.* Books and tracts, particularly, helped spread the vision, hope, and expectancy of renewal. Publications were of two types: Books such as *True Christianity* and *Pia Desideria* which held out a brighter vision of Christian experience and church life, and tracts such as *Pietas Hallensis,* Woodward's *Account* of the religious societies, and the report of the East India mission, which intensified the hope and expectancy of a coming renewal. Francke, Wesley, and the Moravians, especially, published extensively, including devotional

works, sermons, journals, hymnbooks, and tracts. Much of this material was designed for use internally within the movement (especially in the case of the Moravians and Methodists) but had a considerably broader impact as well.

7. Finally, a word may be said about *the role of Scripture and of the primitivist ideal.* All three movements stressed the normative role of the Bible in the life and experience of believers, using Scripture to some extent to critique the contemporary situation of the church. Also, they pointed back to the early church as the model of what church life should be. This primitivist motif seems to have been particularly strong in Francke and Wesley.[9]

These observations suggest that German Pietism, Moravianism, and early Methodism, while certainly distinct and identifiable movements, were interrelated and were in a broad sense part of a larger renewal pattern involving other movements as well. Yet each movement was distinct in that it involved an identifiable group of people led by identifiable leaders and held together in part by identifiable doctrinal emphases and by identifiable patterns and structures of association.

Each of these movements owes much of its character and dynamic to the key leaders who shaped it. The character, vision, and particular decisions of Spener, Francke, Zinzendorf, and John Wesley, especially, significantly extended (or in some cases hindered) the impact which the movement eventually made.

An important observation here is that renewal movements apparently have *no inevitable inherent dynamic* which unfolds automatically, regardless of the behavior, choices, and plans of the people involved. There *are* some inherent dynamics in renewal, as we have been seen. But these dynamics do not simply unfold by themselves. Much depends on the wisdom, vision, sensitivity, foresight, and integrity of the characters in the drama.

This is important for the church today. It means that renewal movements are neither direct, irresistible acts of God nor the mere outworking of inexorable sociological laws or constraints. Much depends on human wisdom and choice. Spener, Francke, Zinzendorf, and Wesley all *intended* to see renewal come to the church and worked self-consciously to achieve it. The impact of the movements they led was due in large measure to the quality of the leadership they provided. If the essential dynamic in movements of spiritual renewal is a fresh personal sense of the reality of God, then the direction a movement takes, and its continuing influence over an extended period of time, depend largely on the human leadership under which the movement develops.

THE FUNCTION OF "LAY" LEADERSHIP AND RENEWAL CELLS

We noted at the beginning that "lay" leadership and small cell groups seem to be important factors in church renewal movements. Much of the discussion throughout this study has focused on the historical and sociological significance of these factors in Moravianism, Methodism, and Pietism, and on the theological issues raised by these factors.

It will be helpful now to look more closely at these two factors, viewing them as both a theological and a structural question.

"Lay" Leadership

The history we have traced yields several insights concerning the importance of "lay" leadership in Pietism, Moravianism, and Methodism:

1. *All three movements made extensive use of "lay" leadership,* though in varying degrees and ways. In general, Methodism and Moravianism used such leadership more extensively than did Continental Pietism, and in more significantly responsible roles. But the use of nonordained leadership in Halle Pietism, especially, and in the network of Pietist house groups (*collegia*) is also notable.

2. *All three movements made structural provision for, and gave theological justification to this use of "lay" leadership.* As we have seen,

the theological justification varied somewhat in each case, but was a significant part of each movement's understanding of the church.

3. *"Lay" Leadership was a key to the vitality of these movements.* This was true in at least two ways. First, nonordained leadership broadened the appeal of the movements by showing that vital spiritual experience and Christian ministry were available to more than just the clergy. Second, it provided an expanding corps of leaders for the movement, beyond the clergy, thus permitting the numerical extension which is essential for the growth of a genuine movement.

4. *"Lay" Leadership was also at the heart of the controversy and opposition which developed around the three movements.* Though this was not the only tension-producing factor, it was a key one because it placed persons in leadership who were not ecclesiastically recognized as "authorized" leaders. This was especially true with regard to Wesley's lay preachers.

5. *The use of "lay" leadership was closely related to the use of cell groups or* ecclesiola *structures,* both theologically and structurally. Structures such as *collegia pietatis,* bands, and classes required leadership, and they also provided the context in which leadership could emerge. Further, in these structures an understanding of Christian faith was taught and caught which encouraged and justified a broader leadership role for all believers.

THE STRUCTURAL QUESTION

The structural issue is simply this: How may all believers be significantly involved in the mission of the church?

The question might of course be put somewhat differently, depending on one's understanding of the Gospel and of normative Christian experience. Is the goal of the church's mission to provide every believer with a genuine inner experience of God, or is it to involve believers in redemptive ministry in the world? Or is it both, or something else? Is the primary focus of the Gospel, and therefore of renewal, inner spiritual experience or outward mission?

Spener, Francke, Zinzendorf, and Wesley all faced this issue as a structural question. When he questioned the manner of theological education in his *Pia Desideria,* Spener was dealing with this issue more or less directly. And Francke's Halle institutions may be viewed, in part, as an attempt to extend renewal and significant ministry beyond the ranks of the clergy.

Zinzendorf viewed the Moravian communities as a means to renew the whole church and provide "soldiers for the Lamb." For Wesley the whole structure of Methodism, and especially the class system and the "lay" preaching itinerancy, were attempts to extend "true religion" of "all inward and outward holiness," involving both renewal and mission, to the whole church.

All three movements viewed the church as needing substantial renewal, a renewal which was not being effected by the existing clergy. Thus the issue was both the renewal of the church (extending renewal from the "renewed" nucleus to the whole church) and the provision of adequate leadership to bring about this renewal. In other words, the issue was the extension of renewal, and leadership for renewal, from the part to the whole.

THE THEOLOGICAL QUESTION

Theologically, unordained or "lay" leaders raise the issue of the priesthood of believers and the gifts of the Spirit. We have encountered spiritual gifts and the universal priesthood already in tracing the ecclesiologies of Spener, Zinzendorf, and Wesley. The theological issues surrounding this question may be summarized as follows.

Renewal movements often manifest a certain "democratizing tendency"—a tendency to extend the "normative" experience of Christianity, however that is understood, to all believers. This, of course, may be conceived of in various ways—as a question of evangelism, of sanctification, of sacramental life, or of leadership and ministry. Conversely, the institutional church often tends over time to restrict the "normative" experience of the faith to a spiritual elite who are in some sense, and in more or less visible ways, especially qualified and empowered for their special role.

It is instructive to view the ecclesiological thinking of Spener, Zinzendorf, and Wesley, especially, from this perspective. Each attempted to give a theological justification for an expanded role for the laity in the church, both in leadership and in spiritual experience. Spener expected "better times" in which the generality of the church would experience holiness, and argued for the giving of leadership roles to common Christians as a means for bringing about this end, as we have seen. Similarly, Wesley argued that Christian perfection was attainable by all Christians *now,* and justified his "lay" preachers (a means to the end) by his view of "extraordinary ministers" and "extraordinary gifts."

More particularly, and in summary, the following points are important:

1. Of the four major figures discussed in this study, Spener gave the most extensive and creative theological treatment to this issue through his doctrine of the priesthood of believers. This was due in part to his theological inheritance from Luther[10] and in part to his own theological creativity. In Luther's doctrine of the priesthood of believers Spener found the vehicle for promoting the spirituality of Arndt, with its implied criticism of dominant Lutheranism.

Spener's doctrine of the spiritual priesthood was a further extension of this doctrine beyond Lutheran orthodoxy, and beyond Luther himself, but in a way that was consistent with Luther. Spener was in harmony with Luther when he wrote in the *Pia Desideria,* "Especially . . . things . . . unrelated to public acts [should] be done continually by all at home and in everyday life."[11] Spener did not interpret the spiritual priesthood so radically as to undercut a distinct ordained ministry, which would have been to break with Luther. But he carried through Luther's thought to the level of practical application, in both theory and practice, in a way Luther never did.

Theologically, Spener went beyond Luther by bringing together Galatians 3:28; Ephesians 4:11–12; and 1 Peter 2:5–9. This gave the spiritual priesthood a practical pastoral turn: Special ministers in the church were charged with the responsibility of equipping the whole church (Eph. 4:11–12) to exercise the spiritual priesthood (1 Pet. 2:5–9). This meant all believers, men and women alike (Gal. 3:28).

2. Spener explicitly applied the doctrine of the universal priesthood to the need for mutual edification in the church. For him, much more than for Luther, this was the real point of the spiritual priesthood. And in calling for mutual edification in the social context of *collegia pietatis,* Spener showed a consciousness of the relationship of the spiritual priesthood and the experience of Christian community that went beyond Luther.

As suggested in chapter 3, these strands in Spener's thought constitute a significant recasting of the concept of the church in more vital and organic, and in less institutional, terms.

3. As a Pietist heir to Spener, Zinzendorf was even more alert to issues of community than was Spener. Presumably because he took Spener's work for granted as foundational, Zinzendorf said little theologically about the spiritual priesthood. But, as we noted in chapter 4, in practice he did not make a strong distinction between clergy and laity and expected to see all Moravians not only spiritually renewed but also involved in some form of ministry for the Lamb.

4. Spener and Wesley make a particularly interesting study at this point. Wesley spoke more of the gifts of the Spirit than did Spener, but said virtually nothing about the priesthood of believers. Spener occasionally mentioned gifts (as did Luther), but did not deal with them extensively nor link them fundamentally with the spiritual priesthood.

Wesley, as we saw, apparently had no knowledge of Spener's stress on the spiritual priesthood and knew Luther very imperfectly. He seems to have been unaware of the Pietist stress on the priesthood of believers as an issue of ecclesiology.

This issue is significant for today, however. Theologically, spiritual gifts and the universal priesthood are related and mutually supportive doctrines, though none of the figures we have been considering made this connection in any very explicit way. These two emphases, and the three movements we are studying, could be positioned on a continuum, the two poles being the spiritual priesthood and spiritual gifts. Pietism would be placed at the spiritual priesthood side; Methodism at the gifts side; and Moravianism between the two but closer to Methodism.

According to the priesthood of believers, every Christian is a priest before God. Similarly, the New Testament passages concerning charismatic gifts (particularly Rom. 12:5–8; 1 Cor. 12; 1 Peter 4:10–11) seem to suggest a general diffusion of the *charismata* among all believers. Combining these emphases yields a doctrine of Christian ministry which stresses its universal reach to all believers, constituting a general Christian priesthood whose function is to be understood as the exercise of the variety of spiritual gifts arising in, and made normative by, the Christian community.[12]

Interestingly, we see here how Spener and Wesley dealt with essentially the same issue (both historically and theologically) in different and yet basically compatible ways. It is my own view that Spener's doctrine of the universal priesthood is a sounder argument, both biblically and logically, than Wesley's reliance on the notion of "extraordinary" gifts and ministries, and that Wesley's ecclesiology would be stronger if it incorporated Spener's stress on the spiritual priesthood.

Renewal Cells

The history of Moravianism, Pietism, and Methodism suggests the following general conclusions about the use of *ecclesiola* structures or renewal cells in the three movements:

257

1. *All three movements employed a variety of small-group structures as renewal cells, and these structures seem to have been at the heart of the social dynamic of the movements.* The use of such structures was much more varied and extensive in Moravianism and Methodism than in Continental Pietism, where *ecclesiolae* were almost exclusively in the form of various kinds of *collegia*, or small nurture groups.

2. *Methodism and Moravianism were in fact* ecclesiolae *in a broader sense, in that they became rather extensive churchlike structures, as organized movements, within the larger church.* As we have seen, both movements developed several levels of such groups, ranging from the Moravian "band" or the Methodist "Select Society" to the larger renewal community (Moravian settlement or Methodist "society"), to the whole movement itself as an organized entity.

3. *All three movements gave theological justification to their use of renewal cells, recognizing the issue as a question of ecclesiology.* Wesley, especially, appealed to the New Testament and the early church as bases for his use of *ecclesiolae*. Primitivism was to some degree part of the rationale in Moravianism and Pietism as well. None of these renewal leaders claimed (to my knowledge) that their use of *ecclesiola* structures was based precisely on biblical models, but argued that such structures were necessary in order to have biblically authentic Christian experience and community in the church. James 5:16 was often appealed to.

4. *As was true with the "lay" leadership issue, this factor was central to the opposition and controversy which developed around the three movements.* The movements became increasingly controversial as they took on visible social form. As noted previously, the use of renewal cells and provisions for various kinds of "lay" leadership were closely related in this and other ways.

THE STRUCTURAL AND THEOLOGICAL SIGNIFICANCE OF ECCLESIOLAE

Renewal cells functioned in somewhat parallel ways in all three movements, despite significant differences in structure and function. Such structures appear to be significant to the dynamics of church renewal at several levels. We may draw the following general conclusions about the function of such structures in the church.

1. These structures provided an immediately available social context for the stabilizing of new converts and for leading to conversion those who had been "awakened" through other means. In the case of Methodism, especially, the class meeting was a key evangelistic structure. Here many were converted or received the "witness of the Spirit." Presumably, a significant proportion of those affected by the Methodist preaching would not have become converts, or Methodists, but for the class meeting.

2. Relatedly, the class meeting and similar structures conserved evangelistic fruit by stabilizing new converts or adherents who otherwise would likely have become discouraged or disaffected and fallen away. This happened through the discipline and accountability, as well as instruction, built into the group structure and, perhaps equally, through the sense of community and fellowship which developed.

3. Vital, disciplined *ecclesiola* structures tended to keep the movement dynamic and its identity and mission clear. They provided the context for nurturing and sustaining the movement's sense of mission in the world. This was especially the case with Moravianism and Methodism; less so with Pietism.

4. In Methodism and to some degree in Moravianism, such structures seem to have been especially well suited for reaching the poorer masses of society. This was true in at least three ways. First, these groups were open and accessible to the poor. Unlike the more institutionalized, less mobile established church, *ecclesiola* cells, in their simplicity and mobility, provided a readily available

structure for the poor. Second, these structures were especially adapted to the poor. They were a structure not requiring special training, social skills, dress-up clothes, or socioeconomic status. In Methodism, particularly, the structure went to the people rather than requiring the people to go to the structure.

Third, these structures provided a mechanism of social cohesion and social power among the poor. Sociologically and spiritually, and soon even economically, the *ecclesiola* structures provided an effective means of empowering the poor. In England, Methodist small-group structures provided a ready vehicle for building social cohesion and opening avenues for leadership among the poor working classes.[13] It was the intuitive sensing of this dynamic, it seems, which led the upper classes to fear the possible impact of Methodism.

It was not such structures alone that led to the impact of Methodism, and to a lesser degree Moravianism, among other poor, however. Pietism never had such an extensive impact. This impact seems to have been due rather to other factors, such as field preaching and the intentional strategy of its leaders. But once a movement among the poor began, the *ecclesiola* structures became important to its continuance and growth.

5. The *ecclesiola* structures maintained and nurtured the vitality of the movements over time. They sustained a network of primary relationships which served to prolong the dynamism of the movements, providing continuity while acting as a check against institutionalism and legalism.

6. *Ecclesiola* structures appear to have played a significant role evangelistically. They provided the indispensable context or environment for translating Christian faith into practical action, creating and sustaining a community of faith which was inherently dynamic, attractive, and thus potentially evangelistic. Viewed psychologically, such structures enabled the integration of the cognitive, affective, and volitional aspects of human behavior. Viewed sociologically, these structures enabled and stimulated the primary, face-to-face relationships which give the church social

cohesion and power. Viewed theologically and biblically, these structures provided the context for experiencing the fellowship of the Holy Spirit and the convicting, correcting, discerning, and encouraging work of the Spirit and the Word (2 Tim. 3:16, Heb. 4:12).

In other words, the *ecclesiola* structures provided spiritual integration. Through them faith and action, personal responsibility and group accountability, and the concerns of mind and heart were joined.

7. This analysis suggests that *ecclesiolae* may have an important function as "mediating structures." That is, they may provide the opportunity for the church to develop intensity of community without disengagement from the world. This happened in early Methodism but to a lesser degree in Moravianism and Pietism, and herein may lie an important difference between the three movements.

The hypothesis here would be that small *ecclesiola* structures such as the Methodist classes and bands which operate without removing members from the normal flow of civic life are more evangelistically potent than similar structures operating within a closed religious community, such as a Moravian settlement. In the former case believers continue in vital, daily contact with the general populace while being continually nourished in the counter-cultural values and ways of the faith. In the latter case (i.e., Moravianism and similar communities) where believers are part of a closed, total religious community, normal, natural day-by-day contact and communication with the world becomes virtually nonexistent. Nonmembers may still be attracted by the quality of community life and thus wish to join (this was Zinzendorf and the Moravians' conscious strategy), but history seems to suggest that the Methodist strategy, where members do not withdraw from the normal life of the larger social community, is more evangelistically dynamic.

In this sense, Methodism stands more or less midway between Continental Pietism and Moravianism. In general, Methodist "societies" were more intense and coherent, distinct communities than were Pietist groups, but were more directly engaged in the normal flow of society than were Moravian settlements. It seems to me that this "mediating posture" of Methodism was one of the keys to its evangelistic dynamism and internal cohesion.

These considerations lead us to ask more fundamentally about an overall theology of renewal in the church.

NOTES

[1] Particularly in F. Ernest Stoeffler, *The Rise of Evangelical Pietism* (Leiden: E. J. Brill, 1965).

[2] Blaise Pascal, mathematician, scientist, and the leading literary figure associated with Jansenism in France, lived from 1623 to 1662.

[3] Richard Paul Heitzenrater, "John Wesley and the Oxford Methodists, 1725–35" (Ph.D. diss., Duke University, 1972), 417.

[4] See F. Ernest Stoeffler, *Continental Pietism and Early American Christianity* (Grand Rapids: Eerdmans, 1976); Lovelace, *The American Pietism of Cotton Mather* (Washington, D.C.: Christian University Press; Grand Rapids: Eerdmans, 1979).

[5] Geoffrey F. Nuttall, "Continental Pietism and the Evangelical Movement in Britain," in J. Van Den Berg and J. P. Van Dooren, eds., *Pietismus und Reveil* (Leiden: E. J. Brill, 1978), 209.

[6] Bernard Semmel, *The Methodist Revolution* (New York: Basic Books, 1973), 21.

[7] Ibid., 33.

[8] Arthur W. Nagler, *Pietism and Methodism* (Nashville: M. E. Church, South, 1918), 15.

[9] Martin Schmidt, *John Wesley: A Theological Biography,* 2 vols., trans. Norman Goldhawk (New York: Abingdon, 1962), 1:141.

[10] See for example the early pages of Luther's 1520 tract "To the Christian Nobility of the German Nation," found in Luther's *Works,* ed. Ulrich Leopold (Philadelphia: Fortress, 1965) and in Martin Luther, *Three Treatises* (Philadelphia: Fortress, 1970).

[11] Philip Jacob Spener, *Pia Desideria,* trans. Theodore G. Tappert (Philadelphia: Fortress, 1964, 1977), 92–93.

[12] See chapter eight of my book, *Liberating the Church: The Ecology of Church and Kingdom* (Downers Grove, Ill.: InterVarsity Press, 1983), 168–80.

[13] See Robert F. Wearmouth, *Methodism and the Common People of the Eighteenth Century* (London: Epworth, 1945), especially 217–38; and his *Methodism and the Working-Class Movements of England 1800–1850* (London: Epworth, 1937).

Toward a Theology of Renewal

Chapter Seven

Toward a Theology of Renewal

In this chapter I wish to propose a model for church renewal which draws on the history of Pietism, Moravianism, Methodism, and similar church renewal movements. This, I think, will show some of the ways such movements are relevant to the question of church renewal today and is a way of reflecting theologically on the meaning of renewal movements for the life and vitality of the church.[1]

PIETISM, MORAVIANISM, AND METHODISM AS MOVEMENTS

In chapter 2, I defined a "renewal movement" as a sociologically and theologically definable religious resurgence which arises and remains within, or in continuity with, historic Christianity, and which has a significant (potentially measurable) impact on the larger church in terms of number of adherents, intensity of belief and commitment, and or the creation or revitalization of institutional expressions of the church. Continental Pietism, the renewed Moravian Church, and early Methodism clearly were renewal movements in this sense.

It is clear also that these three religious groups were "movements" in the sociological sense, as defined by Gerlach and Hine in *People, Power, Change: Movements of Social Transformation.*[2] All the movements exhibited the five key factors of a movement indicated by these authors: (1) "a segmented, usually polycephalous, cellular organization"; (2) "face to face recruitment by committed individuals" from already existing social relationships; (3) personal commitment distinguishing the convert from the prevailing order and conforming him or her to the movement's norms; (4) an integrating and motivating ideology; and (5) "real or perceived opposition."[3]

The seven interpretive frameworks discussed in chapter 2 are all of some use in analyzing and understanding the dynamics of Pietism, Moravianism, and Methodism. I have found the *ecclesiola in ecclesia* conception, the revitalization movement approach, and the Catholic Anabaptist typology especially useful, partly because of their relatively broad scope and their helpfulness in illuminating the social-structural dynamics of the three movements. We will refer again to these particular interpretive frameworks in the final section of this chapter.

Anthony Wallace's concept of "mazeway reformulation" and Thomas Kuhn's reference to "paradigm shifts" seem particularly appropriate in understanding the initial dynamic in the rise of renewal movements. Wallace posits six stages in the course of a revitalization movement, of which the first is "mazeway reformulation" (i.e., a changed basic model, metaphor, or perspective) by a prophetic figure, and the last is the "routinization" or establishment and institutionalization of the movement.[4] Functionally, as applying to the initial dynamics of church renewal movements, "mazeway reformulation" and "paradigm shift" seem to be equivalent. Renewal movements seem to start in the church when a key figure (or figures) proposes a new way of understanding the faith which strikes an immediate response in a growing number of people. This response is not a mere intellectual exercise, of course; it goes to the heart of people's self-understanding and experience of the faith. But this is the nature of a genuine paradigm, root metaphor, or fundamental model, especially in religion. It gives meaning to life.

This seems to be what happened in the cases of Pietism, Methodism, and Moravianism. All three made a "new discovery" of the faith, or a rediscovery of aspects of the faith which were at the time obscured. Spener rediscovered the personal experience of regeneration (rebirth) as the subjective meaning of justification by faith and reformulated his concept of the church in accordance with this shift in emphasis. Zinzendorf, building on a Pietist foundation, rediscovered the sense of the church as a missionary community. In Wesley the "paradigm shift" is particularly clear: Prior to Aldersgate he was seeking sanctification without the foundation of justification or the new birth. From Aldersgate on, Wesley preached justification by faith as the necessary prerequisite for sanctification (understood by Wesley not primarily as a state but as the process of sanctifying or being sanctified). With this marked shift in emphasis came also a vivifying of Wesley's understanding of the nature of the church.

A similar analysis could be extended to other movements in the history of the church, including Montanism. Renewal movements generally "rediscover" some element or accent in the church or in Scripture. Whether this is a genuine recovery or a heretical or eccentric aberration is, of course, often the point of controversy. Examples here could include the quest for perfection and the discovery of community in early monasticism; Luther's reappropriation of justification by faith; or the experience of glossolalia in segments of American Protestantism at the turn of the last century and again in Roman Catholicism at the beginning of the contemporary Catholic charismatic renewal. Many other examples might be given. A comparative analysis of many such cases might yield additional insights into the initial dynamics of church renewal movements. A related issue would be the question (implicit in the "revitalization movement" approach) of the degree to which the dynamics of church renewal movements parallel various secular or non-Christian renewal, revitalization, or reform movements.

With this by way of background and introduction, we may now outline a conceptual model for church renewal.

A MODEL FOR CHURCH RENEWAL

Typically questions of church renewal have been viewed in one of two ways. They have been seen either from what may be called the *institutional* perspective, or the *charismatic* perspective (understanding neither term pejoratively).

The Institutional View

In this perspective, the church is God's saving institution on earth. Church history is seen positively as the unfolding drama of God's purposes. The given structures of the church (theological and especially organizational) are not to be questioned. Periods of decline or unfaithfulness in church history stem from the personal character of church leaders or external factors, but not from the church-as-institution. In fact, the institutional stability and survival of the church in spite of periods of decline, opposition, or weakness are seen as part of the glory of the church. They reveal God's providence in establishing the church as the institution of salvation.

Thus from a Roman Catholic perspective the survival of the papacy in spite of periods of corruption or weakness attests to the validity of the church. Or similarly, from a Protestant perspective, the endurance of preaching or the "ministerial office" is seen as a source of God's renewing work even when many people are unfaithful.

From this perspective, nothing is ever fundamentally wrong with the church. The question of church renewal, therefore, is exclusively (or nearly so) a question of the spiritual renewal of individual persons or of the general body of believers as the mere aggregate of individual members. Thus one of Spener's opponents could argue, "It is not the Church but the ungodly in the Church that must be reformed."[5] The problem is simply that people fail to believe or act as the church tells them to. Renewal, however it comes, means restoring people to the level of belief or action defined by the church as normal. Any genuine renewal is seen as beginning with the ecclesiastical leaders and affecting the whole church more or less evenly.

From the institutional perspective, any kind of renewal movement immediately provokes suspicion, if not actual hostility. A new structure dedicated to church renewal is intuitively, and correctly, perceived by the keepers of the institution as calling into question (at least potentially) the validity of the institutional church itself, at least in its given form. Thus tension is inevitable, and the results are predictable. The renewal body will either (1) become increasingly radicalized and eventually leave or be forced out of the institutional church, as with the Waldensians, the Montanists, and the Methodists (and inevitably, it seems, forces are at work on both sides tending toward schism or separation); (2) lose its vitality to the point where it is no longer a threat to the institutional church (the Continental Pietists); or (3) become accommodated to the institutional church by being given a recognized but limited place within the structure (as with Catholic religious orders and some of the contemporary expressions of the charismatic renewal within Roman Catholicism and some Protestant denominations). All three of these options seem to be compatible with a greater or lesser degree of renewing impact on the church by the renewal structure or movement.

The Charismatic View

In the charismatic view, the church in any age must be in direct contact with God and a clear channel of his grace (*charis*) in order to have life and power. The church is essentially a spiritual organism and community, whatever its institutional form may be. Institutional forms are viewed ambivalently or totally rejected.

The charismatic view naturally sees church history in a different light. History and tradition do not automatically validate the present form of the church. Since the focus is on immediate and direct spiritual life, history is evaluated according to evidence of such life at various points in the past and according to whether past events are seen as contributing to or undermining the church's spirituality.

The charismatic view is especially attracted to the picture of the primitive church in the New Testament, or to an idealized model of that picture, and typically measures the history and present state of the church by this picture (primitivism). Since any substantial decline from the New Testament ideal must be explained without calling God's existence, sovereignty, or immediate agency into question, this line of reasoning leads naturally to some theory of the fall of the church and to the present need to restore the church to its primitive purity (restitutionism).

Because of its emphasis on vital experience and its religious idealism, the charismatic view is typically concerned with the whole experience of the church and with the visible expression of the church as a renewed community and people, and not only with private, individual experience. This places it in conflict with the institutional view, because champions of the charismatic view typically perceive (often correctly) that many of the obstacles to renewal are enshrined in traditional and institutional forms. Either these forms must change, or, failing that, a more renewed and virile form of Christian community must be implanted within the institutional church so that the charismatic ideal may become a reality (*ecclesiola*; the Pietist *collegium pietatis*; the Moravian communities and bands; the Methodist societies and classes).

Thus the same three options emerge. Depending partly on the radicalness of the charismatic group and its critique of the institutional church, and partly on the response or reaction from the institutional church, the renewal group will either: (1) form a totally separate body or sect, (2) gradually fade away; or (3) strike a deal with the institutional church which allows it some autonomy in exchange for its recognition of the authority and validity of the institutional "powers that be." Again, which of these options occurs depends not just on the spiritual temperature of the renewing body but also on other factors, including the response or reaction of the institutional church to the would-be renewers.

A Mediating Perspective

Is there any middle ground here? Can both views be incorporated into one understanding of the church and church renewal which affirms both the necessity of a present, vital experience of Christian community and discipleship and also the validity of the church in its more institutional form?

In the first place, both the institutional and charismatic views are open to criticism. The institutional view is often blind to the great gulf between the church's profession and its possession, and to its own institutionalism and self-interest in keeping the status quo. Consequently it often underrates the truth of the charismatic claim and misreads the importance of the renewal movement. Thus it finds itself in the unfortunate position of fighting in practice the very things it favors in theory.

But the charismatic view has similar problems. The renewers often have no sense of history (or force history into an ideological framework) and too easily identify God's purposes exclusively with their side in the renewal debate. They are typically naive concerning institutional and sociological realities and blind to the institutional dimensions of their own movement. In their concern with present experience they may fall prey to bizarre apocalyptic, dispensational, or millennial views which are unbiblical and unrealistic and may lead to extreme hopes, claims, or behavior.

On the other hand, both views have their strengths. Whatever

273

the church's state of decline, it still carries (except in the most extreme cases) the Scriptures, the sacraments, and a deposit of Christian doctrinal truth. The very birth of a renewal body is presumptive evidence that some spiritual life still remains in the old church. And if one takes history seriously, some real continuity—and therefore validity—must be granted to the institutional church. Otherwise the renewal movement would have to be seen as a *totally* new, unique, and unprecedented phenomenon, a church *sui generis* or one generated uniquely by the Spirit's action unrelated to history. Such a view would be unbiblical as well as sociologically and historically naive.

Similarly, the charismatic view cannot be totally rejected on either biblical or sociological grounds. Institutions decline and need periodic renewal. When the institution is the church, the renewal certainly must spring from or result in a new or renewed *experience* of God's grace, whatever other features it may have. Further, the charismatic stress on community and on charismatic (rather than institutional) leadership often points to real problem areas in the institutional church.

One cannot deny the internal dynamism of many renewal movements nor that, in many cases, this dynamism has contributed largely to the renewal or rebirth of the institutional church itself (for example, the Franciscan movement). This dynamism must be accounted for in some way. If evaluated spiritually, it presumably is either good or bad. If the renewal is in fact biblically based, shows the marks of the New Testament church, and sparks new life throughout the church, it presumably will be evaluated favorably by most Christians, whatever its weaknesses. And even if evaluated on purely sociological grounds, the beneficial impact of the renewing force on the institutional church would presumably have to be admitted.

This line of reasoning logically points toward a theory of church life and renewal which *combines* insights from the institutional and charismatic views. This would point toward a mediating model of the church which seeks not merely to steer a middle course between the two views but to incorporate the truth of both.

Such a mediating model would need, then, to see both the institutional church (even in periods of decline) and also renewal movements and forces as in some sense valid and perhaps even normal. (From Wallace's anthropological revitalization movement perspective, the institutional church would correspond to the particular society within which a movement occurs. Thus the existence and "life" [even if declining] of the host society is assumed.)

Obviously not all renewal movements are equally beneficial. From a Christian theological standpoint the validity of particular renewal movements would have to be settled on primarily biblical grounds. But a mediating model would expect renewal movements to arise and would anticipate their making a genuine biblical and spiritual contribution to the life of the church.

A biblical analogy may be useful here. Most biblical figures for the church are figures from life—body, tree, vine, marriage, and so forth. A particularly interesting figure is found in Isaiah 11:1 (cf. Job 14:7; Isa. 6:13): the figure of an old, partially deadened growth sending forth new shoots. Renewal movements seem almost instinctively drawn toward such analogies. The movement represents "new life," a sprouting forth of new growth. But the analogy necessarily implies that some life still remains in the old stump; that both have sprung from the same roots. In short, this is a mediating figure.

The stump-and-branch metaphor suggests an interdependence or symbiosis between the institutional church and the renewal movement. It recognizes that, for whatever reason, the old tree has lost its earlier vigor and may appear dead, but that it still has life and, therefore, hope. And it recognizes that the new branch has not sprung into being simply on its own but to some degree has its source (whatever other influences may be at work) in the old stump.[6]

Marks of a Mediating Model

Such a mediating model, then, combines elements of both the institutional and charismatic perspectives. The model assumes the existence and value of some form of the institutional church as well as the need for repeated renewal through more or less distinct renewal movements. The problem is to conceive of a renewing structure which brings new life to the larger church without either compromising its own validity or causing a split. It must be a structure which can be seen as normative; that is, whose appearance and impact are seen not as an aberration but as part of the working of the Spirit of God in the church. (This is not to imply that the decline of the church is ever "normative," but only that, given conditions of decline, one may expect certain patterns of "renewal.")

The following model appears to fit these requirements. All the elements described below were found (in the early stages at least) in Pietism, Moravianism, and Methodism, and could be illustrated as well from other renewal movements.

1. *The renewal movement "rediscovers" the Gospel.* Initially one or more persons discover, both experientially and conceptually, what they consider to be a new dynamic in the Christian faith. This experience alters their perception of the nature of the faith, or of its essential core, thus constituting or leading to a new model or paradigm of the Gospel and of the church (a "paradigm shift"). The initial renewal cell consists simply of those who have gained this altered experience and/or perception of the faith. It seems that renewal movements are made up primarily of those who have gained the new *experience,* with varying degrees of understanding, but also, interestingly, of a certain number of people (often more or less on the fringes) who have had the *conceptual* conversion but not yet the new "spiritual" experience.

Francke and Wesley illustrate such an intense personal religious crisis; Spener and Zinzendorf less so. Spener and Zinzendorf's altered perceptions of the faith seem to have come more or less gradually and to have been less linked to a personal spiritual crisis. Yet clearly those two figures, quite as much as Wesley and Francke, set forth a conception of the faith which, though formally orthodox, was also distinctly different from the prevailing conception—different at least in the placing of accents or in the basic models and paradigms used.

It is my conclusion, based on the study of Pietism, Methodism, and Moravianism and the comparison of these movements with others in the history of the whole, that this is a distinctive factor in renewal movements and should therefore be a key element of any mediating model.

2. *The renewal movement exists as an* ecclesiola. That is, it is a smaller, more intimate expression of the church within the church. It sees itself not as the true church in an exclusive sense, but as a form of the church which is necessary to the life of the larger whole, and which in turn needs the larger church in order to be complete. It understands itself as necessary not merely because of a perceived lack in the larger church but also because of a conviction that the Christian faith can be fully experienced only in some such "subecclesial' or small-church form.

3. *The renewing movement uses some form of small-group structure.* It is an *ecclesiola* not merely in a vague or general sense, but it takes on a specific small-group form within the local congregation. It is an *ecclesiola* not only as a group within the Christian church at large but also in the more restricted sense of a movement expressing itself in specific small communities within the local congregation. While the size and structure of these small groups may vary, they generally are composed of a dozen or less persons who meet regularly once a week.

4. *The renewal movement has some structural link with the institutional church.* This is crucial if the renewal structure is to exercise a revitalizing impact without bringing division. Some kind of tie between the two structures is worked out. This may mean ecclesiastical recognition as a religious order, ordination of renewal leaders (for example, Zinzendorf's Lutheran ordination),

or some organizational linkage. It may follow the model of official recognition of and liaison with the renewal body, as in the Anglican recognition of the Moravian Church or the current case of official Roman Catholic links with the Catholic charismatic renewal.

It was especially this structural tie which was lacking in the case of Methodism and the Waldensians. Count Zinzendorf sought such a tie, with limited success, in the case of the Moravians; Francis of Assisi fully achieved one by gaining papal approval for his order.[7]

5. Because it sees itself not as the total church but as a necessary part of the church, *the renewal structure is committed to the unity, vitality, and wholeness of the larger church.* It will be concerned first of all with the life of that branch of the church which forms its most immediate context (for example, a denomination or a theological or ecclesiastical tradition), but it will also have a vision for the universal church and a concern for its unity and united witness.

6. *The renewal structure is mission-oriented.* It senses keenly its specific purpose and mission, conceived in part as the renewal of the church and in part as witness to the world. It will stress practical ethics, attempting to combine faith and love; to link belief with everyday life. In the movements studied here, the sense and definition of mission varied somewhat, but all three groups had a strong sense of mission.

Some renewal movements see their mission simply as the promotion or extension of the renewal itself, while others may understand their mission as evangelism, church unity, or social reform. Presumably those renewal movements are most socially transforming which conceive of their mission more broadly than the mere extension of spiritual renewal. If the central dynamic of the renewal is compromised or lost sight of, however, the movement will likely lose the very power which fundamentally undergirds its socially transforming role.

7. *The renewal movement is especially conscious of being a distinct,*

covenant-based community. It knows it is not the whole church; it senses its own incompleteness. But it sees itself as a visible form of the true church. It does not attempt to carry on all the functions of the church but is a restricted community of people voluntarily committed to each other. Based on a well-understood covenant, it has the capability of exercising discipline, even to the point of exclusion, among its members. As a community the renewal prizes face-to-face relationships, mutuality, and interdependence. It especially stresses Scriptures which speak of *koinonia,* mutual encouragement, and admonition within the body, and sees itself as a primary structure for experiencing these aspects of the church.

8. *The renewal movement provides the context for the rise, training, and exercise of new forms of ministry and leadership.* Out of its experience of community comes a practical stress on the gifts of the Spirit and the priesthood of believers. This consciousness combines with the natural need for leadership within the movement and the outward impulse of witness and service to produce both the opportunity and the enabling context for new forms of ministry. Similarly, it produces new leaders who arise not through the more restricted, established ecclesiastical channels (typically, education and ordination, restricted to males), but through practical experience and the shared life of the group. This happened in Methodism as well as in other renewal movements.

The renewal group provides both opportunities for leadership and service and a natural, practical environment for training new leaders. Partly for this reason, a disproportionately high number of future church leaders often comes from the ranks of a renewal movement if it is not cut off from the established church. (One thinks here of the renewal popes who came from the ranks of religious orders.)

9. *Members of the renewal movement remain in close daily contact with society, and especially with the poor.* Church renewal movements do in fact vary considerably at this point, as can be seen in the case of Pietism, Moravianism, and Methodism (and as noted in chapter 6). Some renewal movements clearly arise among or appeal

directly to the poor; others do not. Here one might contrast, for example, the Franciscan movement and the contemporary charismatic movement. The early Franciscan revival (like early Methodism) was largely a movement of the poor or the lower classes; the charismatic movement (like Continental Pietism) was more a movement of the middle or upper classes.

My conclusion here is that movements which appeal to and spread among the poor are both more radical and more socially transforming than those which do not, though this might require some qualification in particular contexts.[8]

10. *Finally, the renewal structure maintains an emphasis on the Spirit and the Word as the basis of authority*. It is both Christological and pneumatological in this sense. It stresses the norm of Scripture and the life of the Spirit and maintains both of these in some tension with the traditionalism of the institutional church. If it veers to the right or the left at this point, it will become either a highly legalistic sect or an enthusiastic cult liable to extreme or heretical beliefs.

The renewal movement stresses the Spirit and the Word as the ultimate ground of authority, but within limits also recognizes the authority and traditions of the institutional church.

In summary, this is a model for renewal which assigns normative roles both to the institutional church and to movements and structures for renewal. Obviously no actual instance of a renewal movement in an institutional church perfectly fits the model. It is possible, however, that the model could be useful in comparing and evaluating various renewal movements, including contemporary ones.

It is important to note, finally, that this model is capable of including (at least conceptually) not only renewal movements which remain within the institutional church but also the Believers' Churches or other groups which become independent sects. It can include many of the medieval "heretical" sects, or at least those whose only heresy was to separate from Rome. In the first place, the model provides some help in understanding why such groups do in fact become independent. More importantly, if one's understanding of "church" includes broadly all the people of God in the various communions, all those who confess Jesus Christ as Savior and Lord, then such independent churches and sects may still be seen as *ecclesiolae* within the church of Christ, even though they are independent of any particular ecclesiastical structure larger than themselves.

All this is, of course, highly conceptual and theoretical. Does it have any practical value?

I believe it does. It should give Christian leaders—both denominational leaders and leaders in renewal movements—some breadth and perspective in seeing their own place and role. This may provide more tolerance and room for the Spirit to work. And with this foundation, we may move now to some of the more practical questions of church renewal.

NOTES

[1] This chapter is a further elaboration of the main part of chapter 10 of my book *The Radical Wesley and Patterns for Church Renewal* (Downers Grove, Ill.: InterVarsity Press, 1980; Grand Rapids: Francis Asbury Press, Zondervan, 1987).

[2] L. P. Gerlach and V. H. Hine, *People, Power, Change: Movements of Social Transformation* (New York: Bobbs-Merrill, 1970), xvi–xvii.

[3] Ibid.

[4] Anthony F. C. Wallace, "Revitalization Movements: Some Theoretical Considerations for Their Comparative Study," *American Anthropologist* 58 (April 1956): 268–75.

[5] Quoted in Isaac Dorner, *History of Protestant Theology,* trans. George Robson and Sophia Tucker (Edinburgh: T. and T. Clark, 1871), 2:211.

[6] Roman Catholic theologian Rosemary Ruether suggests essentially this model in her essay, "The Free Church Movement in Contemporary Catholicism," in Martin E. Marty and Dean G. Peerman, eds., *New Theology No. 6* (New York: Macmillan, 1969), 269–87.

[7] This is in contrast to Ruether's suggestion that renewal communities exist "autonomously and without any specific kinds of institutional ties" (Ruether, "Free Church Movement," 286). My

conclusion is that some form of institutional tie is normally necessary to prevent (or lesson the likelihood of) schism.

[8]See Norman Cohn, *The Pursuit of the Millennium: Revolutionary Millenarians and Mystical Anarchists of the Middle Ages,* rev. ed. (New York: Oxford University Press, 1970).

Five Dimensions of Renewal

Five Dimensions of Renewal

How does renewal come to the church? We have examined historical examples and seen some of the dynamics at work. Yet renewal, like the church itself, remains a mystery.

The study of Scripture and church history do tell us much, however, about how God renews the church by his Spirit. And we will understand renewal better as we see that renewal has more than one dimension. In this chapter we will examine five dimensions of renewal.

PERSONAL RENEWAL

When we think of renewal, we usually mean *personal* spiritual renewal. Many of us have experienced individual renewal at some point in our Christian lives. Our spiritual life was deepened; God became closer and more personally real. Personal renewal may be a dramatic, decisive experience or simply a deepening that gives us greater peace and joy.

A few years ago, a friend reported that more or less on her own she had come into a new peace with God and a richer sense of God's presence. She calls this her "rise"; that's the best way she can describe it. This was her personal renewal, a deeper experience which came after a number of years as a Christian.

Whatever else renewal is, it surely must be personal. We are human persons made to experience God in all his fullness. Nothing can substitute for this. First through the new birth, then through the deepening work of the Holy Spirit, God wants every son and daughter of his to know the joy of deep, fulfilling communion with himself. This is, in fact, the heart of the Christian faith.

Renewing individual believers is only part of the story, however. God wants to see the whole body of Christ renewed.

CORPORATE RENEWAL

We may call the broader renewing work of the Spirit *corporate renewal,* the renewal of the whole body (remembering that "corporate" means "having to do with the body"). God wants to renew his church in all its members, until the whole community of believers takes on a corporate renewed life.

Many of us have experienced such renewal times in our lives. God's Spirit moved graciously over the whole church, and everyone was touched. This may have been marked by a dramatic spirit of revival sweeping the church, or simply by a gentle quickening of the church's life which affected the whole group of believers. Either way, it is the work of the renewing Spirit.

I remember several times when, as a teenager, I experienced the Holy Spirit's deep stirring in my home church and on the college campus in Spring Arbor, Michigan. One Sunday worship service especially stands out. The sanctuary was filled with some 150 or so people. Someone sang "The Love of God" as a special number. By the end of the song many were weeping, and the sense of God's presence was preciously close.

As the pastor rose to preach, a woman in the congregation

stood and asked to share a word. She told how God's presence had been especially close the past week, and that God had led her to fast and pray for the church from the previous Sunday until Wednesday noon. When she sat down, a man rose and told how God had led him to fast and pray from Wednesday noon until Sunday. Others began to share, and people began going forward to pray at the altar.

Eventually the service was dismissed, but most people stayed for the prayer time around the altar and for the time of testimonies that followed. I was about thirteen at the time. I still remember vividly the strong sense of God's presence that day, and the strange blend of joy, peace, excitement, and awe we felt.

I remember another occasion when I was almost sixteen. It was Tuesday morning, January 17, 1956. With about 300 other high school and junior college students I took my place in Hart Chapel, Spring Arbor, Michigan, for the daily chapel service. When the service finally ended four hours later we knew revival had come. I wrote in my diary, "In chapel period God broke loose and an altar service lasted until 2:00 P.M., and almost all the Spring Arbor students were saved." And the next day: "In the student vesper service God again broke loose while a large number testified and [one of the students] told of his vision of heaven" the night before. This began a dramatic, seemingly spontaneous revival that shook the whole community. People coming on campus said they could feel the Spirit of God.

Corporate renewal is not always this dramatic, nor need it be. The point isn't how we feel but rather the freedom of the Spirit among us. Where renewal becomes corporate, touching the whole body, it reaches a deeper, broader level than when it remains the experience of a few individuals only.

In corporate renewal, the whole is more than the sum of its parts. A renewed congregation is more powerful in God's hands than a collection of isolated Christians, no matter how deeply revived. Combined, the glowing coals of renewal burst into flame and tend to burn longer.

CONCEPTUAL RENEWAL

Renewal may also come *conceptually,* as God gives new vision of what the church can and should be.

Conceptual renewal is a new vision for the church's life and mission. It comes primarily in the area of our thoughts, ideas, and images of the church. Each of us has a set of ideas—a certain "model" or "paradigm"—of what we feel the church should be. Our models are a combination of our experience and our study of Scripture. Conceptual renewal comes when our models are challenged, and we are forced to rethink what the church is really all about. In this book we have seen examples of this in the early stages of renewal movements.

I began to experience this kind of renewal in seminary and later while pastoring in Detroit. The process came into focus especially when my family and I went to Brazil as missionaries. Studying, thinking, praying, and reflecting on more than twenty-five years in the church, I came to a new understanding. I found a new model: the organic community pictured so forcefully in the New Testament. For me, this was a conceptual renewal—my "conversion" to a more biblical understanding of the church.

It is important to see that God works in our minds as well as in our hearts. Conceptual renewal can be just as much the work of the Spirit as is a powerful revival. God wants the eyes of our understanding to be enlightened so that we may comprehend the breadth of what he is doing in and through the church (Eph. 1:17–18).

Many people have experienced conceptual renewal without experiencing personal renewal. They have a new vision of what the church can become, but they haven't experienced it yet. This easily leads to frustration. The key is to not give up on the vision but to become part of a community of believers that is open to the work of the Spirit in all its dimensions. In this context one's vision is clarified and sharpened even while one's heart is warmed. New avenues of ministry open up.

We need conceptual and theological renewal in the church as surely as we need personal and corporate renewal. Jesus warned the Pharisees that they were voiding the Word of God by their traditions. He said new wine needs new wineskins. The same principles hold today. We need an understanding of the church that is based on Scripture *first,* on practical reason and experience *second,* and only *thirdly* on tradition. What promotes revival, renewal, and faithful kingdom witness in the church should be kept; what does not should be scrapped.

It is easy to miss the importance of this aspect of renewal, and yet it is often crucial to the work of the Spirit. We can be imprisoned by our concepts as surely as we are imprisoned by our habits. In fact, concepts *are* habits—habitual ways of understanding and viewing things. God's Spirit may be hindered by wrong or rigid ideas as well as by cold hearts.

Church history shows that conceptual renewal has often been at the heart of revival movements. By God's Spirit, people have been led to a deeper understanding—a new model or vision, a new paradigm—of what the Gospel is or what the church should be. Luther's rediscovery of justification by faith was as much a new concept in his day as a new experience. When John Wesley said, "Christianity is a social religion" and began organizing cell groups, he was teaching a new concept of the church as community. Yet both Luther and Wesley were simply rediscovering what Scripture teaches. This was part of God's renewing work.

Every age needs to reinterpret the biblical understanding of the church for its time and unique needs if renewal is going to go as far as God intends. I believe God is at work today, weaning us away from old, static views of the church to new, dynamic visions of the committed, intimate covenant community.

STRUCTURAL RENEWAL

A fourth dimension of renewal has to do with forms and structures. It is the dimension of renewal concerned with the way we, as believers, live out our lives together. It is the question of the best wineskins for the new wine.

Renewal often dies prematurely for lack of effective structures. The new wine flows through the cracks of our own forms and is soon lost. Renewal becomes a fond memory, not a new way of life.

Structural renewal is simply finding the best forms, in our day and age, for living out the new life in Christ. History is full of examples of structural renewal becoming a key to extending renewal beyond the passing moment. Early Christians discovered the usefulness of homes for church gatherings, and through history the rediscovery of the house church has often been a part of renewal movements. Wesley created the class meeting, the band, the Methodist society, and a team of "lay" preachers who served as wineskins to carry the wine of renewal. It worked! Many other examples could be cited, including the contemporary rediscovery of small groups for growth or for mission, one-on-one discipling, and other nontraditional forms of church life and witness.

It seems to be a principle that traditions and structures outlive their usefulness and become more a hindrance than a help. Nothing in Scripture, for instance, says churches must have a Sunday school, a midweek service, or leadership primarily in the hands of only one or two persons. Nor is there any biblical reason for most activities to happen in a church building rather than in homes. Many other examples could be cited. The point is that *any* traditional form, structure, or practice that helps us be alive and faithful should be kept and improved. Any that insulate us from the fresh fire of the Spirit should be modified or retired.

True enough: We cannot bring renewal by changing forms. But we can stifle it by putting forms above life. Renewal is less likely to come and more likely to die in a tradition-bound group where everything happens routinely in the church building and there is little freedom to innovate. Renewal is more likely when believers begin to share their faith together in homes, when traditional forms are periodically reevaluated, and when the structural vitality and flexibility of the early church are rediscovered.

MISSIOLOGICAL RENEWAL

A fifth dimension of renewal is *missiological renewal*—the renewal of the church's sense of calling and passion. A church needing renewal is focused inward. A renewed church focuses outward to mission and service in the world. It is moved to carry on the very works Jesus did, for the sake of his kingdom.

Sometimes renewal actually begins here, with a new sense of mission. Some people catch a vision for a new ministry in the church, the neighborhood, or the world. "Here is a need we can meet," they say. Faith takes hold; resources are brought together. In finding those in need, a church may find itself and the renewing of the Spirit.

Jesus told us to seek first the righteousness and justice of God's kingdom (Matt. 6:33); to pray that the kingdom may come *on earth* (Matt. 6:10). The church, Emil Brunner said, exists by mission as fire exists by burning. Genuine renewal will include missiological renewal. A renewed, creative sense of mission is as much a part of renewal as is personal or corporate renewal. A church has not really been renewed until it has found its unique mission for God's kingdom in the here and now.

THE RENEWAL PROCESS

We see, then, several sides to renewal: personal, corporate, conceptual, structural, and missiological. We can say several things about how these dimensions interconnect when God's Spirit renews the church.

291

1. *Renewal may begin in any one or more of these five ways.* While we most commonly think of renewal as personal or corporate, history shows that renewal has often begun initially at one of the other points. We should watch for and welcome the renewing work of the Holy Spirit wherever and however it comes.

2. *Renewal must become personal and corporate to be genuine.* A new vision for the church, new structures, or a renewed sense of mission won't carry us very far unless hearts are warmed and changed. Similarly, warm hearts will not fully renew the church unless the church becomes a *renewed community.* In Paul's words, it is the whole body that must "be built up" and "reach unity in the faith" as it "grows and builds itself up in love" (Eph. 4:12–16). Renewal is not really renewal in the full, biblical sense until it is both personal and corporate.

3. *Renewal must become conceptual and structural to be long lasting.* Too often renewal fails precisely here. More than once I have seen the Spirit move upon a congregation until nearly every person was changed—but then the renewal aborted because believers did not understand what was happening and lacked appropriate structures to nurture the new life. Spiritual babies suffered malnutrition, and in short order the new life was stifled by institutional business as usual.

The great renewals in history that shaped the face of society, such as the Wesleyan Revival, reached the conceptual and structural levels. They were based on a recovered biblical vision of the church, and they found appropriate structures to sustain the new life of the Spirit. There probably have been many hundreds of revivals in the history of the church, but only a relative handful were carried through to the conceptual and structural levels.

4. *Renewal must reach the missiological level to be biblically dynamic.* A church is not really renewed until it discovers its mission in the world. God's goal, after all, is not just to renew the church but to reconcile the world. As agents of reconciliation, we are to find our own crucial role in the overall plan of God "to

bring all things . . . together under one head, even Christ" (Eph. 1:10).

In fact, when these five dimensions are all integrated into the renewal of the church, the church becomes God's agent of reconciliation in the earth. Renewal moves out like concentric ripples in a pond, reaching beyond the Christian community to the whole human community. Biblical Christians, in fact, will be satisfied with nothing less: personal renewal, which becomes church renewal, which reaches to social renewal, which sweeps on to become world renewal. Here is a vision for world-wide *shalom*. Though the vision may sound utopian, it is in fact biblical and practical. Jesus spoke of the kingdom sprouting like a seed and spreading like leaven (Matt. 13:31–33).

PRACTICAL IMPLICATIONS

If renewal comes in these varied ways, what can we do? In the final chapter I will propose a renewal strategy for the local church. But some personal application is in order here.

First, we should remember that all Christians have a part to play in renewal. We can be open to the Spirit and the Word—not only in our hearts but in our minds and actions as well. That openness is born from an understanding of the church and God's kingdom plan for his people. Careful Bible study can help, especially if carried out in small groups where people have opportunity to learn, share, and pray together. Particularly useful portions of Scripture for this kind of study include Ephesians, Acts, 1 Corinthians, the four gospels, Hebrews, and Isaiah. More broadly, it is useful to trace God's acts in forming a people in the Old Testament, leading to Jesus Christ and the birth of the church in the New Testament.

One way or another, every Christian should be part of a small committed cell group where she or he can grow and develop, learning new openness to others and to the work of the Spirit.

Alert pastors will make the forming and nurturing of such groups a high priority.

These approaches, supplementing the accepted, necessary disciplines of prayer, worship, and personal Bible study, can be used of God to bring renewal to our lives and to the church—renewal in all its dimensions.

Building a Renewal Strategy for the Local Church

Chapter Nine

Building a Renewal Strategy for the Local Church

Pastor Fred went to a church leadership conference to learn how to make his church grow. The conference was sponsored by a successful suburban church and featured numerous seminars on all aspects of church life. Fred learned about evangelism, discipling, publicity and promotion, media, church finances, and long-range planning. He soon had a whole notebook of ideas.

The highlight of the conference was the evening session when the host pastor told the exciting story of his church's renewal and growth. It was a very inspiring time, and Fred left with new hope and vision for his rather lethargic church.

But on the flight home, Pastor Fred had some second thoughts. Sipping a second cup of coffee, he began thinking back over what he had heard—especially the story told by the senior pastor. The conference had been full of ideas, principles, and strategies—good stuff.

But gradually a new thought occurred to Fred. The host church had surely grown, and was doing many things right. But what was the real secret? He remembered what the senior pastor had said. He told of his own call and vision, of conversions, and of the coming together of circumstances which had brought growth. It was remarkable and refreshing.

But Fred's new thought was this: This church really had a unique story, largely unrepeatable. Surely there were principles he could learn and apply. But at some fundamental level, the story could never be imitated or replayed. The particular setting; the unique gifts and personality of the senior pastor; the conversions of particular people; the adding of particular staff—this church's story was as individual and unique as any one person's biography. He couldn't go home and repeat the same success story in his church.

THE GREAT SEMINAR FALLACY

By this one insight, Pastor Fred escaped the frustrations of falling prey to the Great Seminar Fallacy. The Great Seminar Fallacy is that one can copy in one's own unique circumstances what has transpired elsewhere.

Usually one can't. And the attempt to do so often leads to frustration and disillusionment.

Any viable strategy for church renewal must start with the unique personality, setting, history, and challenges of the particular church. Principles of renewal are valid only to the extent that they are not only scripturally sound but also sensitive to the particular place.

This is also true with history. The story of church renewal movements has much to tell us about local church life and renewal today. But it would be a mistake to try to derive surefire formulas for church renewal based on what we learn from history. Rather, the historical record raises issues and offers insights which can assist churches in designing their own strategy, one as unique to the particular church as a set of specially tailored clothes or a pair of prescription eyeglasses.

This chapter offers, then, not a formula for renewal, but some suggestions for building a renewal strategy which is at once biblically sound, historically informed, and specially tailored to the particular situation.

RENEWAL: THE POSSIBLE MIRACLE

New Testament writers repeatedly address instructions, exhortations, and encouragements to the church, the community of believers. They say things like "Make every effort to live in peace with all men and to be holy" (Heb. 12:14); "Confess your sins to each other and pray for each other so that you may be healed" (James 5:16); "Love one another, for love comes from God" (1 John 4:7); and "Share with God's people who are in need. Practice hospitality" (Rom. 12:13). Jesus himself said things like, "Love your enemies and pray for those who persecute you" (Matt. 5:44) and "Love each other as I have loved you" (John 15:12).

In the light of all that has been said in this book, two things are immensely striking about such biblical statements.

First, they are not addressed primarily to individuals, but corporately to the church, the community of Jesus' disciples. In all the above cases the New Testament Greek uses *you* in the plural, not the singular, form. All these and literally dozens of similar passages are saying, in effect, "Here is the way to truly be Jesus' disciples. This is what it means to be the church."

But something else is equally striking about such exhortations. *All assume that Christians are in fact able to obey,* to exhibit the kinds of behaviors which make them authentically a community of discipleship. The biblical writers assume that, enabled by Jesus' Spirit, believers have the opportunity and the responsibility to cooperate in sustaining and extending the life and vitality of the church.

How then does God renew the church? As we have sought to answer this question throughout the book, we have seen the complexity of the factors involved in the church's life and renewal.

299

Yet whatever else the history of renewal movements shows, it reveals that the church cannot escape responsibility for its own renewal. The church which assumes it can do nothing to renew itself—that says it must simply wait passively for God's sovereign intervention—is fundamentally no different from the individual Christian who abdicates responsibility for his or her own spiritual discipline and growth.

This means that we can appropriately talk about renewal strategies for local churches. We need to know *what* can be done, and how to do it. In these final pages I wish to sketch briefly some of what this means.

A PRACTICAL APPROACH TO RENEWAL

The first and perhaps most critical beginning point for renewal is to understand that *the church has an inborn tendency to grow.* Growth is in its genes. Whatever its pathologies, every church has a vital urge toward its own health and renewal. The reason for this is simple, and simply profound: The church is the body of Christ. The very Spirit of Jesus is at work in his church, always prodding and drawing it toward life and renewal. The key to renewal therefore is always a matter of identifying and removing the hindrances to vitality, never a matter of simply finding the right method, program, or success formula.

Since this is true, we may identify several keys to building a viable renewal strategy in local churches. In most cases, examples of these can be found in the renewal movements we have studied in this book. The goal is to build a healthy, vital congregation which is marked by wholehearted love for God and warmhearted love for all people. Nothing less deserves to be called "renewal."

Here are ten keys to developing a renewal strategy in the local church. These are not arranged in a given order or sequence; it will take discernment to know what the right "mix" and relative priority should be in each particular case. But each element has a vital place.

1. Begin With Life

Renewal begins with recognizing the sparks of life already present in the church and then fanning those sparks into flame. The principle is basic and self-evident: Life begets life.

We have seen (for example, in Spener's view of the church) the importance of understanding the church as a living organism, and therefore of using organic images and models of the church. To say that renewal should begin with existing life is to underscore pragmatically that the church is fundamentally an organism, not an organization. In both language and structure, renewal must maintain this organic basis, never subverting the principle that life begins with life.

In the local church, this means finding the life and vitality already present in both individuals and structures. Who are the *people* in the congregation who demonstrate by their lives that they truly know God and are ready to put Jesus Christ and his body first? Or at least who show genuine spiritual hunger and openness? Who are those that are hungering and thirsting for righteousness? Here is the starting point for renewal, as it was for Jesus and his disciples, and for John Wesley when he brought together those who were in earnest to know God and "flee from the wrath to come."

But not only who are the *people:* Also, what are the *structures* which are life giving or life sustaining? Is there any functioning life-support system in the congregation? It may show up in surprising places. It may be an *ad hoc* group of members who meet and support each other spiritually. It may be some family networks. It may even be a committee or other group, or even the choir, which has discovered a deeper, spiritual life-giving purpose to meeting together, so that it is the key structure for spiritual growth to its members. A renewal strategy begins with recognizing and affirming such structures. This is a first step.

For example, suppose Pastor Fred notices three men in his congregation who really seem to know God, and who find themselves together a couple of times each week because of their involvement in the work of the church. He sees that they are in effect a mutual support group, though they don't see themselves that way. So he spends an evening with them, shares a little of his own spiritual journey, opens the Word with them, prays with them. Soon—without any fanfare and hardly even any self-consciousness about what is happening—Pastor Fred has a vital discipleship group which begins subtly to spark new life in the congregation and also encourages and feeds him.

Renewal often begins by testing the wind: discerning where God is already at work and becoming willing co-laborers with him (2 Cor. 6:1).

2. Don't Attack Entrenched Institutional Patterns

The question often arises in renewal discussions: What do you do about institutionalism? What do you do about entrenched patterns and traditions which clog the channels of God's renewing work?

I will say more about the special problem of institutionalism shortly, but here we need to nail down a vital point: Don't attack institutional obstacles directly. Bypass them, if possible. The thing that institutions do best is defend themselves. Attacking entrenched patterns usually raises defenses instead of furthering renewal.

This is not the same as passivity or surrender. Where institutional barriers impede renewal, these must be faced squarely and eventually changed. But by beginning with life rather than focusing on barriers, one sets in motion the process which will lead to less stressful opportunities for counteracting institutionalism. Sometimes institutional barriers gradually become obsolete and simply wither on the vine and drop off. Or, to change the image, sometimes the stream of renewal simply cuts a new path around the dam.

Most folks have a high investment in stability. For many

Christians the church is a source of security, so any talk of change is threatening. A wise renewal strategy recognizes this, and says it is all right. So, rather than calling initially for major changes in tradition or structure and thus provoking opposition, a wise strategy values patience in this area while it works to rebuild the life of the church on a more organic model.

Wesley and the German Pietists exemplified this principle. By the judicious use of small groups and personal discipling, these reformers in effect bypassed many institutional obstacles and rebuilt a vital church from within. Many things in Anglicanism irritated Wesley (and at times he pointed them out), but rather than attack the dead institutionalism around him he built new relationships and structures of renewal.

3. Seek to Pastor All the People

Pastors or elders will normally be the key people in developing and implementing a renewal strategy, and they should understand that they must pastor all the people. Not everyone will favor renewal; some may actively oppose it. But wise pastoral leaders can often change the whole climate and win over hardened opponents simply by being available to and pastoring all the people.

Sometimes opposition turns to support when a church member passes through crisis and the pastor is there, showing the servant spirit of Jesus. Wesley relates in his *Journal* times when some of his most outspoken critics changed their views because he befriended or visited them in illness or crisis. Demonstrated caring is often more powerful than persuasive argument.

Pastors bent on renewal face the temptation of, in effect, playing favorites, focusing on those who are open to their renewal agenda and ignoring others. Careful strategy *does* require investing especially in those most open to renewal, as Jesus' own ministry shows. But it also means not neglecting anyone, and particularly not shutting anyone off. Some will never favor renewal and some may eventually leave, but faithful shepherds show concern for all the sheep.

4. Build a Balance of Worship, Community, and Witness

The church is a living organism, and the major components of its life are worship, community, and witness.[1] Healthy churches grow, and health is a balanced vitality of worship celebration, community building, and witness in the world. Effective renewal strategizing asks: Are we providing believers with the opportunities and the structures for these key aspects of their life together?

Worship—The church's highest calling is to worship God. Worship can be a key to renewal. Believers need both joyous celebration of God's acts and promises and opportunities to hear and respond faithfully to God's Word proclaimed and demonstrated. Worship forms and styles may vary considerably, but the key questions is whether people are really encountering God.

Community—The church is by definition the community of God's people. But what is true spiritually must be acted out in space, time, and structure. We are to "encourage one another daily" (Heb. 3:13) and "consider how we may spur one another on toward love and good deeds" as we meet together (Heb. 10:24). This is community, and it is basic to renewal. An effective renewal strategy concentrates on building vital community, understanding that community is the environment of the Spirit's working and that ministry grows out of community.

Witness—A church's renewal is ultimately only as vital and authentic as its witness. Healthy churches give healthy witness in evangelism, service, and justice ministries. This is, in essence, what was termed "missiological renewal" in chapter 8. Regardless of how good Christians may feel about themselves and their church, their life is not really demonstrating biblical vitality if it doesn't issue in consistent outflow in witness.

Renewal strategizing means examining each of these areas and their interdependence. The heart of a renewed church is always a healthy, functioning balance of worship, community, and witness.

5. Provide Small Groups and Home Meetings

Pietism had its *collegia pietatis;* the Moravians had their bands; Methodism had its classes and other groups. Vital renewal movements, it seems, not only rediscover community but develop practical structures to build the *koinonia* of the Spirit.

A pragmatic renewal strategy will use some form of small groups as *basic structure* in congregational life.[2] The precise form of such groups may vary and will need to fit the particular setting. Usually renewal movements have found the practical value of meeting in homes as a more informal and "family" setting for experiencing Christian community. Often it is practical to supplement such meetings with cell groups which meet wherever is most convenient.

The principle is this: The small group is a basic structure which is universally, crossculturally relevant and necessary, but the specific form of such groups is culturally relative.

In the church I helped lead in Chicago, we found midweek house church gatherings (what we called "home fellowships") to be basic and essential, along with a network of smaller cell groups. The church had about fifteen cell groups in a congregation of about eighty people. The cells averaged three or four people in number, most meeting for a couple of hours or so weekly. Cells would meet in such diverse places as living rooms, coffee shops, and offices, and at hours ranging from early morning to late at night.

A wide literature is available on small groups, and leaders will want to become familiar with it, but the basic guidelines are simple. In my view, the main keys to effective small groups and house meetings are these: Effective groups normally 1) meet weekly; 2) provide for adequate time (usually at least one and one-half to two hours); 3) meet consistently, each member seeing the group as one of the most fundamental commitments of the week; 4) meet over a long enough period of time (months or years) to build trust and a healing sense of community; 5) involve some combination of prayer, Bible study, and mutual sharing and encouragement; and 6) integrate themselves into the larger life of the church so that they nurture the congregation. In my experience, groups which don't meet these criteria are much less vital.

The size of groups can vary a lot, depending on purpose and function. In my recent experience in Chicago, what worked best for us was cells from about three to six people and home fellowships from fifteen to thirty. As we saw, early Methodist bands seemed to average about six or seven persons each, and the class meetings averaged about a dozen or less.

In building a renewal strategy, churches may want to experiment with some of these factors, particularly size and specific purpose of groups. The main danger to avoid is a half-hearted or halfway attempt to use such groups. Whenever I have encountered churches which say, "We tried small groups and they didn't work," I have usually found the reason for failure quite easily. The above guidelines were fundamentally violated. Failure seems to result most often from three causes: lack of serious commitment on the part of group members; meeting on a less-than-weekly basis; or trying to add such groups to an already full schedule without cutting out other activities of lower priority. The Wesleyan class meeting was so vitally successful for a century chiefly because it was a first-order discipleship commitment, not something to be added on after several other activities. It was not optional.

6. Affirm the Ministry of All Believers

Early Pietism, as we saw, gave Luther's emphasis on the priesthood of believers new depth and practicality. It meant a call to ministry; a vocation to encourage and disciple one another. Combined with the New Testament teaching on spiritual gifts and on servanthood in following Jesus, the priesthood of believers provides a vital key for church renewal: All believers are called, and should be equipped and empowered, for ministry.

Pastors may not realize it, but this teaching is dynamite. I have seen what happens when believers finally come to realize that they *really are* ministers of the Gospel, not second-class "laymen" in the church. Their whole self-perception changes, and with this often comes a new sense of responsibility to be servants and ministers for Jesus.

As part of a renewal strategy, this emphasis calls for several things: Teaching on spiritual gifts and the universal priesthood; modeling this in speech and structure; and providing training and opportunities for leadership development. The ministry of all believers needs to be demonstrated visibly in the three areas of worship, community, and witness. Perhaps most basically, this emphasis means conceiving of the pastoral role essentially as one of equipping believers for ministry (Eph. 4:11–12). This ties in naturally with the use of small groups, which are an essential discipling and equipping structure.

The ministry of all believers moves from theory to fact when it becomes visible in the congregation. A good place to start, I have found, is to develop a team of people to serve as worship leaders. This provides diversity within unity and shows we mean what we say about gifts and ministries.

7. Move Toward the Biblical Model of Leadership

A natural corollary to the ministry of all believers is biblically defined leadership. It is striking how clear the New Testament is on spiritual leadership and yet how massively these biblical teachings are ignored in the contemporary church. Renewal becomes deeper and longer-lasting as a congregation increasingly implements biblical patterns of leadership. So this is basic in a serious renewal strategy.

By the biblical model of leadership I mean essentially three things: leadership based on the Scriptural qualifications of character and giftedness; pastoral leadership defined primarily as equipping for ministry; and team or plural leadership in each congregation. Key passages here are Acts 6:1–4; 20:28; 1 Corinthians 12:1–28; Ephesians 4:7–16; 1 Timothy 3:1–13; 2 Timothy 2:2; Titus 1:5–9; Hebrews 13:17; James 5:13–16; and 1 Peter 5:1–3.[3]

An effective renewal strategy understands that ministry grows out of community and that leadership grows out of discipleship. It seeks to demonstrate the servant leadership of Jesus Christ, not only in spirit but also in strategy and direction, following the example of Jesus with his disciples and of Paul with his fellow workers.

This obviously means that pastors will need to begin by examining their own lives in the light of New Testament teachings about leadership. Then it means beginning to develop a core of spiritual leaders and disciples who demonstrate and model biblical leadership. The final result should be an effective pastoral leadership team in each congregation, regardless of what it is called or precisely how it is structured.

In several years of team leadership experience in our church in Chicago, I learned the values and strengths, as well as the problems, of this model. Two things have particularly impressed me. First, team leadership is not a weak model but rather a strong one, despite stereotypes of the "strong" individual leader. Second, I learned how important it is to have women as well as men in pastoral leadership. Repeatedly I saw how leadership was stronger, more balanced, and more sensitive because we had both men and women on our pastoral team.

8. Help the Congregation Discover Its Own Identity

Implementing a renewal strategy based on the above points gives a congregation a strong sense of identity as the body of Christ and as a ministering community. It is important however that a congregation's identity be based on its own unique personality, culture, and range of gifts, rather than being imposed by the pastoral leadership.

Pastors have authority and responsibility to lead, based on the biblical model. But that very model says that Jesus, and he alone, is the Head of the church, and that pastors are themselves fellow members of the body. The function of pastors, then, is to help the whole body "grow up into . . . Christ" (Eph. 4:15), finding its identity in him.

From a renewal standpoint, this means pastors are the key catalysts in helping a congregation discover its own unique identity and mission within the framework of the biblical Gospel of the kingdom. This is part of the discipling, equipping task. It relates to what was described as "conceptual renewal" in the previous chapter.

Discovering self-identity is in part a natural by-product of the other things we have been discussing here. A congregation finds its identity as it ministers, grows, and discovers its gifts. But this process can be made more intentional and self-conscious through teaching and preaching, Bible studies in cells and home groups on the nature of the church, annual church retreats, seminars and classes, and similar things. Church retreats can be an especially useful way to build identity through a combination of study, recreation, worship, and fellowship.

9. Work to Ensure that Financial Stewardship Authentically Reflects the Church's Mission and Self-Identity

It is true, as often said, that the use of money shows what one's *actual* priorities are. Church finances may end up betraying the church's renewal and identity unless consciously brought under the lordship of Christ and into line with the church's stated mission.

The whole area of finances should be seen in relation to the biblical image of the church and of New Testament discipleship. In the Sermon on the Mount, Jesus tells us where our priorities should lie. Matthew 6:33 applies as much to church finances as to personal priorities: We are to seek first God's kingdom and justice. If we do, other matters will take care of themselves.

In other words, spiritual and pastoral priorities should determine financial goals and strategies. As the renewal and mission of the church become increasingly its central focus, this will be reflected in church finances. Often in this process some major redirection may be necessary, a shifting of priorities from property and program toward people and ministry. God unfailingly provides the material resources when the church's priorities are straight. Then finances become a delight and a source of blessing rather than a burden and a problem. What joy to relax and see God provide; to see overflow funds available for mission to the world when previously finances always meant a tight twisting inward.

10. Help the Church Catch a Kingdom Vision

This is in some ways the most important thing, though it relates to all the above points. The congregation needs a *vision* of God's kingdom—what God is doing and what he has promised to do. This is a vision for community and worship, but also a vision for reconciling ministry in the world in which evangelism, discipling, and justice are inseparable strands in the fabric of ministry. Ongoing vitality is grounded in both the *vision* and the *practice* of consistent, continuous evangelism and compassionate, effective social transformation. It's a beautiful thing when a congregation gets beyond the evangelism/justice hang-up and, at the practical level of ministry, does both, virtually unconscious of the distinction. But reaching this point requires an overarching biblical vision of the kingdom of God.

Here again, teaching is important. This is a key role for pastoral leadership. Leaders must both model and teach a life centered on the hope and reality of God's reign.

A kingdom vision gives life and focus to the church's

worship, community, and witness. Worship is "reality therapy" in which the church affirms, against all visible signs to the contrary, God's present and ultimate victory in Jesus Christ. Kingdom vision makes worship the very center of the church's life.

A kingdom vision gives added meaning to the church's community life as well. It gives meaning to the church as a kingdom community, an outpost and foretaste of the age of *shalom* which is coming. Jesus' words become life and fire: "Fear not, little flock, for your Father delights to give you the kingdom" (Luke 12:32, translation mine).

And a kingdom vision gives impulse and coherence to the church's outward witness. It is the hope of Christ's kingdom which holds together the evangelistic and prophetic dimensions of the church's mission and keeps the church laboring for that which as yet remains largely unseen.

Church renewal can turn inward; it can be understood and experienced in pretty subjective and narcissistic terms. A kingdom vision is an antidote to this danger. Church leaders concerned about balanced, long-lasting renewal will do well to develop and instill the vision of God's reign as a basic part of a renewal strategy. Much of the dynamic of Pietism, Moravianism, and Methodism was due to their overarching vision of God's renewing work.

THE SPECIAL PROBLEM OF INSTITUTIONALISM

Institutionalism in its various forms is often a fundamental obstacle to renewal, and has been throughout history. It was largely the institutional barriers to renewal efforts that provoked Philipp Spener to call for reform in his *Pia Desideria* of 1675. To avoid unnecessary frustrations, we must be realistic about institutionalism.

At this point the church is much like any other social institution. Institutions resist change and therefore renewal.

Why is this? There are at least seven reasons. First, an institution is structured for continuity, stability, and routinization and against the unpredictable. Second, institutions partake of human fallenness. An institution may not be inherently evil, but can become the repository and tool of human evil. Third, institutions rely on *technique,* not grace. Grace is uncontrollable and forgiving while technique is always consistent: the same things done the same way. Fourth, an institution exists as an objective structure to which people must conform. It conforms people to itself, not vice versa. Fifth, institutions become repositories of vested interests, providing power and security, not easily given up, for those who wield institutional power. Sixth, institutions divide people up according to institutional power and status. Generally institutions make it very clear just where everyone fits— what your place is, and how it compares to those above or below. Finally, institutions tend to create their own mythology and morality. They define reality in *their* terms. Right becomes, by definition, what the institution wants, and evil is to oppose the institution.[4] This is true of all institutions, but it becomes especially invidious in religious institutions, which take on the aura of the sacred. As Gilbert James used to say, any institution may become demonic—and especially a church institution!

But there are effective ways to work for institutional renewal. Some of these are suggested above, and some hints were given in the previous chapter. I would add here, however, by way of summary and extension, the following clues in working for institutional renewal:

1. Don't attack head-on. That produces reaction, strife, and the institutional discrediting of the renewal effort.

2. Recognize the inevitability and positive value of the institution. Institutions are functional, or they would not exist. Recognize the legitimate functions they fulfill.

3. In institutional renewal, begin with life, not with organization or organizational tinkering. The points made previously in the discussion of renewal strategies apply here.

4. Make community the context for renewal. Seek to create a sense of community, or subcommunity, within the institution, using *ecclesiola* structures.

5. Transfer institutional functions to community functions wherever possible. Do informally or in community what has been overly formalized or institutionalized.[5]

6. Work to create structures based on community and consensus rather than on hierarchy and delegated authority. In other words, work to change the model.

CONCLUSION

God's remarkable strategy to redeem the world centers in Jesus Christ—his birth, life, death, resurrection, and reign. And Jesus' remarkable strategy for the kingdom relies heavily on that strange, weak, often unfaithful "little flock," the church.

History provides abundant evidence of that weakness and infidelity. But we see also the fascinating, recurring story of renewal.

The story has not ended. Jesus is always a step ahead of us. His Spirit is always bidding us to follow, to be renewed and enlivened for our life task. Great renewals have occurred in the past.

And the age of renewal is not over. Jesus still has glorious surprises for any church that will hear his words and be his body.

NOTES

[1] See in particular my *Liberating the Church: The Ecology of Church and Kingdom* (Downers Grove, Ill.: InterVarsity Press, 1983), 68–93, where a model based on these three components is elaborated.

[2] See "The Small Group as Basic Structure" in my book, *The Problem of Wineskins* (Downers Grove, Ill.: InterVarsity Press, 1975), chap. 11.

[3] See Howard Snyder and Daniel Runyon, *Foresight: 10 Major Trends That Will Dramatically Affect the Future of Christians and the Church* (Nashville: Thomas Nelson, 1986), 81–94.

[4]Jacques Ellul has written brilliantly on this last point. See, for example, *To Will and To Do,* trans. C. Edward Hopkin (Philadelphia: Pilgrim Press, 1969), 185.

[5]This relates to the trend today "from hierarchies to networking" described by John Naisbitt in *Megatrends* (New York: Warner Books, 1982, 1984), 211–29.

Select Bibliography

Addison, William George. *The Renewed Church of the United Brethren 1722–1930*. London: SPCK, 1932.

Allen, W. O. B., and Edmund McClure. *Two Hundred Years: The History of the Society for the Promoting of Christian Knowledge, 1698–1898*. London: SPCK, 1898.

Arndt, John. *Of True Christianity: Four Books*. Translated by Anthony William Boehm. London: Downing, 1712, 1714.

———. *True Christianity*. Translated by Peter Erb. Classics of Western Spirituality. New York: Paulist, 1979.

Baker, Frank. *John Wesley and the Church of England*. Nashville: Abingdon, 1970.

Barrett, David D., ed. *World Christian Encyclopedia*. Nairobi: Oxford University Press, 1982.

Bebb, E. Douglas. *Wesley: A Man with a Concern*. London: Epworth, 1950.

Benham, Daniel. *Life and Labours of the Rev. John Gambold, A.M. of Christ Church College, Oxford, First Bishop of the United Brethren in England*. London: Mallalieu, 1865.

———. *Memoirs of James Hutton; Comprising the Annals of His Life, and Connection with the United Brethren*. London: Hamilton, Adams, 1865.

Beyreuther, Erich. *Geschichte des Pietismus*. Stuttgart: Steinkopf Verlag, 1978.

Bindley, T. Herbert. *The Epistle of the Gallican Churches Lugdumum and Vienna*. London: SPCK, 1900.

Bloesch, Donald G. *Wellsprings of Renewal: Promise in Christian Communal Life*. Grand Rapids: Eerdmans, 1974.

Bonhoeffer, Dietrich. *The Communion of Saints* [1927]. Translated by R. Gregor Smith. New York: Harper and Row, 1960.

Borgen, Ole E. *John Wesley on the Sacraments*. Nashville: Abingdon, 1973.

Bost, A. *History of the Bohemian and Moravian Brethren*. Translated from the French, abridged, with appendix. London: Religious Tract Society, 1834; 2d ed., 1836.

Bovet, F. *The Banished Count*. London: E. T. J. Gill, 1865.

Brown, Dale. "The Problem of Subjectivism in Pietism: A Redefinition with Special Reference to the Theology of Philipp Jakob Spener and

August Hermann Francke." Doctoral dissertation, Garrett Theological Seminary and Northwestern University, 1962.

_____. *Understanding Pietism*. Grand Rapids: Eerdmans, 1978.

Browning, Wilfrid R. F. *The Anglican Synthesis: Essays by Catholics and Evangelicals*. Derby: Peter Smith, 1964.

Cairns, Earle E. *An Endless Line of Splendor: Revivals and Their Leaders from the Great Awakening to the Present*. Wheaton, Ill.: Tyndale, 1986.

Cannon, William Ragsdale. *The Theology of John Wesley, with Special Reference to the Doctrine of Justification*. New York: Abingdon, 1946.

Carpenter, S. C. *Eighteenth Century Church and People*. London: John Murray, 1959.

Cell, George Croft. *The Rediscovery of John Wesley*. New York: Holt, 1935.

Chadwick, Henry. *The Early Church*. Middlesex, England: Penguin, 1967, 1976.

Church, Leslie F. *More About the Early Methodist People*. London: Epworth, 1949.

Clark, Stephen B. *Unordained Elders and Renewal Communities*. New York: Paulist, 1976.

Clarke, William Kemp Lowther. *A History of the Society for Promoting Christian Knowledge*. London: SPCK, 1959.

Cohn, Norman. *The Pursuit of the Millennium: Revolutionary Millenarians and Mystical Anarchists of the Middle Ages*. Rev. ed. New York: Oxford University Press, 1970.

Crantz, David. *Ancient and Modern History of the Brethren*. Translated by B. LaTrobe. London, 1780.

Cross, F. L., and E. A. Livingstone, eds. *The Oxford Dictionary of the Christian Church*. 2d ed. London: Oxford University Press, 1974.

Curie, Robert, Alan Gilbert and Lee Horsley. *Churches and Churchgoers: Patterns of Church Growth in the British Isles Since 1700*. Oxford: Clarendon, 1977.

Dallimore, Arnold. *George Whitefield: The Life and Times of the Great Evangelist of the Eighteenth-Century Revival*. Vol. 1. London: Banner of Truth Trust, 1970.

Deeter, Allen C. "An Historical and Theological Introduction to Philipp Jakob Spener's *Pia Desideria:* A Study in Early German Pietism." Doctoral dissertation, Princeton University, 1963.

Dimond, Sydney, G. *The Psychology of the Methodist Revival*. Oxford: Oxford University Press, 1926.

Durnbaugh, Donald F. *The Believers' Church: The History and Character of Radical Protestantism*. New York: Macmillan, 1968.

Edwards, Jonathan. *A History of the Work of Redemption Containing the Outlines of a Body of Divinity in a Method Entirely New*. Edinburgh, 1774; Philadelphia: Presbyterian Board of Education, n.d.

Edwards, Maldwyn. *John Wesley and the Eighteenth Century: A Study of His Social and Political Influence*. London: Epworth, 1933; rev. ed., 1955.

Emerick, Samuel, ed. *Spiritual Renewal for Methodism: A Discussion of the Early Methodist Class Meeting and the Values Inherent in Personal Groups Today*. Nashville: Methodist Evangelistic Materials, 1958.

Finney, Charles G. *Reflections on Revival*. Compiled by Donald W. Dayton. Minneapolis: Bethany, 1979.

———. *Revivals of Religion*. Westwood, N.J.: Revell, n.d.

Ford, J. Massyngberde. *Which Way for Catholic Pentecostals?* New York: Harper and Row, 1976.

Francke, August Hermann. *Pietas Hallensis*. 2d ed., enlarged. London: Downing, 1707.

———. *A Short Introduction to the Practice of Christian Religion*. London: Downing, 1708.

———. *Three Practical Discourses*. London: Downing, 1716.

Frend, W. H. C. *The Rise of Christianity*. Philadelphia: Fortress, 1984.

Fulneck Jubilee Committee. *Celebration of the Centenary Jubilee of the Congregations of the United Brethren in Wyke, Mirfield, Gomersal, and Fulneck, April, 1855*. London: Mallalieu, 1855.

Gerlach, L. P. and V. H. Hine. *People, Power, Change: Movements of Social Transformation*. New York: Bobbs-Merrill, 1970.

Gibson, Elsa. *The "Christians for Christians" Inscriptions of Phrygia*. Missoula, Mont.: Scholars, 1978.

Gill, Frederick C. *Charles Wesley the First Methodist*. New York: Abingdon, 1964.

———. *In the Steps of John Wesley*. London: Lutterworth, 1962.

Gollin, Gillian Lindt. *Moravians in Two Worlds: A Study of Changing Communities*. New York: Columbia University Press, 1967.

Gradin, Arvid, *A Short History of the United Brethren*. London: Hutton, 1743.

Greschat, Martin, ed. *Zur Neueren Pietismusforschung*. Darmstadt: Wissenschaftliche Buchgesellschaft, 1977.

Gryson, Roger. *The Ministry of Women in the Early Church*. Trans. Jean LaPorte and Mary Louise Hall. Collegeville, Minn.: Liturgical Press, 1976.

Halévy, Elie. *The Birth of Methodism in England*. Translated and edited by Bernard Semmel. Chicago: University of Chicago Press, 1971.

Hamilton, J. Taylor, and Kenneth G. Hamilton. *History of the Moravian Church*. Bethlehem, Pa.: Inter-Provincial Board of Christian Education, Moravian Church in America, 1976.

Hamilton, Kenneth G., ed. and trans. *The Bethlehem Diary, vol. 1, 1742–1744*. Bethlehem, Pa.: The Archives of the Moravian Church, 1971.

Harmon, Nolan B., ed. *The Encyclopedia of World Methodism*. 2 vols. Nashville: United Methodist Publishing House, 1974.

Hasse, E. R. *The Moravians*. 2d ed. London: National Council of Evangelical Free Churches, 1913.

Heitzenrater, Richard Paul. "John Wesley and the Oxford Methodists, 1725–35." Doctoral dissertation, Duke University, 1972.

Hilbert, Gerhard. *Ecclesiola in Ecclesia: Luthers Anschauugen von Volkskirche und Freiwilligkeitskirche in ihrer Bedeutung für die Gegenwart*. Leipzig: P. Deichert, 1920.

Holmes, John. *History of the Protestant Church of the United Brethren*. 2 vols. London: J. Nisbet, 1825.

Hone, Richard B. *Lives of Eminent Christians*. London: Parker, 1839–42.

Hutton, Joseph E. *A History of the Moravian Church*. 2d ed. revised. London: Moravian Publication Office, 1909.

Johnson, Paul. *A History of Christianity*. New York: Atheneum, 1976.

Kelley, Dean M. *Why Conservative Churches Are Growing*. New York: Harper and Row, 1972.

Kidder, Richard. *The Life of the Reverend Anthony Horneck, D.D.* London: J. H. for B. Aylmer, 1698.

Kirkpatrick, Dow, ed. *The Doctrine of the Church*. New York: Abingdon, 1964.

Knox, Ronald A. *Enthusiasm: A Chapter in the History of Religion*. London: Oxford University Press, 1950.

Kraft, Charles H. *Christianity in Culture: A Study in Dynamic Biblical Theologizing in Cross-Cultural Perspective*. Maryknoll, N.Y.: Orbis, 1979.

Kuhn, Thomas S. *The Structure of Scientific Revolutions*. 2d ed. enlarged. International Encyclopedia of Unified Science, 2:2. Chicago: University of Chicago Press, 1970.

Langton, Edward. *History of the Moravian Church: The Story of the First International Protestant Church.* London: Allen and Unwin, 1956.

Lawson, A. B. *John Wesley and the Christian Ministry: The Sources and Development of His Opinions and Practice.* London: SPCK, 1963.

Lewis, A. J. *Zinzendorf the Ecumenical Pioneer.* Philadelphia: Westminster, 1962.

Lindt, Andreas, and Klaus Deppermann, eds. *Pietismus und Neuzeit. Ein Jahrbuch zur Geschichte des Neueren Protestantismus.* Bielefeld: Luther-Verlag. Band I, 1974; Band II, 1975; Band III, 1977.

Littell, Franklin Hamlin, *The Anabaptist View of the Church: A Study in the Origins of Sectarian Protestantism.* 2d ed., revised. Boston: Starr King, 1958.

Lovelace, Richard F. *The American Pietism of Cotton Mather.* Washington, D.C.: Christian University Press; Grand Rapids: Eerdmans, 1979.

―――. *Dynamics of Spiritual Life: An Evangelical Theology of Renewal.* Downers Grove, Ill.: InterVarsity Press, 1979.

McLoughlin, William Gerald. *Revivals, Awakenings and Reform: An Essay on Religion and Social Change in America, 1607–1977.* Chicago: University of Chicago Press, 1978.

McNeill, John T. *A History of the Cure of Souls.* New York: Harper and Row, 1951.

―――. *Modern Christian Movements.* Philadelphia: Westminster, 1954.

Mellis, Charles J. *Committed Communities: Fresh Streams for World Missions.* South Pasadena, Calif.: William Carey Library, 1976.

Mezezers, Valdis. *The Herrnhuterian Pietism in the Baltic and Its Outreach into America and Elsewhere in the World.* North Quincy, Mass.: Christopher, 1975.

Miller, Perry. *Jonathan Edwards.* N.p.: William Sloane Associates, 1949.

Monk, Robert C. *John Wesley: His Puritan Heritage.* Nashville: Abingdon, 1966.

Myers, Elizabeth Lehman. *A Century of Moravian Sisters: A Record of Christian Community Life.* New York: Revell, 1918.

Nagler, Arthur Wilford. *Pietism and Methodism, or The Significance of German Pietism in the Origin and Early Development of Methodism.* Nashville: M. E. Church, South, 1918.

Oden, Thomas C. *The Intensive Group Experience: The New Pietism.* Philadelphia: Westminster, 1972.

Orr, J. Edwin. *Evangelical Awakenings in Africa.* Minneapolis: Bethany, 1975.

_____. *The Second Evangelical Awakening in Britain*. London, 1949.

Outler, Albert C., ed. *John Wesley*. New York: Oxford University Press, 1964.

Overton, John Henry. *The Evangelical Revival in the Eighteenth Century*. 2d ed. London: Longmans, Green, 1891.

_____. *Life in the English Church (1660–1714)*. London: Longmans, Green, 1885.

Pinson, Koppel S. *Pietism as a Factor in the Rise of German Nationalism*. New York: Columbia University Press, 1934; reprint, New York: Octagon, 1968.

Richard, Marie E. *Philip Jacob Spener and His Work*. Philadelphia: Lutheran Publication Society, 1897.

Ritschl, Albrecht. *Three Essays*. Translated by Philip Hefner. Philadelphia: Fortress, 1972.

Robinson, J. Armitage. *The Passion of St. Perpetua*. Cambridge, England: The University Press, 1891.

Robinson, William. *Completing the Reformation: The Doctrine of the Priesthood of All Believers*. Lexington, Ky.: The College of the Bible, 1955.

Rouse, Ruth, and Stephen C. Neill. *A History of the Ecumenical Movement 1517–1948*. 2d ed. Philadelphia: Westminster, 1967.

Russell, Jane Elyse. "Renewing the Gospel Community: Four Catholic Movements with an Anabaptist Parallel." Doctoral dissertation, University of Notre Dame, 1979.

Sattler, Gary R. *God's Glory, Neighbor's Good*. Chicago: Covenant, 1982.

Schattschneider, David Allen. " 'Souls for the Lamb': A Theology for the Christian Mission according to Count Nicolaus Ludwig von Zinzendorf and Bishop Augustus Gottlieb Spangenberg." Doctoral dissertation, Chicago Divinity School, 1975.

Schmidt, Martin. *John Wesley: A Theological Biography*. Translated by Norman Goldhawk. 2 vols. New York: Abingdon, 1962, 1972.

_____. *Pietismus*. Stuttgart: Kohlhammer, 1978.

_____. *Wiedergeburt und Neuer Mensch*. Witten: Luther-Verlag, 1969.

Semmel, Bernard. *The Methodist Revolution*. New York: Basic Books, 1973.

Sessler, Jacob John. *Communal Pietism among Early American Moravians*. New York: Henry Holt, 1933.

Simon, John S. *John Wesley and the Methodist Societies*. London: Epworth, 1923.

————. *John Wesley and the Religious Societies*. London: Epworth, 1921.

Smaby, Beverly Prior. *The Transformation of Moravian Bethlehem From Communal Mission to Family Economy*. Philadelphia: University of Pennsylvania Press, 1988.

Smith, Timothy L. *Revivalism and Social Reform*. New York: Abingdon, 1957.

Spangenberg, August Gottlieb. *The Life of Nicholas Lewis Count Zinzendorf, Bishop and Ordinary of the Church of the United (or Moravian) Brethren*. Translated by Samuel Jackson. London: Holdsworth, 1838.

Spener, Philipp Jakob. *Pia Desideria*. Translated by Theodore G. Tappert. Philadelphia: Fortress, 1964, 1977.

————. *The Spiritual Priesthood*. Translated by A. G. Voight. Philadelphia: Lutheran Publication Society, 1917.

Stein, K. James. *Philipp Jakob Spener: Pietist Patriarch*. Chicago: Covenant, 1986.

Stevens, Abel. *The History of the Religious Movement of the Eighteenth Century, Called Methodism, Considered in Its Different Denominational Forms, and Its Relations to British and American Protestantism*. 3 vols. New York: Carlton and Porter, 1858–61.

Stoeffler, F. Ernest *German Pietism in the Eighteenth Century*. Leiden: E. J. Brill, 1973.

————. *The Rise of Evangelical Pietism*. Leiden: E. J. Brill, 1965.

Stoeffler, F. Ernest, ed. *Continental Pietism and Early American Christianity*. Grand Rapids: Eerdmans, 1976.

Telford, John. *The Life of John Wesley*. New York: Phillips and Hunt, 1886.

Todd, John M. *John Wesley and the Catholic Church*. London: Hodder and Stoughton, 1958.

Towlson, Clifford W. *Moravian and Methodist. Relationships and Influences in the Eighteenth Century*. London: Epworth, 1957.

Tyerman, Luke. *The Life and Times of the Rev. John Wesley, M.A., Founder of the Methodists*. 3 vols. New York: Harper and Brothers, 1872.

Urlin, R. Denny. *The Churchman's Life of Wesley*. London: SPCK, 1905.

————. *John Wesley's Place in Church History*. London: Rivingtons, 1870.

Visser 't Hooft, W. A. *The Renewal of the Church*. London: SCM, 1956.

Vulliamy, C. E. *John Wesley*. New York: Scribner, 1932.

Watson, David Lowes. "The Origin and Significance of the Early Methodist Class Meeting." Doctoral dissertation, Duke University, 1978.

Watson, Richard. *The Life of Rev. John Wesley, A.M.* New York: Carlton and Phillips, 1853.

Waugh, W. T. *A History of the Fulneck School.* Leeds: Richard Jackson, 1909.

Wearmouth, Robert F. *Methodism and the Common People of the Eighteenth Century.* London: Epworth, 1945.

_____. *Methodism and the Working-Class Movements of England 1800–1850.* London: Epworth, 1937.

Weborg, John. "Spener's Doctrine of the Church." Thesis, North Park Theological Seminary, 1961.

Weinrich, William C. *Spirit and Martyrdom: A Study of the Work of the Holy Spirit in Contexts of Persecution and Martyrdom in the New Testament and Early Christian Literature.* Washington, D.C.: University Press of America, 1981.

Wesley, Charles. *The Journal of the Rev. Charles Wesley, M.A.* London: John Mason, 1849; repr. Grand Rapids: Baker, 1980.

Wesley, John. *Explanatory Notes upon the New Testament.* London: Epworth, 1958.

_____. *Explanatory Notes upon the Old Testament.* 2 vols. Bristol: William Pine, 1765; repr. Salem, Ohio: Schmul, 1975.

_____. *The Journal of the Rev. John Wesley, A.M.* Edited by Nehemiah Curnock. 8 vols. London: Culley, 1909.

_____. *The Letters of the Rev. John Wesley, A.M.* Edited by John Telford. 8 vols. London: Epworth, 1931.

_____. *The Works of John Wesley.* 3d ed. Edited by Thomas Jackson. 14 vols. London: Mason, 1829–31.

_____. *The Works of John Wesley.* Edited by Frank Baker. Vol. 11, *The Appeals to Men of Reason and Religion and Certain Related Open Letters.* Edited by Gerald R. Cragg. London: Oxford University Press, 1975.

Whitehead, John. *Life of Rev. John Wesley.* London, 1793; Boston: Dow and Jackson, 1845.

Williams, Colin W. *John Wesley's Theology Today.* New York: Abingdon, 1960.

Williams, George Huntston, ed. *Spiritual and Anabaptist Writers.* Library of Christian Classics, vol. 25. Philadelphia: Westminster, 1957.

Winter, Ralph D., and R. Pierce Beaver. *The Warp and the Woof: Organizing for Mission.* South Pasadena, Calif.: William Carey Library, 1970.

Wood, A. Skevington. *The Burning Heart: John Wesley, Evangelist.* Grand Rapids: Eerdmans, 1967.

Woodhouse, H. F. *The Doctrine of the Church in Anglican Theology 1547–1603.* London: SPCK, 1954.

Woodward, Josiah. *An Account of the Rise and Progress of the Religious Societies in the City of London, etc., and of Their Endeavours for Reformation of All Manners.* 3d ed., enlarged. London, 1701. 4th ed., enlarged. London: Downing, 1712.

Zinzendorf, Nicolaus. *Maxims, Theological Ideas and Sentences, Out of the Present Ordinary of the Brethren's Churches. His Dissertations and Discourses from the Year 1738 till 1747.* Extracted by J. Gambold. London: Beecroft, 1751.

————. *Nine Publick Discourses upon Important Subjects in Religion, Preached in Fetter-lane-Chapel at London, in the Year MDCCXLVI.* Translated from the German. London: James Hutton, 1748. Republished as *Zinzendorf: Nine Public Lectures on Important Subjects in Religion.* Edited and translated by George Forell. Iowa City: University of Iowa Press, 1973.

————. *Sixteen Discourses on the Redemption of Man by the Death of Christ* [1738]. Translated from the German. London: Hutton, 1740.

————. *Twenty One Discourses or Dissertations upon the Augsburg Confession, Which is also the Brethren's Confession of Faith: Deliver'd by the Ordinary of the Brethren's Churches before the Seminary.* Translated by F. Okeley. London: Bowyer, 1753.

Shorter Writings

Benz, Ernst. "Pietist and Puritan Sources of Early Protestant World Missions (Cotton Mather and A. H. Francke)." Translated by Luise Jockers. *Wesley Historical Society* 7:5 (March 1910): 101–02.

Chamberlayne, John H. "From *Sect* to *Church* in British Methodism." *British Journal of Sociology* 15 (1964): 139–49.

Cho, John Chongnahm. "John Wesley's View on Baptism." *Wesleyan Theological Journal* 7:1 (Spring 1972): 60–73.

Duffy, Eamon. "The Society of Promoting Christian Knowledge and Europe: The Background to the Founding of the

Christentumsgesellschaft." In *Pietismus und Neuzeit* 7:28–42. Gottingen: Vandenhoeck and Ruprecht, 1981.

Durbin, Linda M. "The Nature of Ordination in Wesley's View of the Ministry." *Methodist History* 9:3 (April 1971): 3–20.

Gerdes, Egon W. "Pietism: Classical and Modern. A Comparison of Two Representative Descriptions." *Concordia Theological Monthly* 39 (1968): 257–68.

———. "Theological Tenets of Pietism." *The Covenant Quarterly* 34:1–2 (February May 1976): 25–60.

Hamilton, Kenneth Gardiner. "John Ettwein and the Moravian Church during the Revolutionary Period." In *Transactions of the Moravian Historical Society*, 7, 85–429. Nazareth, Penn.: Whitefield, 1940.

Heitzenrater, Richard P. "The Oxford Diaries and the First Rise of Methodism." *Methodist History* 12:4 (July 1974): 110–35.

Hutton, J[oseph], E. "Methodist Bands: Their Origin and Nature—A New Discovery." *Wesleyan Methodist Magazine* 134 (March 1911): 197–202.

Kincheloe, Joe L. "European Roots of Evangelical Revivalism: Methodist Transmission of the Pietistic Socio-Religious Tradition." *Methodist History* 18:4 (July 1980): 262–71.

Kissack, R. "Wesley's Concept of His Own Ecclesiastical Position." *London Quarterly and Holborn Review* 186 (January 1961): 57–60.

Klawiter, Frederick C. "The Role of Martyrdom and Persecution in Developing the Priestly Authority of Women in Early Christianity: A Case Study of Montanism." *Church History* 49 (September 1980): 251–61.

Kohl, Manfred Waldemar. "Pietism as a Movement of Revival." *The Covenant Quarterly* 33:3 (August 1975): 3–23.

———. "*Wiedergeburt* as the Central Theme in Pietism." *The Covenant Quarterly* 32:4 (November 1974): 15–35.

"Life and Labors of Francke." *The Evangelical Quarterly* 19:74 (April 1868): 277–98.

Littell, Franklin H. "The Discipline of Discipleship in the Free Church Tradition." *Mennonite Quarterly Review* 35 (April 1961): 111–19.

Metzler, E. A. "Spener on Baptism." *Quarterly Review of the Evangelical Lutheran Church* 23:4 (October 1893): 533–50.

"Minutes of Conference for 1749, 1755, 1758. From John Wesley's MS. Copy." *Supplement to the Proceedings of the Wesley Historical Society* 4 (1904): 63–75.

Novak, Michael. "The Free Churches and the Roman Church." *Journal of Ecumenical Studies* 2 (1965): 426–47.

―――. "The Meaning of 'Church' in Anabaptism and Roman Catholicism: Past and Present." In D. B. Robertson, ed., *Voluntary Associations: A Study of Groups in Free Societies*, 91–107. Richmond, Va.: John Knox, 1966.

Nuttall, Geoffrey F. N. "Continental Pietism and the Evangelical Movement in Britain." In J. Van Den Berg and J. P. Van Dooren, eds., *Pietismus und Reveil. 209–22.* Kerkhistorische Bijdragen, 7. Leiden: E. J. Brill, 1978.

Outler, Albert C. "John Wesley as Theologian—Then and Now." *Methodist History* 12:4 (July 1974): 63–82.

Parkinson, Fred. M. "Methodist Class Tickets." *Proceedings of the Wesley Historical Society* 1:5 (1898): 129–35.

"The Pietistic Controversy." *The Quarterly Review of the Evangelical Lutheran Church* 4:2 (April 1879): 278–301.

Reist, Irwin. "John Wesley's View of the Sacraments: A Study in the Historical Development of a Doctrine." *Wesleyan Theological Journal* 6:1 (Spring 1971): 41–54.

Ruether, Rosemary. "The Free Church Movement in Contemporary Catholicism." In Martin E. Marty and Dean G. Peerman, eds., *New Theology No. 6,* 286–87. New York: Macmillan, 1969.

Stampe, George. "Note by Mr. George Stampe." *Proceedings of the Wesley Historical Society* 1:5 (1898): 135–37.

Stoeffler, F. Ernest. "Tradition and Renewal in the Ecclesiology of John Wesley." In Bernd Jaspert and Rudolf Mohr, eds., *Traditio–Krisis– Renovatio aus theologischer Sicht,* 298–316. Marburg: Elwert, 1976.

Tappert, Theodore G. "Orthodoxism, Pietism, and Rationalism 1580– 1830." Harold C. Letts. ed., *Christian Social Responsibility,* 2:36–88.

Tholuck, A. "Philip Jacob Spener." Translated by F. A. Muhlenberg. *Evangelical Quarterly Review* 14:53 (October 1862): 68–96.

Verney, John H. "Early Wesleyan Class Tickets: Comments and Catalogue." *Proceedings of the Wesley Historical Society* 31 (1957–58): 2–9.

Wallace, Anthony F. C. "Revitalization Movements: Some Theoretical Considerations for Their Comparative Study." *American Anthropologist* 58 (April 1956): 264–75.

Wallmann, Johannes. "Pietismus und Chiliasmus. Zur Kontroverse um Philipp Jakob Speners 'Hoffnung besserer Zeiten.'" *Zeitschrift für Theologie und Kirche* 78:2 (1981): 235–40.

_____. "Wiedergeburt und Erneuerung bei Philipp Jakob Spener." In Andreas Lindt and Klaus Deppermann, eds., *Jahrbuch 1976 zur Geschichte des Neueren Protestantismus*, 7–31. Bielefeld: Luther-Verlag, 1977.

Walsh, John. "Origins of the Evangelical Revival." In G. V. Bennett and J. D. Walsh, eds., *Essays in Modern English Church History*, 132–62. New York: Oxford University Press, 1966.

Ward, W. R. "Power and Piety: The Origins of Religious Revival in the Early Eighteenth Century." *Bulletin of the John Rylands University Library* 63:1 (Autumn 1980): 231–52.

Winter, Ralph D. "The Two Structures of God's Redemptive Mission." *Missiology* 2:1 (January 1974): 121–39.

Wright, Joseph G. "Class and Band Tickets." *Proceedings of the Wesley Historical Society* 5:2 (1905): 33–44.

Index

SIGNS OF THE SPIRIT